Dora Komnenović

Reading between the Lines
Reflections on Discarded Books and
Sociopolitical Transformations in (Post-)Yugoslavia

Literatur und Kultur im mittleren und östlichen Europa

herausgegeben von Reinhard Ibler

ISSN 2195-1497

17   *Magdalena Baran-Szołtys, Monika Glosowitz,*
     Aleksandra Konarzewska (eds.)
     Imagined Geographies
     Central European Spatial Narratives between 1984 and 2014
     ISBN 978-3-8382-1225-8

18   *Adam Jarosz*
     Der Spiegel und die Spiegelungen
     Über Geschlecht und Seele im Werk von Stanisław Przybyszewski
     ISBN 978-3-8382-1246-3

19   *Šárka Sladovníková*
     The Holocaust in Czechoslovak
     and Czech Feature Films
     ISBN 978-3-8382-1196-1

20   *Julia Spanberger*
     Grenzen und Grenzerfahrungen in den Texten Viktor Pelevins
     Eine Analyse seiner frühen Prosa
     ISBN 978-3-8382-1460-3

21   *Magda Dolińska-Rydzek*
     The Antichrist in Post-Soviet Russia:
     Transformations of an Ideomyth
     ISBN 978-3-8382-1545-7

22   *Martina Napolitano*
     Sasha Sokolov: The Life and Work of the Russian "Proet"
     ISBN 978-3-8382-1619-5

23   *Astrid Maria Ottilie Shchekina-Greipel*
     Deutsch-sowjetischer Kulturtransfer unter totalitären Bedingungen
     Heinrich Böll und Günter Grass in der Sowjetunion (1953–1985)
     ISBN 978-3-8382-1660-7

Dora Komnenović

READING BETWEEN THE LINES
Reflections on Discarded Books and
Sociopolitical Transformations in (Post-)Yugoslavia

Bibliografische Information der Deutschen Nationalbibliothek
Die Deutsche Nationalbibliothek verzeichnet diese Publikation in der Deutschen Nationalbibliografie; detaillierte bibliografische Daten sind im Internet über http://dnb.d-nb.de abrufbar.

Bibliographic information published by the Deutsche Nationalbibliothek
Die Deutsche Nationalbibliothek lists this publication in the Deutsche Nationalbibliografie; detailed bibliographic data are available in the Internet at http://dnb.d-nb.de.

Cover picture: Photo taken at the exhibition/action "Otpisane". © Ivan Kuharić

Gießener Dissertation im Fachbereich Kultur- und Sozialwissenschaften

ISBN-13: 978-3-8382-1643-0
© *ibidem*-Verlag, Stuttgart 2022
Alle Rechte vorbehalten

Das Werk einschließlich aller seiner Teile ist urheberrechtlich geschützt. Jede Verwertung außerhalb der engen Grenzen des Urheberrechtsgesetzes ist ohne Zustimmung des Verlages unzulässig und strafbar. Dies gilt insbesondere für Vervielfältigungen, Übersetzungen, Mikroverfilmungen und elektronische Speicherformen sowie die Einspeicherung und Verarbeitung in elektronischen Systemen.

All rights reserved. No part of this publication may be reproduced, stored in or introduced into a retrieval system, or transmitted, in any form, or by any means (electronical, mechanical, photocopying, recording or otherwise) without the prior written permission of the publisher. Any person who does any unauthorized act in relation to this publication may be liable to criminal prosecution and civil claims for damages.

Printed in the EU

Abstract

(Public) libraries are expected to regularly weed and/or to discard parts of their collection. International standards and national regulations make sure it is carried out appropriately and that no book gets permanently lost. The perception that non-librarians have of discarding is often diametrically opposed to the way professionals think about it. In fact, the weeding and discarding that ensued after the collapse of communism were seen as a "de-ideologization" of library holdings by some and as "bookicide" by others. This research project, anchored in the field of (post-)Yugoslav studies, investigates the modalities of book removal from public libraries in Croatia and Slovenia in the 1990s and the sociopolitical implications thereof.

While the post-1989 "cleansing" of libraries might not be a (former) Yugoslav idiosyncrasy, certain developments in Croatia make this case stand out. A study on the topic, abundant newspaper accounts and meagre quantitative data available on the discarding of books in Croatia are confronted with personal recollections and figures from Slovenia in order to determine the extent to which this standard library practice was affected by the political, social and economic transformations concomitant with the dissolution of Yugoslavia. Based on interviews and the close reading of documents, reports and newspaper articles, this volume offers an empirically founded study of the inconsistencies and lack of implementation of regulations in the field of librarianship and of the media representations thereof in Croatia, as opposed to a seemingly more synchronized environment in Slovenia.

Imprudent political statements, terminological unclarity, the lack of reaction from professional librarians' associations to cases of inappropriate discarding and the overall polarization of society partially (but not exclusively) due to the War of Independence are identified as the main reasons for the politicization of the issue and the subsequent antagonism between librarians and non-librarians. The second part of the book focuses on the fate of discarded volumes and by doing so provides an innovative and original interpretation of postsocialist transition and post-Yugoslav memory. Whether on the shelves of a library, in film or as objects in exhibitions and artistic performances, two books in particular and "the discarded" in general are analyzed as "memory triggers" and thus potential vehicles for a critical examination of the recent past.

Table of Contents

Abstract 5
List of Figures 9
List of Tables 10
Abbreviations and Acronyms 11

Preface and Acknowledgments 13

Introduction 19

1. Yugoslavia, Europe and the World After 1989 43
   1.1. Blooming Mythscapes, Languishing Landscapes:
        Eastern Europe in Postsocialism 44
   1.2. The Multiple Transitions in (Post-)Yugoslavia 50
   1.3. "Europe Now!" 55
   1.4. A Spectre is Haunting Croatia – The Spectre of
        Yugoslavia 59
   1.5. A for Another, B for Balkanization: Language in
        (Post-) Yugoslavia 65
   1.6. The "Spirit of Renewal" is Sweeping Libraries 71

2. The Discarding of Books in the 1990s: A Fact, a
   Perception, a Metaphor 83
   2.1. My Approach to the Topic 84
   2.2. The Theory and Practice of Weeding and Discarding
        in Public Libraries 88
   2.3. Newspaper Accounts about the Discarding of Books
        from Croatian Libraries 97
   2.4. Ante Lešaja's *Libricide* and Other Sources 107
   2.5. Discarding in Public Libraries in Slovenia: Data and
        Perceptions in Comparison 115

2.6. The Discarding of Books in Public Libraries in Croatia and Slovenia during Transition: Possible Lines of Interpretation 130

3. **The Afterlife of Discarded Books between Dumps, Library Shelves and Art** 137

    3.1. The Hedgehog in Search of a Home 140

    3.2. Reusing Discarded Books 146

        3.2.1. The Book as Artistic Object: the Project "Odpisani" ("The Written-Offs") at the Maribor University Library 147

        3.2.2. The Opening of the Serbian Central Library in Zagreb 148

    3.3. In War and Revolution: An Experimental Documentary Film by Ana Bilankov 150

    3.4. The Discarding of Books in the 1990s in Croatia as an Inspiration for Artists: Exhibition-Action "Discarded" 155

4. **In Lieu of Conclusions: On Discarded Books, Memory and Dealing with the Socialist and Yugoslav Legacy Thirty Years Later** 169

Bibliography 181

List of Figures

Figure 1.	Somewhere in Rijeka, 2016. Photo by Dora Komnenović	64
Figure 2.	Ana Bilankov: In War and Revolution. Still frame. © VG Bild-Kunst, Bonn 2022	151
Figure 3.	Ana Bilankov: In War and Revolution. Still frame. © VG Bild-Kunst, Bonn 2022	152
Figure 4.	Ana Bilankov: In War and Revolution. Still frame. © VG Bild-Kunst, Bonn 2022	155
Figure 5.	Exhibition "Discarded". Zagreb, June 2015. Photo by Dora Komnenović	157
Figure 6.	Ante Lešaja's categories of "exclusionism". Photo by Dora Komnenović	157
Figure 7.	The exhibited books. Photo by Dora Komnenović	159
Figure 8.	The scanner with which the books were scanned during the exhibition. Photo by Dora Komnenović	159
Figure 9.	Siniša Ilić's wall painting. © Ivan Kuharić, 2022	160
Figure 10.	Siniša Labrović's performance. © Ivan Kuharić, 2022	162
Figure 11.	Performative installation by Božena Končić Badurina. © Ivan Kuharić, 2022	163
Figure 12.	Antonio Grgić's performance. © Ivan Kuharić, 2022	164
Figure 13.	One of the readers in *Osluškivanje*. © Ivan Kuharić, 2022	165
Figure 14.	Rescuing books. A small section of the exhibition in Leipzig, February 2019. Photo by Dora Komnenović	171
Figure 15.	A book sterilizer in the Rijeka City Library, March 2021. Photo by Dora Komnenović	180

List of Tables

Table 1.	Collection development in public libraries in Zagreb between 1988 and 1998	100
Table 2.	Discarded material from public libraries in Slovenia in the year 1990.	120
Table 3.	Discarding from public libraries in Slovenia in 1993.	122
Table 4.	The development of the collection in Slovenian public libraries in the period 1990–2000	130

Abbreviations and Acronyms

ALA	American Library Association
CEE	Central-Eastern European
COBISS	Cooperative Bibliographic Systems and Services
EU	European Union
FRY	Federal Republic of Yugoslavia *(Savezna republika Jugoslavija)*
HDZ	*Hrvatska demokratska zajednica* Croatian Democratic Union)
HKD	*Hrvatsko knjižničarsko društvo* (Croatian Library Association)
HNS – LD	*Hrvatska narodna stranka – liberalni demokrati* (Croatian People's Party – Liberal Democrats)
ICJ	International Court of Justice
ICTY	International Criminal Tribunal for the Former Yugoslavia
IFLA/FAIFE	International Federation of Library Associations and Institutions / Freedom of Access to Information and Freedom of Expression Advisory Committee
IUC	Inter-University Center Dubrovnik
JNA	*Jugoslovenska/Jugoslavenska Narodna Armija* (Yugoslav people's Army YPA)
LDS	*Liberalna demokracija Slovenije* (Liberal Democracy of Slovenia)
NAM	Non-Aligned Movement
NATO	North Atlantic Treaty Organization
NSK	*Nacionalna i sveučilišna knjižnica* (National and University Library)
NSM	New social movements
SDP	*Socijaldemokratska partija Hrvatske* (Social Democratic Party of Croatia)
SDP	*Stranka demokratične prenove* (Party of Democratic Reform)
SFRY	Socialist Federal Republic of Yugoslavia

SKD	*Slovenski krščanski demokrati* (Slovene Christian Democrats)
SECI	Southeast European Cooperative Initiative
SR	Socialist Republic
UGM	*Umetnostna galerija Maribor* (Maribor Art Gallery)
UNESCO	United Nations Educational, Scientific and Cultural Organization
USA	United States of America
ZKS	*Zveza komunistov Slovenije* (League of Communists of Slovenia)

Preface and Acknowledgments

> "Culture is essentially a graveyard for books and other lost objects. Scholars are currently researching how culture is a process of tacitly abandoning certain relics of the past (thus filtering), while placing others in a kind of refrigerator, for the future. Archives and libraries are cold rooms in which we store what has come before, so that the cultural space is not cluttered, without having to relinquish those memories entirely."
> Umberto Eco[1]

In 1989 the Berlin wall fell, Yugoslavia won the Eurovision song contest, Ayatollah Ruhollah Khomeini issued a fatwa calling for the death of Salman Rushdie for having published the novel *The Satanic Verses* (1988), and Francis Fukuyama proclaimed the end of history. If someone else were to write this sentence, the selection of events that marked 1989 would probably be somewhat different. The multiplicity of perspectives would nevertheless converge towards the fact that the year is generally remembered as a turning point in history, marking the end of state socialism in Europe and therefore the beginning of a new era, that of postsocialism. Around the same time, the process of disintegration of the Socialist Federal Republic of Yugoslavia (SFRY) culminated in a decade of wars. Consequently, former Yugoslav countries are simultaneously postsocialist, post-Yugoslav and post-conflict societies that in the past quarter century faced multiple transformations. While the political, economic and social dimensions of what is commonly referred to as transition, i.e. the shift to market economy and political pluralism have been more or less successfully studied, mostly within the paradigm of Europeanization, the transformations in the realm of culture have been predominantly approached by deploying nation-building as the primary interpretative framework. What such analyses often exclude, however, are non-state actors, as well as local forms of organization, which operate in a globalized and increasingly interdependent world that in the meantime underwent the Internet revolution. In fact, to the abovementioned list of singular events that marked the year 1989 the invention of the World Wide

---

1 In Carrière, J.C. and Eco, U. (2011). *This is Not the End of the Book. A conversation curated by Jean-Philippe de Tonnac.* London: Harvill Secker, 63.

Web (WWW) by the British computer scientist Tim Berners-Lee could be added.

When a country disappears, it leaves behind material and immaterial signs of its (past) existence. Some of these buildings, institutions, monuments, books, documents, festivities, practices or rituals are then preserved, stored, or musealized; others are torn down, removed, or abolished. Some outlive the defunct country in unchanged form, while the function and meaning of others change. Still others disappear forever, or until they resurface again in the future. The outcome of these processes undoubtedly influences national identity, narrative and image, but who does the "filtering" and on what grounds? Is it even possible to talk about a rational selection process? In those circumstances, what is the fate of the material legacy of a vanished state? What role does it play?

Objects as "carriers" or "triggers" of memory are as important for groups, which do not have a memory of their own, as they are for individuals because memory "exists only in constant interaction not only with other human memories but also with 'things', outward symbols" (J. Assmann 2008, 111). In the novel *Museum of Unconditional Surrender*, Dubravka Ugrešić writes that "if the country has disappeared, then so has collective memory. If the objects that have surrounded us disappear, then so has memory of the everyday life that we lived" (Ugrešić 1998, 243). But how do these objects disappear? Can their disappearance actually induce a form of remembrance or, rather, a (critical) examination of the past?

Such changes are rather complex and cannot be unequivocally attributed to "the state" and to a top-down course of action analyzed *ex post facto* through a "before" and "after" comparison. It is solely the tension and interplay between inclusion and exclusion, memory and forgetting, the spoken and the unspoken, the lost and the found that do justice to the multi-directionality of the power discourse that underlies each sociopolitical transformation. The renegotiation of these categories during the "Autumn of Nations" in 1989 and the transition to market economy produced residues in the form of statues, street signs, memorabilia, furniture, books: "cultural remains" that covered Eastern European streets together with fallen leaves. In the following years they began to inhabit museums, flea markets, landfills, or other less likely places. At an abstract level, among these objects' books stand out because of their non-negligible symbolic weight, as they are universally associated with knowledge, wisdom, and, more broadly, culture and memory. Even if stained and with a couple of pages missing, a book in the rubbish dump is more likely to provoke disgust than an object of everyday use spotted at the same place. Furthermore, due to their double nature as objects and symbols, throughout history books have been targets of violence directed at their authors, their contents, their language, and, consequently, the culture they are associated with. This is particularly the case in times of sociopolitical upheaval and armed conflict like the situation in the former Yugoslavia.

The demise of this multinational, multilingual, multiconfessional, politically non-aligned and economically self-managed country, the ensuing wars and different attempts at nation and state-building left their mark on books and libraries across the region. The destruction of the cultural heritage, including libraries and invaluable manuscripts, during the Yugoslav wars in the 1990s is widely known and researched. But what happened with books that became "outdated" once the country ceased to exist, such as *The Selected Works of Josip Broz Tito*, volumes on the People's Liberation Struggle, disquisitions on workers' self-management, and books on Yugoslavia in general? Is there such a thing as an outdated book? The overall impression one gets from conversations with people at different levels of familiarity with librarianship and the book industry, but who all lived through the dissolution of Yugoslavia, is that in the 1990s countless books were thrown away by individuals and institutions. At the same time, school and public libraries were increasingly reviewing their collections in order to adapt them to the new sociopolitical reality. In Croatia the first public reactions to the "cleansing" of libraries started appearing almost concurrently with the numerous newspaper reports about the libraries destroyed in war-affected areas. However, opinions differed as to the cause of the "cleansing", ranging from the need to "cleanse" the Croatian culture and language of Serbian influences to an absolute civilizational barbarism. A number of newspaper articles, a couple of lawsuits and a book on the topic ensued. These clearly emphasized the Croatian case, but to what extent was the situation in this post-Yugoslav country different from what happened in other postsocialist countries, where large cultural institutions and publishing houses were massively dumping unsold books and libraries and making room for western publications by discarding so-called "red literature"?

These were more or less the questions that I had, and the little that I knew about the topic, before reading a volume published by Ante Lešaja in 2012: *Libricide: The Destruction of Books in the 1990s in Croatia*. In it, sporadic newspaper reports about library "cleansing" in the 1990s acquire a new meaning and are placed within a different context: the destruction of books is a phenomenon, argues the author, a symptom of the exclusionism *(isključivost)* that reigned in Croatia in the 1990s. Such exclusionism consisted in the antagonization of Yugoslavia, anti-fascism, the working class, the Serbs as well as dissenters and was the main criterion for the removal of books from primarily public and school libraries, and it applied to books on Yugoslavia, socialism, the National Liberation War and anti-fascism, the Serbs, and the working class, and, finally, to any books expressing disagreement with existing policies (Lešaja 2012, 502). The idea of libraries removing "unsuitable" *(nepodobne)* books started progressively attracting my attention. Are libraries not, in Eco's words, "cold rooms in which we store what has come before", and frequently considered as belonging to the same category as mnemonic institutions like archives and museums? Even mnemonic institutions, public libraries in particular, are compelled to discard certain materials from time to time, but this should not be regulated by ideological criteria. Through the mandatory periodic review of their collections, libraries often face the dilemma of what to keep and what to discard, which could be regarded as a synecdoche of larger, societal processes, of what Eco calls "filtering". However, is there any difference in the criteria used in the process? Discarding is a regular library procedure that usually passes unnoticed to most of the population. It becomes an issue when it is carried out in an inappropriate manner, is contrary to professional regulations, and/or is turned into a (political) scandal. In Croatia most citizens have heard of library "cleansing", but what exactly is implied by this term? How did library "cleansing" even become a topic if, as most librarians insist, politically motivated discarding occurred, if at all, only in isolated cases? Is the Croatian case a *unicum* in former Yugoslavia? Other, more general questions started piling up: To what extent do the acquisition and particularly the discarding of books in public libraries reflect sociopolitical and value changes on a national and local level and do they concomitantly act upon them? What is the degree of control the state—that is, the responsible ministry (in the case of public libraries, the ministry of culture)—exerts in this domain? Or is it, rather, the individual librarian who decides what is to be weeded (moved to a second level of access usually not open to the public), discarded (permanently withdrawn from stock) and acquired? In other words, is it a political (enforced by the state/local authority), economic (regulated by the market) or professional/individual (initiated by the librarian) decision? How do developments in the publishing industry influence libraries? Is it possible to draw any conclusions on the Yugoslav dissolution and/or the process of dealing with the socialist and Yugoslav past by looking at library practices? These are some of the questions I tackle in the first part of the volume, where the accent is on discarding in public libraries in the transition period by using examples from Croatia and Slovenia. It is preceded by an overview of the salient features of postsocialist, post-Yugoslav and post-conflict transformations, namely, the framework within which the removal of books was taking place and was being discussed. In the second part I turn my attention to books, whose lives do not necessarily end once they are discarded. How does the value of books change with the changing of the sociopolitical context? Do books have a limited lifespan like other objects and turn into rubbish? What role do garbage dumps and rubbish have in the definition of identity? To what extent can books (and libraries) be regarded as a materialization of memory?

The present study is an attempt at answering these and other questions, the product of four years of research and several creative breaks, reflection and incessant journey through the legacy of Yugoslavia and the intricacies of post-Yugoslavia. This book is a revised version of my PhD dissertation, which would not have been possible without the help and support of the wonderful people who walked with me the long road to its completion. I am deeply indebted to my supervisors, Prof. Dr. Andreas Langenohl and Prof. Dr. Mitja Velikonja, who magnanimously shared their knowledge, experience and patience with me. A big thank you goes to all those who agreed to devote their valuable time to answering my questions and who helped me with the collection of sources and materials. I also wish to express my gratitude to all colleagues, friends, and acquaintances who in various ways contributed to this project. Finally, I am grateful to the International Graduate Centre for the Study of Culture and Justus Liebig University for having materially and institutionally sustained this project.

All errors, inadvertencies and omissions are nevertheless my own.

Introduction

> "Similar scenes are appearing from Sofia to Riga, and probably even more to the East, the classics of Marxism and local theoreticians are abandoning library shelves and offices or are being sold for pennies [...] Books and monuments, as the ideological furniture of the previous epoch, now have recycling or museums as options."[2]

These lines, written in December 1990 by the Croatian journalist Jasmina Kuzmanović, capture a common sight on the streets of many East European cities and towns following the first multiparty elections. A series of mostly peaceful revolutions, sometimes referred to as the "Autumn of Nations", brought an end to real existing socialism. Yugoslavia was in turmoil: the Albanians in Kosovo were on a general strike after the Parliament of Serbia had abolished the Parliament of Kosovo, the Croatian Serbs raised barricades and proclaimed their autonomy in Croatia, Slobodan Milošević called for a military action against Croatia, the proposal for a confederation put forward by Croatia and Slovenia was rejected ... In mid-October 1990 an article in *The Economist* saw a possible solution to the "Yugomess" in the split, or the creation of a North-Western province aptly called "Crovenia" (Croatia and Slovenia) and a larger, Southern region dubbed "Greater Serbia".[3] The events that followed have proven the prediction wrong; however, the presumed borders of "Crovenia" match today's external borders of the European Union. In fact, the former westernmost republics of Yugoslavia and later independent states continued to perform better economically and went through a swifter Euro-Atlantic integration process than their southern neighbors. Slovenia joined NATO and the EU in 2004, Croatia in 2009 and 2013 respectively, while their

---

2 Jasmina Kuzmanović. "Epoha na smetlištu" (Epoch on the Junkyard). *Danas*, December 4, 1990. My translation. All translations from Bosnian-Croatian-Serbian and Slovenian are my own unless otherwise indicated.
3 "Disintegration in the Balkans could be foretaste of things to come in the USSR". *The Economist*, vol. 317, n. 7676, October 13, 1990.

neighbors find themselves at different stages of the pre-accession process.[4]

The two countries followed slightly different transitory patterns after the dissolution of Yugoslavia, but both were characterized by a strong drive towards distancing themselves as much as possible from the Socialist Federal Republic and the Balkans, perceived as symbols of underdevelopment, periphery, and barbarism. In both Croatia and Slovenia, the delegitimization of socialism coincided with the delegitimization of the common state (Yugoslavia) and the "othering" of former compatriots (principally Serbs in Croatia and "Southerners"[5] in Slovenia) in the public sphere. How did Yugoslavia undergo the transformation from a socialist federation based on "brotherhood and unity" to a totalitarian "prison of nations"[6] in the collective *imaginarium* of "Crovenes"? This question is badly formulated for a number of reasons. Firstly, it implies a certain uniformity of the *imaginarium*, namely, that everyone believed what was publicly declared, and no discrepancy existed between dominant rhetoric and personal convictions. Similarly, it suggests that there was an agreement on what this entity that underwent the transformation was. Moreover, it is a general and broad question that labels the given change as a finished action, rather than a long-term, still ongoing process. Finally, it does not give any indication as to when the transformation could have occurred, nor does it contemplate the possibility of it occurring only temporarily, and being dismissed afterwards. Nevertheless, this badly formulated query is what implicitly guided me through the research process and writing of this book. In fact, I was hoping it

---

4 At the time of writing, all other Yugoslav successor states are EU candidate countries, except for Bosnia that submitted its application in mid-February 2016 and is still a potential candidate. Montenegro joined NATO in June 2017. Kosovo/Kosova continues to be a disputed territory and a partially recognized state.

5 It is interesting to note that the Other in Slovenia is a generalized, an abstract entity. For more insights on the topic see for instance Skrbiš (2017).

6 This syntagm was previously associated with the Austro-Hungarian Empire and certainly not the only reference to the latter. A.J.P. Taylor has in fact argued in 1948 that Tito was the "last Habsburg", argument that was later reused by other scholars such as Griffith (1964), Kuljić (2007) and Jović (2009).

would help me to find answers or, even more blatantly, to pose the right questions.

In the past twenty or more years, a lot of scholarly attention has been given to the causes of the breakup of Yugoslavia, the subsequent wars, and the Europeanization and democratization processes, but the underlying cultural transformation did not always receive an equally attentive scrutiny.[7] Together with new insights and approaches, novel studies advance different perspectives that are considerably conditioned by the historical moment they are conducted in. Today the Yugoslav past is no longer confronted with an uncertain, undoubtedly bright future ahead, but with almost thirty years of post-Yugoslav (crony) capitalism and political corruption. In other words, dealing with the past necessarily implies dealing with the present that is increasingly looking into the transnational past for alternatives.[8] Three decades after the end of state-socialism in Europe, despite the nominal incompleteness of transition[9], former socialist countries are entirely integrated into the capitalist world in a semi-peripheral role, and their impoverished citizens feel excluded from the decision-making process (Horvat and Štiks 2015, n.p.). As it becomes clear that promises for a better future have been broken, the past and all that has been rejected in the name of bright prospects start regaining currency. Mitja Velikonja wrote in a recent text that the Yugoslav successor states went through a phase of negation and demonization of all ties with Yugoslavia (period of ex- or former Yugoslavia), through the rebuilding of certain, particularly informal connections (Yugosphere) to a period of consumerist, pop-cultural depictions of the socialist federation (post-Yugoslavia) (Velikonja 2017, 11–12). In the past couple

---

7   On the idea of a Yugoslav nation and its failure see Wachtel (1998).
8   See for instance Petrović (2014).
9   A disquisition about the beginning, development and end of postsocialist transition goes beyond the scope of this introduction. Suffice it to mention that Thomas Carothers declared "the end of the transition paradigm" in a paper of that title published in 2002. There he wrote that "what is often thought of as an uneasy, precarious middle ground between full-fledged democracy and outright dictatorship is actually the most common political condition today of countries in the developing world and the postcommunist world" (18). Horvat and Štiks (2015) argue that extending transition has the purpose of reaffirming the need for tutelage of these countries and avoiding facing its consequences.

of years, the term "post-Yugoslavia" asserted itself in academic circles and in the works of authors examining current cultural practices in the region and their potential in dealing with the often-stigmatized socialist past. Starting with *After Yugoslavia: The Cultural Spaces of a Vanished Land* (Gorup ed., 2013), the field was enriched by contributions such as *Post-Yugoslavia: New Cultural and Political Perspectives* (Abazović and Velikonja eds., 2014) and *Post-Yugoslav Constellations: Archive, Memory, and Trauma in Contemporary Bosnian, Croatian, and Serbian Literature and Culture* (Beronja and Vervaet eds., 2016). The "attractiveness" of the term is given by its spatial (Yugoslavia) and temporal (post) meaning and the relation with Yugoslavia the "post" implies: both a break from socialist Yugoslavia and continuity with its legacy (Beronja and Vervaet 2016, 5) that is still present, despite the attempts at ethno-nationalization the region underwent in the past three decades. If break and continuity were two extremes in relation to Yugoslavia, where would the region find itself today? More "spice" to this rhetorical question could be added with Stuart Hall's interpretation of the "post" as "anti", which is how the author defines the initial phase of postcolonial politics. Quoting Hall, Zsuzsa Gille writes that "in the first stage of postcolonial politics, the *post* is primarily synonymous with *anti*, valorising the *other* side of the coloniser/colonised dichothomy" (Gille 2010, 28). More specifically, what are the frames within which, to use Sharon Macdonald's term, the Yugoslav past is "negotiated"? Macdonald calls the process of dealing with a difficult heritage "negotiating", which implies both a physical (material) and a discursive practice. "Negotiating is a more active process in which spaces, identifications, alignments and even objects are positioned and given recognition" (Macdonald 2009, 19). The prevalent model in public discourse perpetuated by the political elites is to suppress the Yugoslav past or to present it in a negative way, while private reminiscences tend to differ greatly, ranging from exaltation to demonization. Public statements about the past and personal memories tell as much about the present moment and the political convictions of the person as they do about the past. The material traces of bygone times are in some ways more difficult to conceal, but even that is a double-sided coin: while five-pointed stars and monuments might be easy to remove and the renaming of streets might be regarded as just a formality, the Yugoslav legacy is also reflected in architecture, urbanscapes and infrastructure.

The removal of what Kuzmanović defines as "ideological furniture" in Eastern Europe after 1989 meant a (material) break with the past. However, does removal necessarily imply forgetting, also considering that many of these objects were relocated and as such they did not disappear completely? In her book about difficult legacy Susan Macdonald writes that "substantiating [history] through material culture [is] the dominant mode of performing identity-legitimacy" (2009, 2). In this respect it could be argued that removal and/or relocation corresponds to delegitimization, while memorialization happens at a second level, through the (re)negotiation of frames within which certain discussions take place. As Victor Buchli and Gavin Lucas write in their *Archaeologies of the Contemporary Past*,

> "it is not just that memorials commemorate and iconoclasm causes forgetfulness; the relation between remembrance and forgetfulness is not a linear process but a struggle, a tension—in every memorial, something has been left out or forgotten, in every removal, something is left behind, remembered" (Buchli and Lucas 2001, 80).

It is precisely this entanglement between continuity and discontinuity, memory and forgetting, presence and absence that provided background for my research. I set myself the task of examining the modalities of removal of "socialist" and "Yugoslav"[10] books from public libraries in Croatia and Slovenia after the dissolution of Yugoslavia and the sociopolitical implications thereof. In other words, I was curious about the extent to which this was another way of "legitimizing identity" and "othering" the rest of Yugoslavia, or if it was "just" a de-ideologization (as the librarian Dragutin

---

10 I am using quotation marks here because it is not entirely clear what exactly a Yugoslav or a Serbian or a socialist book is. Is the content of the book that matters, the language/dialect/pronunciation or the script in which it is written, or the ethnic and ideological background of the author? All these terms, together with the more generic "unsuitable" were used in the public discussion about the occurrence in Croatia.

Katalenac once classified it)[11] of library collections to be treated in a "business as usual" fashion. Furthermore, considering that discarded books in many cases continued circulating, I decided to analyze two books in particular, and "the discarded" in general, using the children's book *The Hedgehog's Home*, the experimental documentary *In War and Revolution* by Ana Bilankov, and the exhibition -action "Discarded. On the occasion of the 20th anniversary of operation Storm". It was clear right from the start that this was going to be rather asymmetric research, considering that the "cleansing" of libraries or "libricide" became a topic in Croatia after a couple of unprofessionally executed weeding instances became publicly known in the 1990s, while in Slovenia the accounts of the disappearance of books could be counted on the fingers of one hand. When, in the late summer of 1997, the acting director of the library "Ivan Vidali" in Korčula threw a number of books into a nearby trash can, the debate about the weeding of library collections in Croatia spilled over from professional circles to the public sphere and received considerable media coverage. The discussion soon polarized between those defining the removal of "socialist" and "Yugoslav" books as something normal and necessary and those that called it a "libricide/bookicide" and compared it with the Nazi book burnings, with an ever-decreasing involvement of professional librarians in the argument.

A decisive contribution to the debate came from one of its initial participants, Ante Lešaja, a retired economics professor and amateur librarian from Korčula. In 2012 Lešaja published his voluminous book *Libricide. The Destruction of Books in the 1990s in Croatia (Knjigocid. Uništavanje knjiga u Hrvatskoj 1990-ih)*. The daily newspaper *Jutarnji list* greeted the publication of Lešaja's book with this sensational headline: "In the 1990s 2.8 million 'unsuitable' books were destroyed in Croatia".[12] What Lešaja (280) actually writes, however, is that 2.8 million is the estimated number by which the

---

11 See Katalenac (1994).
12 Adriana Piteša, "Lešaja: Devedesetih smo uništili 2,8 mil. 'nepoćudnih' knjiga". *Jutarnji list*, July 13, 2012, https://www.jutarnji.hr/kultura/knjizevnost/lesaja-devedesetih-smo-unistili-28-mil.-%E2%80%98nepocudnih%E2%80%99-knjiga/1540434/. Last accessed on April 18, 2019.

collections in Croatian public, special, school and general scientific libraries shrank (the exceptions are the National and University Library—NSK, university and academic libraries), with the biggest oscillations recorded in the period 1990–1995. By comparing the total number of books registered in the various types of libraries every three years by the Croatian Bureau of Statistics *(Državni zavod za statistiku)*, the retired economics professor established that the biggest reduction in the size of the collections happened in school libraries (55 percent of the total), while that observed in public libraries amounted to 2.4 percent. Only from the year 1998 did libraries register a constant increase in the number of registered volumes. These numbers are estimates because the data about discarding is not available at the National and University Library (central libraries started systematically collecting this data, which are then compiled on a national level at the NSK, from the year 2000).[13] According to the author, the recorded oscillations are most likely the result of the "cleansing of libraries", which confirms that the writings in the press about the occurrence were not "mere phantasms". What this statistical verification does not provide, however, is the type of books that were discarded from libraries. The removal of books — often without respecting professional weeding guidelines, argues Lešaja — was made possible by the cultural climate in the 1990s, characterized by "exclusionism" *(isključivost)*, which was nothing but an expression of the fundamental social conflict, a change in the economic system that allowed a very limited number of people to grow rich at the expense of a much wider population. It was a period marked by anomie, the absence of social norms and dysfunctional institutions, which promotes deviant behavior (Lešaja 2012, 417). Such exclusionism was directed at Yugoslavia, socialism, the National Liberation War and anti-fascism, the Serbs, the working class and, finally, those who disagreed with the existing policies (502). The expressions that Lešaja uses to denote the phenomenon

---

13 This is regulated by the Regulation on the bibliographic activity of libraries in the Republic of Croatia *(Pravilnik o matičnoj djelatnosti knjižnica u Republici Hrvatskoj)* (NN 43/2001). On pages 273-274 of his book Lešaja mentions that he got the data for 2000, 2001 and 2002, but the tables did not contain any information about discarding.

are "libricide" and "destruction". "Libricide" was first used by the political weekly *Feral Tribune* in their articles about the librarian from Korčula who threw a number of books into the waste bin (the so-called "Korčula case"). "Destruction" is employed as an umbrella term comprising

> "all handling of library collections—that is, books—that led to their destruction, regardless if it consisted of 'throwing books into the trash bin', 'sending them to paper recycling facilities', 'throwing books onto the streets', 'leaving them on the porch', 'burning' etc. and regardless of the formal explanations given for the destruction of a particular collection such as 'outdatedeness', 'uselessness', 'unfitness', 'redundancy' etc., because generally standard library practices and rules were not respected in the process, and if they were, they were most often used to justify the removal of 'unnecessary' and 'unsuitable' books" (23).

Syntagms like "the burning of books" or "the destruction of libraries" are now to be found in on- and offline publications and they belong to the standard "repertoire" of attacks against cultural heritage during and after the dissolution of Yugoslavia. However, even a quick web search reveals that there is no consensus on what is meant by these expressions and how they should be interpreted. For instance, a Wikipedia page on "bookicide in Croatia" was until recently available in English and Serbian language.[14] The entry was unequivocally inspired by Lešaja's book, and it does not feature a Croatian version. What can still be found is a Croatian site titled "book burning" *(spaljivanje knjiga)* with a section on "book burning as a result of the Greater-Serbian aggression" *(spaljivanje knjiga kao dio velikosrpske agresije)* where it is stated, among other things, that "Croatian books were burned back in Yugoslavia when the novels of unsuitable writers and unwanted authors of orthography books

---

14 "Bookocide in Croatia". https://web.archive.org/web/20190328152312/https: //en.wikipedia.org/wiki/Bookocide_in_Croatia. Last accessed on April 2, 2019. Update September 2021: the said web page is no longer available except in archived versions. Update November 2021: the following two pages can be found online: https://en.everybodywiki.com/Destruction_of_books_in_post-independence_Croatia and https://sr.wikipedia.org/wiki/Fenomen_uni%C5 %A1tavanja_knjiga_u_Hrvatskoj_1990-tih. I wish to thank my anonymous reviewer for drawing my attention to these websites.

Introduction   27

were destroyed".[15] What is more, the term "destruction" (sometimes in combination with "culturecide", "ethnocide" and "libricide")[16] was used in the media to denote the demolition of cultural heritage during the wars in Bosnia and Herzegovina and Croatia, but this is also the term used in professional weeding manuals addressing the issue of the disposal of discarded books: "destruction should be used for materials in the worst physical condition, the absolutely hopeless cases, and then only as a last resort if the books cannot be recycled or sold for pulp" (Larson 2012, 86). Ante Lešaja employs the same term to describe all actions that for whatever reason ultimately led to the destruction of books, from throwing them into the garbage to burning them. He writes that what inspired him to apply the term "destruction" to what was happening with books in the 1990s was the press reaction in October 1991 to how books were handled in the publishing house Logos in Split. Instead of donating them to libraries or selling them at discounted prices, the responsible people in the publishing house decided to send excess books to a paper recycling center (Lešaja 2012, 161–162). One more example that was quoted in newspaper articles[17] is that 40,000 copies of the *Encyclopedia of Yugoslavia (Enciklopedija Jugoslavije)*, a project ideated and edited by the writer Miroslav Krleža[18], were sent for recycling. The Director of the Institute of Lexicography, Dalibor Brozović, stated, however, that it was done for business and economic reasons, such as the lack of space in the storage room (233). The publishing sector, on the other hand, obeys a different logic from that of libraries, which are a public service. Unlike other Eastern European countries, after the split with the Soviet Union in 1948 Yugoslavia developed a decentralized, market-based and competitive book publishing system. Publishing in socialist Yugoslavia

---

15 "Spaljivanje knjiga" (Book burning). https://hr.wikipedia.org/wiki/Spaljiva nje_knjiga. Last accessed on April 2, 2019.
16 See, for instance, Branka Džebić. "Otpor librocidu". *Vjesnik*, October 16, 1991.
17 See Milan Kangrga, "Hrvatski knjigocid. Barbarizam i renesansa" (Croatian libricide. Barbarism and renaissance). *Feral Tribune*, March 30, 1998. Lešaja (2012) mentions that this was first exposed publicly in 1995 by Svetozar Livada (166).
18 For an analysis of the circumstances that led to the foundation of the Institute of Lexicography of Yugoslavia (today the Miroslav Krleža Institute of Lexicography) and its main project see Roksandić (2015).

enjoyed state subsidies, large print runs, low retail prices and accessibility by the population. The disintegration of the common Yugoslav market and the transition to market economy led to a decrease of state subsidies, lower print runs, higher sale prices, a drop in demand and literature's loss of social status due to the imperative to survive in market conditions by searching for business opportunities.[19] Apart from use of the terms "libricide" and "destruction", the press sometimes resorted to the term "book burning" when reporting about cases of actual burning—such as the one in Velika Gorica, where the librarian of the Nikola Hribar Elementary school allegedly ordered the incineration of 400 books in the school furnace[20]—but also metaphorically, when talking about the "Korčula case" where books were trashed. For Lešaja, this is irrelevant, because if books end up in the dump, they are either incinerated or levelled by bulldozers. To recapitulate, various words have been used to designate the discarding of books from libraries in Croatia in the 1990s: in the media outlets that reported about it (such as *Feral Tribune*, *Zarez* or *Novi list*), the discarding of books from libraries was referred to as "destruction" *(uništavanje)*, "burning" *(paljenje)*, "bookicide" *(knjigocid)*, "bibliocide" *(bibliocid)*, "libricide" *(libricid)* or, more broadly, "culturecide" *(kulturocid)*. These are also the terms that Lešaja uses in his book. Another concept that sometimes appears in connection with the phenomenon is "cleansing" *(čišćenje)*, a word that featured prominently in the (political) vocabulary of the 1990s. As Dubravka Ugrešić wrote in her 1992 essay *Čisti hrvatski zrak* (Clean Croatian Air)[21], "the newly established value system was based on the clean-dirty dichotomy" (Ugrešić 1999, 74): cans of *clean Croatian air* were sold on the streets

---

19 For an overview of publishing in the Yugoslav successor states (except Croatia) in the period 1990–2000 see Biggins (2000).
20 As reported in the special edition of "Prosvjeta" dedicated to "libricide" (2005). Reports differ on whether the burning took place in front of the pupils (as it is claimed on page 9 of the special issue) or not.
21 First published in German as *Saubere kroatische Luft* on October 23, 1992, in *Die Zeit*, followed by the English version "The Dirty Tirany of Mr. Clean" on December 5th of the same year. The Croatian text was later published in the collection of essays *Kultura laži* (Culture of Lies) in 1996. On May 30, 2015, the text reappeared on Peščanik.online: http://pescanik.net/esej-koji-putuje-vec-pun e-23-godine/. Last accessed on June 4, 2015.

of Zagreb, (national) hygiene was on the lips of prominent politicians, who in pure Croatian language boasted their pure Croatian blood and expressed their happiness for having clean, non-Serbian and non-Jewish-wives.[22] An even grimmer association is with the term "ethnic cleansing" that accompanied the wars of Yugoslav succession. Some of the abovementioned concepts are symbolically and historically "loaded" since they have been used to denote publicized acts of violent book destruction throughout history, from Alexandria to present-day Iraq, and often allude to another word. For instance, "libricide" (and its synonyms, bibliocide or bookicide) echoes genocide, while "biblioclasm" implies the destruction of books, in particular the Bible.

For the purposes of this volume, which focuses on the removal of books from public libraries, I find the words "removal" and "discarding" (including its synonyms) as most appropriate. The latter term is particularly "convenient" in English because it stands for the standard library practice through which materials are removed from a certain collection, but to "discard" in general means "to get rid of as useless or unwanted"[23], even if it is etymologically related to cards, indicating the act of removing a playing card from a player's hand. And what is discarding for a librarian? Often called discarding, deaccession, reverse selection, deselection, pruning, retirement and relegation,[24] weeding consists in removing books and other materials from a library collection to another location that can range from a larger library to a storage site or a book sale (Doll and Barron 2002, 59). Even if they are sometimes used interchangeably, weeding and discarding are not synonyms since weeding can also

---

22 The reference here is to a well-known statement by Franjo Tuđman at a preelectoral gathering of the Croatian Democratic Union (HDZ- *Hrvatska demokratska zajednica*) in April 1990. In her essay, Ugrešić also cites the intellectual V.G., who once stated he liked "clean" women and of another public figure, who declared it was "common knowledge that for 300 years there was no byzantine blood in his/her family" (Ugrešić 1996, 74).
23 I am using the definition from the Merriam-Webster online dictionary: https://www.merriam-webster.com/dictionary/discard. Last accessed on March 27, 2019.
24 Since these are mostly terms with a negative connotation, there is a tendency to use more proactive expressions such as collection renewal or collection revaluation.

involve storing, i.e., keeping the material at a second level of access usually not open to the public. Put differently, when a book is weeded, it is still property of the library; when it is discarded it no longer belongs to it. There are five basic ways to dispose of discarded materials: selling, donating, trading, recycling, and destroying by incineration or by throwing them into the trash (Larson 2012, 83–86). Professional manuals encourage librarians to use the latter method only as a last resort because it can create the "weeding controversy" since people are shocked by the "waste" of throwing "good books" on the trash heap (86). In other words, it can happen that, even if the process is carried out in full respect of professional standards, non-librarians who are rarely familiar with standard library procedures and are unaware that even libraries must discard from time to time, will interpret this as "destruction of valuable books". However, what is valuable for the reader does not have to be equally valuable for the librarian, let alone for the library accountant. Another important point is that not all books that are "destroyed" are actually destroyed: often they are picked up by a user and end up enriching a private library. One could argue that the period in which books were massively discarded from Croatian libraries was a great opportunity for bibliophiles and readers in general because they could get not-too-worn-out books for free. For instance, some of the library users I had informal conversations with remember that if they were borrowing certain books in the early 1990s the librarians would tell them that they do not have to give them back. Nevertheless, what matters here is the context: if reviews of library collections, with massive discarding as a result, happen repeatedly over a short period of time—a period in which monuments are blown up and people forcefully evicted from their homes or children killed because of their nationality—it is highly unlikely that the citizens misunderstood the reasons why books were found on the streets, in paper bins, etc. In the early 1990s a number of people, mostly of Serbian ethnicity, were forcefully evicted by the Croatian Army, the military police or unidentified people wearing uniforms from apartments that had been allocated to them by the Yugoslav People's Army in socialist Yugoslavia. Despite the protests of local human rights groups, no legal protection

Introduction   31

was given to the tenants.²⁵ The murder of a twelve-year-old girl of Serbian ethnicity, Aleksandra Zec, and her parents, committed by five Croatian militiamen in December 1991 in Zagreb, equally resulted in controversial trials, acquittals and retrials of the perpetrators, who were later given prison sentences for different crimes. In 2004 the Croatian state paid compensation to the surviving two members of the family.

A couple of cases of "murky" discarding conducted by librarians or library employees in Croatia were featured in the media as they were happening, but the one that probably attracted most (media) attention was the so-called "Korčula case". In the summer of 1997, the acting director of the "Ivan Vidali" library in Korčula dumped a number of books²⁶, which the locals found in the bin. A couple of months later the weekly *Feral Tribune* published a reaction to the act by the renowned philosopher Milan Kangrga; both the weekly and Kangrga were later sued for defamation by the librarian responsible for the trashing, Izabel Skokandić.²⁷ The first more systematic analysis of this and other cases was published in the form of a special issue of *Prosvjeta*, the monthly magazine of the Serbian National Council *(Srpsko narodno vijeće)*, titled "Bibliocide-Culturecide: Where One Burns Books, One Will Soon Burn People" in Serbo-Croatian (2003) and English (2005). The special issue of *Prosvjeta* and Lešaja's study will be closely examined further on as

---

25 Human Rights Watch has written about it extensively in its 1995 report on Civil and Political Rights in Croatia, which can be read in its entirety here: https://www.hrw.org/legacy/reports/1995/Croatia.htm. Last accessed on March 7, 2019.
26 The exact number is unknown, as are the titles of these books. Based on the estimation of a resident who took 42 books from the bin, in total there were around 120-150 volumes. In the press, the numbers 150 and 500 were most commonly cited, presumably because the two lists compiled by the responsible librarian, Izabel Skokandić, contain respectively 157 and 400 titles. Ante Lešaja, however, warns that 12 of the 42 books taken from the trash can do not even appear on any of the two lists (Lešaja 2012, 341-343). For a more detailed examination of the case, see Lešaja (2012), 328-355.
27 Kangrga was first found guilty, but the lawsuit against him was finally dismissed in 2002. For a detailed chronology of the process, see also *Kulturocid. Sudski process protiv Milana Kangrge*, (Culturecide. The Court Case against Milan Kangrga), a text by Lešaja published in *Republika*, n. 490-491, 2010.

the only two contributions to the investigation of the fate of books in areas not directly affected by the armed conflict.[28]

The war-related destruction and burning of libraries, archives, churches, and cultural heritage in general in former Yugoslavia has been relatively well documented. In the midst of war, the National and University Library *(Nacionalna i sveučilišna knjižnica* — NSK) in Zagreb published Hrvatske knjižnice na meti: Vodič (Croatian Libraries on target: A Guide), a compendium of approximately 150 destroyed libraries in the besieged regions of Croatia in 1991-1992. A year later, in 1993, the Croatian Library Association *(Hrvatsko knjižničarsko društvo* — HKD) published a similar account, *Wounded Libraries in Croatia*. These two publications provide real-time data about the destruction of Croatian libraries during the War of Independence (1991-1995) and are principally aimed at attracting international donors to reconstruct the library network in the country. However, the lack of coordination between the two (it is unclear, above all, why both the University Library and the Croatian Library Association undertook the same task within a period of one year), the inconsistency and intransparency in presenting and interpreting the collected data, and the use of emotional language cast doubts on their objectivity (Dalbello-Lovrić 1993, 290-294). Considering the circumstances in which they were written, it was to be expected that they would be followed by a more complete compendium after the war ended, which was, however, not the case.[29] Destroyed Bosnian and Croatian libraries and archives are also listed in a document compiled on behalf of the United Nations Educational, Scientific and Cultural Organization (UNESCO) in 1996, *Memory of the World: Lost Memory — Libraries and Archives Destroyed in the Twentieth Century*, which enumerates the libraries and archives destroyed and severely damaged in the course of the

---

28   The following literature review has been partially published in Komnenović, D. (2018). *The "Cleansing" of Croatian Libraries in the 1990s and Beyond or How (Not) to Discard the Yugoslav Past*, in Bevernage, B. and Wouters, N. (eds.), "The Palgrave Handbook of State-Sponsored History After 1945", London: Palgrave Macmillan.

29   Ante Lešaja (2012) likewise mentions this point in his elaborate critique of the two publications on pp. 78-82 of his book.

Introduction 33

twentieth century. In 1998 Nensi Brailo wrote her master's thesis on the destruction of Croatian libraries during the 1991–1995 conflict and the role that UNESCO and other international organizations and programs have in the protection of cultural heritage at times of war.[30] Furthermore, András Riedlmayer has written a number of articles and reports on what a Council of Europe paper[31] has called "cultural cleansing" during the war in former Yugoslavia and its aftermath. He has served as an expert witness before the International Criminal Tribunal for Former Yugoslavia (ICTY) and the International Court of Justice (ICJ). Among the tasks that the ICTY undertook were in fact the investigation and processing of crimes against cultural and religious property during the Yugoslav wars.[32] Miriam Valencia also mentions the Bosnian conflict in her paper on "Libraries, Nationalism and Armed Conflict in the Twentieth Century". In Rebecca Knuth's *Libricide: The Regime-Sponsored Destruction of Books and Libraries in the Twentieth Century,* there is a chapter devoted to Greater Serbia and the wartime destruction of mostly Bosnian-Herzegovinian cultural heritage. In another of her books, *Burning Books and Leveling Libraries: Extremist Violence and Cultural Destruction,* the author resumes her rather simplistic depiction of the conflict in Bosnia and Herzegovina. The list could go on with Fernando Báez's *A Universal History of the Destruction of Books: From Ancient Sumer to Modern-Day Iraq* or Lucien Polastron's *Books on Fire: The Destruction of Libraries throughout History,* and probably many more.[33] Considering their large geographical and temporal

---

30 I wish to thank Florian Bieber for bringing this MA thesis to my attention.
31 "War damage to the cultural heritage in Croatia and Bosnia and Herzegovina presented by the Committee on Culture and Education", doc. 6869, Strasbourg: Council of Europe, Parliamentary Assembly, July 17, 1993.
32 A detailed overview of the ICTY's activities in that field can be found on the website "Targeting history and Memory. The ICTY and the investigation, reconstruction and prosecution of the crimes against cultural and religious heritage": http://www.heritage.sense-agency.com/. This is also where some of Riedlmayer's reports can be read. Last accessed on April 2, 2019.
33 The list could, for instance, include documentary films such as The Destruction of Memory (2016) by Tim Slade or Sam Hobkinson's The Love of Books: A Sarajevo Story (2011) on how rare manuscripts and books from the Gazi Husrev Beg library were saved during the siege of Sarajevo. The aim of this literature review is not exhaustivity, but rather to point to the multiplicity of resources.

scope, these works are not distinguished by a sharp analytical approach to the former Yugoslav area, which constitutes only one of the many cited instances of book destruction. Finally, I shall also mention a documentary film by Branko Lazić, *Biti ili ne, Ivan Hiti* (To be or not to be, Ivan Hiti).[34] The film tells the story of a soldier in the Croatian Army, Ivan Hiti, who in 1992 disregarded the command of his superiors to burn the oldest and largest Serbian Orthodox Church Library in Pakrac. Instead of destroying them, Hiti dispatched the books to the National and University Library in Zagreb, which is why he was discharged from the Army, lost his job as a teacher, and struggled for years to find a new occupation. The film not only tells the story of a single man, who was subjected to insults and ostracized from the community for having saved Serbian books, but it also implies that the destruction of cultural heritage was a policy, and not a "collateral damage" in the war, perpetrated not only by the "Serbian-Chetnik aggressors", but by all sides involved in the conflict. Ivan Hiti was decorated for his act by the Serbian Patriarch Irinej and the Croatian President Ivo Josipović in 2013. To sum up, the demolition of cultural heritage in former Yugoslavia and its most powerful symbol, the burning of the National and University Library in Sarajevo, have secured themselves a permanent presence in the accounts on the phenomenon, which was described very early on with words like "culturecide" or "urbicide".

Apart from the destruction of cultural heritage in war-torn areas, the former-Yugoslav region, and Croatia in particular, sadly became known for the deliberate destruction of partisan monuments, which went from being "a symbol of victory over fascism [...] to a symbol of failed communist dictatorship" (Cipek 2009, cited in Radonić 2012, n.p.).[35] Many of these monuments were

---

For a brief summary of the available literature on on the destruction of cultural heritage during the war in Bosnia and Herzegovina see Lešaja (2012), p. 137.
34   I wish to thank Ante Lešaja for directing my attention to the film.
35   Between 1945 and 1990 approximately 6000 monuments were erected in cities and villages throughout Croatia. In the 1990s "2964 have been demolished, damaged or removed, out of which 731 are monuments and other memorials of high artistic and cultural-historical value" (Hrženjak 2002, xii).

Introduction   35

prime examples of Yugoslav modernist architecture and had a high artistic value. The damaging, dynamiting, graffitiing and neglect of the "spomeniks"[36] have therefore been the object of several scholarly studies, documentary films, exhibitions, and other projects. Suffice it to mention the volume *Rušenje antifašističkih spomenika u Hrvatskoj 1990–2000* (The Demolition of Antifascist Monuments in Croatia 1990–2000), published in 2002 by the Association of Antifascist Fighters of Croatia *(Savez antifašističkih boraca Hrvatske)*, or the documentary films *Udar na sjećanje/Damnatio Memoriae* (The Attack on Memory/Damnatio Memoriae, 2001) by Bogdan Žižić or Irena Škorić's *Neželjena baština* (Unwanted Heritage, 2016). The exhibition "Heroes we Love. Socialist Realism Revisited" *(Naši heroji. Socialistični realizem revidiran)* shown at the Maribor Art Gallery *(Umetnostna galerija Maribor* – UGM) between March and August 2015 also displayed examples (and pieces) of demolished partisan monuments. Nevertheless, one of the first attempts of sensitizing the public to the problem was Siniša Labrović's performance "Bandaging the Wounded" *(Previjanje ranjenika)* on June 22, 2000, in Sinj. On the Day of Antifascist Struggle (celebrated on June 22 in Croatia), the artist filmed himself bandaging the "wounded" monument of a partisan woman holding a wounded soldier that was destroyed in the 1990s.

Now that terminological overlaps have been cleared and an overview of the available literature has been provided, I wish to dwell upon the contents of this volume. Even if it predominantly focuses on Croatia and Slovenia (albeit in an asymmetric way), this research, like all (scholarly) endeavors even vaguely touching upon the topic of Yugoslav disintegration, has to take into consideration the entire *Yugo-Atlantic-grupa*-sphere.[37] Despite the flourishing

---

36 I am borrowing the Anglicized plural of the noun *spomenik* (=monument in Bosnian-Croatian-Serbian) from Donald Nyebil, the creator of the Spomenik Database, a self-funded project conceived as an online database on modernist, abstract monuments built in Yugoslavia in the period 1960–1990. To access the database: https://www.spomenikdatabase.org/. Last accessed on March 6, 2019.

37 In a 2012 interview with Igor Štiks, Tim Judah, the coiner of the term Yugosphere, explained that "the most successful practitioner" of the term is the leading Croatian company in the region, Atlantic Grupa. In fact, it is mostly

commercial ties strengthened by multinational companies such as Atlantic Grupa, the political will to deal with the legacy of the 1990s wars is still lacking in the former Yugoslav region and is limited to the formal satisfaction of EU pre-accession criteria. In most cases the elites are actually drawing their legitimacy from nationalist discourses established in that period, which are used as an interpretative lens for the narration of the history of the whole 20th century. These narratives all have a common denominator — victimization. In the Croatian case, the victimization discourse is complemented by the victory myth: a non-negligible part of the population considers the 1990s a time of "pride and glory" when the Serbian aggressor was defeated and uses it as a legitimizing factor for one's adhesion to the national cause (exemplified by the by now proverbial question, "Where were you in 1991?").[38] The search for sources of legitimacy does not, however, stop in the 1990s, but instead goes back to the 1940s, to the Middle Ages and even to the 7th century, following one pattern: The more pressing the current economic problems are, the more assiduous is the search for historical traces and more fantastic are its results. The political and cultural climate in former Yugoslavia and in Eastern Europe in general after 1989 will thus be the objects of Chapter One. Although Yugoslavia is often approached as a special case due to its political and institutional peculiarities, it did not exist and dissolve in a vacuum. The broader context of postsocialist transition, in fact, must be taken into consideration in order to underscore that neither the discarding of books nor the postsocialist condition are a (former) Yugoslav idiosyncrasy. From Eastern Europe the focus then narrows to the most

---

Croats who prefer using the term Adriatic or Adria instead of Yugosphere: http://www.citsee.eu/interview/citizens-'yugosphere'-and-'united-kingdom s'-interview-tim-judah. Last accessed on November 25, 2014.

38 I have written about it in more detail in Komnenović, D. (2017). The 1990s: A Decade that Never Ended?, *Der Donauraum*, 1-2/2014, IDM, Vienna. Other sources that can be consulted are a series of TV interviews with public figures conducted by the journalist Aleksandar Trifunović *Vraćaju li se devedesete?* (Are the 1990s coming back?), which can be watched online (in BCS) at http://www.6yka.com/, or a text by Dežulović, B. "Gdje ste bili devedeset prve?" (Where were you in 1991?). *Globus*, September 24, 2014. Retrieved from http://www.6yka.com on November 25, 2014.

Introduction 37

important changes that Croatia and Slovenia underwent during and after the dissolution of Yugoslavia and that might be relevant for the analysis of book discarding, such as the political and cultural reorientation towards Europe and language policies. What this examination shows is that these transformations were gradual rather than abrupt, and their origins are to be traced a couple of decades prior to the breakup of the country. Moreover, it calls for a certain caution among researchers when not distinguishing between discussions happening inside particular circles, fields, and professions, and those that are taken over by the media and involve the larger public.

This is also a common thread that can be found in Chapter Two, which provides a more nuanced examination of the practice of discarding in public libraries. In fact, discarding and books have a slightly different meaning for librarians who work with them and for bibliophiles (categories which obviously do not exclude each other, as librarians can be bibliophiles, too). In this chapter, first my methodological approach is outlined, mostly consisting of a close reading of the data obtained at the Research and Education Centre *(Bibliotekarski raziskovalni, izobraževalni in informacijski center)* of the National and University Library *(Narodna in univerzitetna knjižnica)* in Ljubljana and newspaper articles and semi-structured interviews with librarians, used book dealers and other professionals from the book industry, as well as journalists involved in the "libricide" debate. First, the development of the media discussion on "libricide" in Croatia is traced, followed by an analysis of the data from Slovenia. A comparison between the available data on discarding, librarian's views, and public perceptions of the occurrence reveals that many of the accusations, mystifications, and misunderstandings come from a lack of communication between libraries and their patrons.

An example of how to improve communication, in particular with regard to discarding, is given in Chapter Three. It is with this chapter that the focus slowly switches from libraries to books as objects and to the category of discarded books in particular, whose useful lives do not end once they abandon the shelves of a library. Departing from Michael Thompson's *Rubbish Theory: The Creation and Destruction of Value*, in which he writes that "in order to study the attribution of value in a society, there has to be rubbish" (Thompson 1979, 10), I argue that "the discarded" came to form a category on their own and as such they have a potential in triggering a critical examination of the recent past. The inspiration came from the exhibition-action "Discarded. On the occasion of the 20th anniversary of Operation 'Storm'" *(Otpisane, povodom 20. godišnjice Oluje)*, launched by the non-profit organization Multimedia Institute *(Multimedijalni institut MI2)* in cooperation with the curatorial collective What, How and for Whom (WHW) in June–July 2015 in Zagreb. By asking visitors to bring books discarded in the 1990s, which were exhibited in Gallery Nova and later scanned and uploaded on a website, the organizers wished to promote free access to information and knowledge, but also to direct people's attention to the logic that led to the killing of people twenty years earlier. Apart from analyzing the exhibition and the accompanying performances, I reconstruct the vicissitudes of the most popular discarded book, *The Hedgehog's Home*, and examine the experimental documentary *In War and Revolution* (2011) by Ana Bilankov, in which the author also follows the fate of one book, *School in War and Revolution*.

While I was working on this project, a couple of events that happened in different Eastern European cities showed the amount of politicization and violence to which printed books can be subject, even in the highly informatized 21st century characterized by dropping levels of (literary) reading. For instance, in March 2019 the news spread online, corroborated by a photo, that Catholic priests in northern Poland were inciting believers to burn books and other items allegedly connected with magic and the occult. As part of "spring cleaning", three priests were reading from the Bible while burning Harry Potter books, the Twilight novels, and a "Hello Kitty" umbrella, among others.[39] In February 2018 a bizarre incident occurred in Kašteli, close to Split in Croatia, where the

---

39 "Catholic priests burn 'sacrilegious' Harry Potter books and Twilight novels in Poland. *Mail online*, April 1, 2019. I wish to thank Magda Dolińska-Rydzek, Irena Komnenović, Mitja Velikonja and Igor Zemljič for directing my attention to the occurrence.

Introduction 39

organizers of the local Children's Carnival burned a panel representing the LGBT picture book *Moja dugina obitelj* (My Rainbow Family), as part of the traditional burning of the *Fašnik*. The *Fašnik* or *Krnjo* is usually a dummy that is symbolically responsible for everything bad that happened in the previous year and is thus burned at the end of the carnival. Burning a picture book about same-sex families in front of children by hijacking a popular tradition equals an (implicit) call for violence towards the LGBT community and their families, but also an invitation to children to hide and/or to repress their sexual identity. Following the incident, the associations "Zagreb Pride", "LORI", "Dugine obitelji" and "RODA — Roditelji u akciji" filed law suits against the organizer of the carnival, the association "Poklade".[40] The picture book is directed at preschool children and aimed at "strengthening the integration of children raised by same sex couples, the promotion of tolerance and respect towards diversity".[41] It was first presented in Zagreb in January 2018, to which the conservative "Vigilare association" reacted with a letter to the Croatian Minister of Science and Education, Blaženka Divjak, asking her whether she would allow the distribution of the said picture book to kindergartens and schools.[42] Similarly, after the book was presented in Belgrade in late April, the Serbian Minister without portfolio in charge of innovation and technological development, Nenad Popović, promptly reacted by stating on his Twitter page that "the importation of gay picture books from Croatia should be stopped immediately".[43] The

---

40 "Zagreb Pride, Lori, Dugine obitelji i Roda kazneno prijavili organizatora karnevala" (Zagreb Pride, Lori, Dugine obitelji and Roda report the organizers of the carnival to the police). *Večernji list*, February 6, 2018. Retrieved from: https://www.vecernji.hr/vijesti/spaljivanje-slikovnica-zagreb-pride-lori-dugine-obitelji-roda-karneval-1224669. Last accessed on May 24, 2018.
41 Quoted from the web page of the association Dugine obitelji: https://www.dugineobitelji.com/slikovnica/. My translation. Last accessed on May 24, 2018.
42 "Hoćete li dopustiti ulazak slikovnice o tzv. istospolnim obiteljima u vrtiće i škole? (Will you allow the entry of the picture book about the so-called same-sex families into kindergartens and schools?). *Večernji list*, January 4, 2018. Retrieved from: https://www.vecernji.hr/vijesti/udruga-vigilare-blazenka-divjak-istospolne-zajednice-1217836. Last accessed on May 24, 2018.
43 Nataša Latković. "Ministar besan što 'Srbija uvozi' GEJ SLIKOVNICE IZ HRVATSKE [capitalized in the original]: 'Nije u redu da Roko ima dve mame, a Ana dvojicu tata' (Minister furious about 'Serbian import' of CROATIAN PICTURE BOOKS: It is not OK that Roko has two moms, and Ana has two

case of the burning of the picture book *My Rainbow Family* is particularly alarming because it happened in an EU member country, it was an organized event and it happened in front of children. What is more, it "teaches" children intolerance and violence towards people belonging to sexual minorities, but potentially also minorities in general and books. The Minister of Science and Education, as well as the Children's Attorney, immediately condemned the burning, whereas the organizers of the event did not consider it problematic at all. In fact, the president of the Carnival association "Poklade" stated that "when a mom makes a child with a mom or a dad with a dad, we will finance all children's carnivals in the world and will be the children's godfathers at baptism".[44] That books in the 21st century enjoy a considerable symbolic value and can be used as instruments in political disputes was also demonstrated in March 2016, when activists of the Kosovar *Vetëvendosje* (Self-Determination) movement overturned a truck with Serbian products as a reaction to Belgrade's decision not to distribute Kosovar schoolbooks to Albanian children in Serbia because of their political bias.[45] In the same period, some events in Crimea and the Russian Federation tested the limits of the International Federation of Libraries Association (IFLA) postulate based on which "collections and services should not be subject to any form of ideological, political or religious censorship, nor commercial pressures".[46] In late 2014 the director of Feodosia Central Library (Crimea) was

---

dads). *Blic*, May 4, 2018. Retrieved from: https://www.blic.rs/vesti/drustvo/ministar-besan-sto-srbija-uvozi-gej-slikovnice-iz-hrvatske-nije-u-redu-da-roko-ima/nl7nlsd. Last accessed on May 24, 2018.

44 "Javio se predsjednik udruge koja je pred djecom spalila gay slikovnicu, probao je biti duhovit" (The president of the association that in front of children burned a gay picture book comments the event trying to be witty). *Index.hr*, February 4, 2018. Retrieved from: http://www.index.hr/vijesti/clanak/javio-se-predsjednik-udruge-koja-je-pred-djecom-spalila-gay-slikovnicu-probao-je-biti-duhovit/1023773.aspx?fb_comment_id=1730524903635295_1730577726963346#f35eaa6a66190d8. Last accessed on May 24, 2018.

45 Petrit Çollaku, "Kosovo activists overturn Serbian truck in schoolbook protest". *Balkan Insight*, March 3, 2016. Retrieved from: http://www.balkaninsight.com/en/article/ser-bia-s-truck-rolled-over-as-response-to-refused-school-boks-03-03-2016. Last accessed on May 16, 2016.

46 IFLA/UNESCO Public Library Manifesto, available online at https://www.ifla.org/publications/iflaunesco-public-library-manifesto-1994. Last accessed on April 5, 2019.

found guilty of an administrative offense and fined 2000 rubles for displaying 12 copies of a book on *Holodomor*,[47] which is considered extremist by the Russian Federation. Vasyl Marochko's *Ukrainian Genocide. Series: Holodomor 1932–1933* was added to the Federal list of extremist materials in 2011, and, according to the Prosecutor in Feodosia, it "has an anti-Russian orientation […] and calls for and incites hatred against an identifiable group […] and promotes ultra-radical and nationalistic attitudes".[48] Moreover, the director of the library in Kerch was also fined for not having restricted the access to "extremist materials". Finally, I would briefly like to mention another strictly related story, not least because it features some resemblances with the anti-Serbian sentiment in Croatia and how it affected libraries in the 1990s. In June 2017 Natalia Sharina, the former Head of the Library of Ukrainian Literature in Moscow, was declared guilty of inciting hatred and embezzling library funds. She spent 19 months under house arrest because during a search of the library in October 2015 volumes by Ukrainian nationalist Dmytro Korchynsky had been found in a non-indexed pile of books. The librarian denied the charges and characterized the trial as political, but was nevertheless given a four-year suspended sentence. Amnesty International criticized the verdict, stating that

> "the prosecution has exploited the highly charged anti-Ukrainian atmosphere that is prevalent in Russia at the moment, while the court simply dismissed key evidence for the defence, including testimonies that police officers were seen planting the banned books at the library".[49]

Meanwhile, the library's 52,000 volumes were packed up, and Moscow city officials announced that a part of this collection will be given to a new center of Slavonic culture. While some of the

---

47 The Great Famine or Holodomor was an induced famine that killed millions of Ukrainians in 1932–1933. In Ukraine it is considered a genocide operated by the Soviet authorities.
48 "Chief librarian in Feodosia (Crimea) fined for displaying books on Holodomor". *Euromaidan Press*, January 17, 2015. Retrieved from: http://euromaidanpress.com/2015/01/17/chief-librarian-in-feodosia-crimea-fined-for-displaying-books-on-holodomor/#arvlbdata. Last accessed on May 16, 2016.
49 "Russia: Conviction of librarian for holding 'extremist books' demonstrates utter contempt for rule of law". *Amnesty International*, June 5, 2017. Retrieved from: https://www.amnesty.org/en/latest/news/2017/06/russia-conviction-of-librarian-for-holding-extremist-books-demonstrates-utter-contempt-for-rule-of-law/. Last accessed on April 19, 2019.

employees, representatives of the Ukrainian diaspora and Ukrainian Foreign Ministry interpret it as a closure, the Moscow city spokesperson commented that

> "there is no intention to 'destroy' or 'kill something off'. On the contrary, by transferring the books ... we are not only preserving the Library of Ukrainian literature's books, but also believe it will facilitate the popularization of the Ukrainian literary legacy."[50]

A similar divergence of opinion manifested itself when the Serbian Central Library opened in Zagreb in 1996, which is one of the topics addressed in Chapter Three.

All the cited instances clearly show the pressure that libraries are subject to in times of sociopolitical transformations and emphasize the need to engage in research on these public institutions and book policies even outside the field of librarianship.

Last but not least, a couple of words about the structure of this book. It consists of a preface, introduction, three chapters and a conclusion. The preface sets the tone to the volume, while the introduction familiarizes the reader with the covered topics and the local context. While the first chapter should help the reader to locate the topic within the broader context of postsocialist transition, Chapter Two deals with the framing and conceptualization of book removal, including the various levels of analysis the findings could be subject to, and provides a succinct review of the available literature on the removal of "unsuitable" books in former Yugoslavia. It focuses primarily on the two countries that have been taken as case studies, namely, Croatia and Slovenia, and the discrepancies between available data and people's perceptions. Regardless of what the actual figures are, the fate of books in the 1990s has served as inspiration for two artistic initiatives that will be extensively scrutinized in Chapter Three. The two show how a film and a gallery can become alternative arenas for discussion when all other venues are silenced by the rolling of tanks in a victorious military parade. The conclusion summarizes the findings and reflects upon the changing role of public libraries in a neoliberal setting in the digital age.

---

50 Quoted in Andrew Osborn. "Disappearing Books: How Russia is shuttering its Ukrainian library". *Reuters*, March 15, 2017. Retrieved from: https://www.reuters.com/article/us-ukraine-crisis-russia-library-idUSKBN16M0PW. Last accessed April 17, 2018. Ellipses in the original.

1. Yugoslavia, Europe and the World After 1989

The fall of the Berlin Wall on November 9, 1989, symbolically marks the end of "real existing socialism" in Europe, even if it was not the first crack in the Iron Curtain (in the summer of 1989 the border between Hungary and Austria was opened), nor was the "Peaceful Revolution" in East Germany the first time that thousands of people went to the streets demanding reforms in a country of the so-called Eastern Bloc (suffice it to mention the strikes in Poland in 1980–81 and the founding of "Solidarity", the first independent trade union in a Warsaw Pact country). This is just to say that deep-rooted change does not occur overnight and that highly publicized events are only the tip of an iceberg that started forming long ago. Moreover, it is problematic to talk about neat endings and new beginnings, when these are rather rupture points in a constantly liminal state (Bailyn et al. 2018, 1). Translated into more concrete terms, the question "when did communism[51] in Europe end?" can be answered with "in 1989, but …" or "the beginning of the end started in 1980 in Poland when …"; I am assuming that as time goes by more and more creative approaches and propositions will be advanced, some of which might date it back to 1945 or even set it in 2045.[52] Nevertheless, engaging in a deeper discussion on the causes and the end of real existing socialism in Europe goes beyond the

---

51   It is a common practice, especially in Anglophone literature, to use the words "communism" and "socialism" as synonyms, which is why I will be following the same pattern. Nevertheless, in Leninist philosophy socialism was considered to be the path towards communism. In other words, communism was yet to be reached in the countries of "real existing socialism," a phrase which was coined to denote their actual experience as opposed to theory.
52   Rather than being a prophecy, my assumption is triggered by and a reaction to the interpretation of World War I Jay Winter presented at a conference I attended. On January 31, 2018, the acclaimed historian held the keynote lecture "The Second Great War 1917–1923" in the framework of the conference "Central and Eastern Europe after the First World War," organized by the European Network Remembrance and Solidarity (ENRS) at the Embassy of the Slovak Republic in Berlin. As the title of his contribution suggests, Winter talked about the First Great War from 1914–1917 and the Second Great War from 1917–1923.

scope of this chapter, which rather deals with what happened afterwards, and principally in former Yugoslavia. One might in fact even argue that the year 1989 was not as ground-breaking in Yugoslavia as it might have been in the countries of the Eastern Bloc. However, events in Yugoslavia did not unfold in a vacuum, which is why it is important to briefly examine what Kristen Ghodsee calls the "red hangover", that is, "the after-effects of real existing socialism".[53] First, the most salient features of the (global) postsocialist condition will be discussed, followed by a more detailed examination of the Yugoslav case: a multinational, multilingual and multiconfessional federal entity descending into crisis and armed conflict only to greet the new millennium as five (by now seven) underperforming formally independent states. The focus of the chapter then shifts to the westernmost former republics of Yugoslavia—Croatia and Slovenia—united in their attempts at distancing themselves from their southern neighbors and from the idea of Yugoslavia with the help of political declarations and language policies.

1.1. Blooming Mythscapes, Languishing Landscapes: Eastern Europe in Postsocialism

While the first Western beer might have been free for many or at least the "Wall-dancers" in Berlin on the night between November 9 and 10, 1989, what followed was a reality check: a transition to market economy and political pluralism with all the social problems that such a transformation entails—unemployment, inflation, corruption, and income disparity, to name only a few. Despite some differences in addressing these issues, Eastern European countries share the socialist legacy, or, as Maria Todorova puts it, "Eastern Europe is the socialist legacy" (Todorova 2005, 73). Nevertheless, behind the term "Eastern Europe" hides a variety of political developments and responses to the challenges of postsocialism, but also slightly different structural arrangements inherited from the previous system. When it comes to the nature of the regime change, it

---

53 The reference here is to the book *Red Hangover: Legacies of Twentieth-Century Communism* by Kristen Ghodsee, published in 2017 by Duke University Press.

was not equally peaceful and devoid of bloodshed in all the countries that used to call themselves socialist: Romania, the Soviet Union and Yugoslavia are cases in point. Furthermore, the latter two socialist federations, as well as Czechoslovakia, fell apart, while Germany reunited. Among the top priorities of the first democratically elected governments was to privatize previously state-owned assets and to remedy the perceived injustice from the former system. As John Borneman argues, this provided them with an immediate source of legitimacy (Borneman 1997, vii). The process resulted in a number of lustration laws with varying degrees of applicability, implementation and success.[54] Economic transition brought along two basic models: gradual and rapid ("big-bang") reforms. Although some countries enjoyed a better starting position (the less centralized Croatia, Slovenia and Hungary), they all went through a recession, growing unemployment rates, inflation, and a rise in income disparity. A policy analysis of the CATO Institute, prepared on the occasion of the 25th anniversary of the beginning of the reform process, concludes that rapid reformers performed better (Central-Eastern European countries, including Croatia and Slovenia, and the Baltic countries) and that those countries that quickly adopted market liberalization also took the leading role in democratization.[55] Along with retributive justice as a legitimizing factor, postsocialist states needed new narratives recounting the nation's past and its place in the world, which would replace the socialist one. It was mostly nationalistic narratives that "did the job." This is not to say that the year 1989 marked "the release of the genie of nationalism out of a tightly capped bottle," but rather that nationalist discourse no longer needed to conform to the "dominant jargon," while the end of the international status quo made the

---

54 For a more detailed scrutiny see Borneman (1997).
55 "25 Years of Reforms in Ex-Communist Countries. Fast and Extensive Reforms Led to Higher Growth and More Political Freedom". Policy Analysis by Oleh Havrylyshyn, Xiaofan Meng and Marian L. Tupi. *Cato Institute*, July 12, 2016, n. 795. Retrieved from: https://object.cato.org/sites/cato.org/files/pubs/pdf/pa795_2.pdf. Last accessed on April 19, 2019. For a qualitative comparative study of transitory patterns in postsocialism see Norkus (2012). I would like to thank Miglė Bareikytė for reading an early draft of this chapter and for bringing Norkus's work to my attention.

realization of these claims possible (Todorova 1993, 149). In an essay dealing with memory, mythology and national identity, Duncan Bell (2003) uses the notion of the governing myth to define these national narrations, where memory is the "socially-framed property of individual minds" (Bell 2003, 72). Collective (organic) memory or remembrance can be included in the myth, but it can also contradict and challenge its simplifications within the framework of a mythscape, namely, "the temporally and spatially extended discursive realm wherein the struggle for control of peoples['] memories and the formation of nationalist myths is debated, contested and subverted incessantly" (66). The mythscape is determined by institutions and influenced by changes in the power relations (76). I find the concept useful because it stresses the role of human agency and the negotiational character of a myth, instead of presenting it as a reified entity that all social actors unconditionally accept. Rather than writing about governing myths like Bell, the novelist Dubravka Ugrešić, an attentive observer of the events that immediately followed the dissolution of Yugoslavia, uses the term "national memory": "With the breakup of multinational Yugoslavia the process of confiscation of the Yugoslav collective memory started and was replaced by the construct of national memory" (Ugrešić 1999, 251). Due to her sharp observations and figuratively evocative language, Ugrešić became an unavoidable reference for all those writing about memory both in the region and elsewhere. For instance, in the introduction to his book on memory and power in postwar Europe, Jan-Werner Müller quotes her no fewer than four times (Müller 2004, 1–35), not to mention all the (literary) scholars working on Ugrešić's opus proper (see, for instance, Popescu 2007; Vervaet 2011; Hitzke 2014). In Müller's edited volume on the memory-power nexus after 1945 and the interplay between memory, oblivion and myth-making in post-1989 (Eastern) Europe, Tony Judt defines the latter period as an "interregnum, a moment between myths when the old versions of the past are either redundant or unacceptable, and new ones have yet to surface" (Müller 2004, 12, 180). This "in-betweenness" resurfaces once again in Müller's argument when he states, echoing Eric Hobsbawm's notions of the "twilight zone between history and memory" and "no

Yugoslavia, Europe and the World After 1989 47

man's land of time" (24), that the period under communism "seems to have been consigned [again quoting Judt] to a 'limbo between history and memory'" (10).

Be that as it may, the narrative that managed to crystallize itself in all postsocialist states—being institutionally sponsored both on the national and the EU levels—is that of victimization, namely, self-representation on the part of the states as victims of communism that have now returned to Europe. For instance, the European Commission (EC) report on *The State of Integration of East and West in the European Union*, prepared on the occasion of the 25th anniversary of the opening of the Iron Curtain (2015, 17), states that "it is therefore tempting to view the totalitarian period in the area as a 'pause' in history, after which these countries were regained for Western Europe". Describing the socialist period as a "pause in history" is the negation of any attempt at critical historiography or serious public debate. As Ghodsee argues, in Eastern Europe there exists a "prohibition on thinking about the everyday lived experiences of communism," where "with the tacit support of Brussels [...] politicians, scholars, and activists try to drown out other stories about the past by focusing exclusively on the crimes of communism" (Ghodsee 2017, 134–35). Such discourses perfectly fit into the "two totalitarianisms" paradigm, leading to an equation of Nazism and communism. Organizations close to the Platform of European Memory and Conscience,[56] Ghodsee continues, rewrite official history textbooks and influence public debate by using

---

56 Founded in Prague in 2011, the Platform of European Memory and Conscience is an interest association endorsed by the European Parliament and the Council of the European Union. Its members include governmental and nongovernmental organizations from twenty, mostly Eastern European, countries. Interestingly, of the seven post-Yugoslav countries only Slovenia is represented with two member organizations, the Study Centre for National Reconciliation (*Študijski center za narodno spravo*) and New Slovenian Commitment (*Nova slovenska zaveza*). Most of the participating organizations distinguish themselves through their insistence on communist crimes and promote an equation of communism and Nazism. The activities of the Platform include conferences, education and commemoration events, publications and the "Justice 2.0" project, the goal of which is to obtain "international justice for the Communist crimes". More information about the project and Platform can be found on its website: https://www.memoryandconscience.eu/. Last accessed on April 19, 2019.

methods equal to those deployed by communist regimes, the object of their harshest criticism (135). Former Yugoslav countries are no exception, even if the Yugoslav "path to communism" was slightly different from that of the Soviet bloc. What is more, in these countries a second "layer" of victimization is added: there are victims of Serbian aggression (Croatia), victims of Serbian and Croatian expansionistic plans (Bosnia and Herzegovina), victims of discrimination and Slovenian betrayal (Serbia), and victims of a Serbo-Croatian linguistic and cultural hegemony (Slovenia). Due to their geographical position, some countries (for instance, Poland, Serbia, or Croatia) also resort to the *Antemurale* (Bulwark) myth: they stand as a bulwark against Orthodoxy, Islam, communism, barbarism and other "evils". To put it in one sentence, mythscapes are blooming, but can the same be said about landscapes?[57]

Many of today's political crises, Ghodsee (2017, 50) maintains, are a result of the "greedy and self-aggrandizing stance of Western political and economic elites after the collapse of communism". As Katherine Verdery wrote back in the mid-1990s, the stories of postsocialism all include "the knights of Western know-how rushing to save the distressed of Eastern Europe" (Verdery 1996, 204). Salvation comes in two variants: "shock therapy" and the "big bang". While the first treats the Eastern bloc as a mentally ill person that needs to be cured with therapy, the second implies that history began in 1989 and everything that came before is without form (205). Consequently, Western advisors are treated as doctors or Gods *(ibid.)*, or, to use a term inspired by Boris Buden's analysis of the postsocialist condition, educators. In fact, Buden claims that in a political sense people in postcommunism have been put under tutelage, made into children with no critical memory of the past (because

---

[57] In a speech on the day the monetary, economic and social union between the Federal Republic of Germany (FRG) and the German Democratic Republic (GDR) entered into force (July 1, 1990), the Federal Chancellor Helmut Kohl promised that the five new federal states (which until reunification on October 3, 1990 constituted the GDR) would be transformed into blooming landscapes. The phrase was later used to criticize unification policies. The full speech is available in English on the German History in Documents and Images (GHDI) webpage: http://ghdi.ghi-dc.org/sub_document.cfm?document_id=3101. Last accessed on November 27, 2018.

the future is what matters) and finally transformed into political fools (Buden 2010, 8).

While promoting private property and free markets, the "West" fought for political and economic dominance over former socialist countries by simultaneously ignoring the social costs of their policies and the resentments of ordinary people whose existences were turned upside down in the name of freedom. The "losers" of transition started increasingly turning to the far right in search for solutions to their precarious condition. A quarter of a century after the fall of the Berlin Wall, the worldwide upswing of radical right parties is accompanied in Eastern Europe by staunch anti-communism and an undiscussed neoliberal hegemony. Chelcea and Druţă (2016) call this combination "zombie socialism". Now that transition is over, socialism is used as a ghost to gain support for certain economic measures, to justify others, and to frame policy priorities (Chelcea and Druţă 2016, 523). The depiction of state socialism as the "ultimate bogeyman, disciplinary device and 'ideological antioxidant'" has pushed some of these countries to zealously embrace neoliberalism, making them even "more" capitalist than countries that did not go through a socialist *intermezzo* (521). While the defenders of democracy tend to disentangle the ideal from the distortions of neoliberalism, they view socialism solely through the lens of Stalinist crimes. In other words, they claim that one political ideal may suffer from distortions, but they negate the same "right" to another ideal. This hypocrisy hinders the critical analysis of the socialist past, while simultaneously leading to an empowerment of the far right (Ghodsee 2017, xix–xx). As long as the dominant public discourse is pronouncedly anti-communist, no serious process of dealing with the socialist past can take place. A critical examination of the socialist experience, which takes into consideration the achievements of the system without dismissing them *en bloc*, while at the same time remembering the crimes that were committed in its name, is still a distant future for many countries. The question is when this will be possible, considering that the year 2019 marks the thirtieth anniversary of the fall of the Berlin Wall and three decades of what the theorist Mark Fisher (2009) called in his book of the same name "capitalist realism," the idea of neoliberal capitalism as the only game in town. This is what makes postsocialism (or what comes next) a global rather than merely Eastern European issue. With that in mind, in the following section I will provide an overview of the post-Yugoslav transition.

1.2. The Multiple Transitions in (Post-)Yugoslavia

The Socialist Federal Republic of Yugoslavia was a socialist federation made up of six constituent republics—the Socialist Republic (SR) of Bosnia and Herzegovina, SR Croatia, SR Macedonia, SR Montenegro, SR Serbia and SR Slovenia—and two autonomous provinces within Serbia, Vojvodina and Kosovo. This multinational, multilingual and multiconfessional federation distanced itself from the Soviet Union in 1948 and started building its own way to socialism under the strong leadership of Josip Broz Tito, who became life-long president in 1963. Following the Tito-Stalin split, Yugoslavia replaced the Soviet economic model based on central planning and centralized management with workers' self-management *(radničko samoupravljanje)*. The pillar of Yugoslav foreign policy became the Non-Aligned Movement (NAM), of which it was a founding member. The NAM was founded in 1956 on the Brijuni islands in Yugoslavia with a declaration signed by the Indian Prime Minister Jawaharlal Nehru and the presidents of Yugoslavia and Egypt, Josip Broz Tito and Gamal Abdel Nasser. The first summit was held in 1961 in Belgrade. The purpose of the NAM, as outlined in the Havana Declaration (1979), was to represent the interests of developing countries and support their struggle against imperialism and colonialism, while formally maintaining their neutrality in the face of the Soviet and American blocs. After the end of the Cold War the Movement, which currently has more than 100 members, had to reinvent itself and now champions international cooperation and the self-reliance of developing countries against increasing worldwide wealth inequalities. Tito successfully struck a balance between the two superpowers, the United States and the Soviet Union, securing a place for Yugoslavia on the political map and developing close trade relations with the European Economic Community and the United States. Contrary to their counterparts in the Soviet bloc,

Yugoslav citizens enjoyed the freedom to travel and relative economic prosperity, largely financed by international loans. In the 1980s the country's economy entered a period of crisis fuelled by international debt, inflation and unemployment, which together with the rising ethnic tensions after the death of Tito (1980) and the changing international constellation led to the dissolution of the country and a decade of wars.[58] Sabrina Ramet summarizes the elements that led to the Yugoslav dissolution, which she defines as "over determined, but not inevitable," as: structural problems inherent to the Yugoslav system; economic decline and political illegitimacy; the lack of a common interest; and competing national historical narratives based on resentment and blame and the emergence of a "national revitalization movement" in Serbia, led by Slobodan Milošević (Ramet 2007, 27–28). In other words, the factors that led to the disintegration of the country included "widespread discontent, fracture lines along which the country might be dissolved, and leaders prepared to exploit discontent for their own purposes" (69). The ethnic federal system, which accorded high degrees of autonomy to the republics in the spheres of education and the media, increased the tendency within each federal unit to blame another nationality for the difficult economic situation (68).

In Slovenia, the prospect of full national independence started gaining clearer contours in the second half of the 1980s, when the economic and political crisis in Yugoslavia was in full swing. Such an outcome was primarily favored by intellectual circles close to the magazine *Nova revija*, but was underpinned by civil society organizations and alternative youth culture; in addition, it could count on the support of reformist currents within the League of Communists[59] (Repe 2012, 6–7). The national sentiment was further strengthened by two campaigns started in 1984, namely, the fundraising lottery for the national Alpine team *Podarim-dobim* (I give-I receive), which lasted until 1997, and the *Slovenija, moja dežela*

---

58 Numerous articles and books have been written on the causes of the breakup of Yugoslavia. For a succinct review of the various explanatory approaches see Jović (2001).
59 The communist party in Slovenia. The Communist Party of Yugoslavia and its subunits were renamed the "League" at the 6th Party Congress in 1952.

(Slovenia, my country) tourism campaign (Repe 2012, 7–8). Both initiatives made Slovene national conscience stronger and co-created its national image. On the other hand, Croatia after the crackdown of the Croatian Spring in 1971 became known as "the Silent Republic," at least until the late 1980s. The Croatian Spring or MASPOK *(Masovni pokret* — Mass Movement) was a cultural and political movement led by Croatian Party leaders demanding bigger political and economic autonomy for the Republic. The issue that inflamed spirits the most was foreign currency distribution, which provoked a student strike and forced Tito to intervene. In December 1971, the Party leaders were accused of nationalism and liberalism and forced to step down, while student leaders were arrested. Many of these actors would later hold positions of power in independent Croatia.

As questions about the federal order started regaining momentum, old arguments resurfaced regarding Croatian statehood, the sovereignty of its institutions, and an increasingly ethnic understanding of citizenship (Irvine 2008, 173). Even if these issues bore a resemblance to previous Croatian demands for a reform of the Federation, the setting did not: Tito was not there to intervene, and Milošević had already started an aggressive campaign aimed at achieving Serbian national goals *(ibid.,* 172–173), not to mention the changing international constellation and balance of power. The concomitant rise of competing national revisionist historiographies and victimization narratives paved the way for a war over history which soon after became a war over territory and resources and is today a war over memory (Müller 2004, 17). A day after the European Community recognized Croatia's and Slovenia's independence, on January 16, 1992, the *New York Times* wrote: "While Slovenia looks forward to a relatively secure future as a comparatively prosperous Alpine republic, the joy in Croatia was tempered by uncertainty"[60]. Indeed, while independence in Slovenia was achieved relatively peacefully (apart from the ten-day conflict with the Yugoslav Peoples' Army), Croatia went through a war, the so-called

---

60 "Breakup of Yugoslavia Leaves Slovenia Secure, Croatia Shaky" (January 16, 1992), *New York Times*.

"Homeland War" from 1991–1995. With a population consisting of more than 90 percent ethnic Slovenes, Slovenia was one of the most ethnically homogeneous republics, whereas in Croatia the second largest group (constituent nation in Yugoslavia, later national minority) were the Serbs, forming 12.6 percent of the population in 1991. Following operation "Storm," this number dropped to 4.54 percent in 2001 and 4.36 percent in 2011.[61] Operation "Storm" was one of the last major battles in the Croatian War of Independence. Launched on August 4, 1995, to restore Croatian control over a large part of the territory, it provided the setting for various crimes against civilians. It also forced most of the remaining Serbian population to flee the country.

Slovenia's transition into a liberal democracy was among the smoothest in Eastern Europe and in former Yugoslavia due to several factors. While the country's ethnic homogeneity and higher level of prosperity might have contributed to its relative success, in a report for the Wilson Center Sabrina Ramet argues that what had a decisive impact was a transition towards pluralism initiated in the mid-1980s by the League of Communists and the development of a liberal political culture. The latter was promoted by different associations, including pacifist, punk, environmentalist and gay and lesbian groups in a period when in Serbia an increasingly nationalist culture was nurtured.[62] Žiga Vodovnik dissects the process even further by identifying new social movements (NSMs) active between the late 1970s and the mid-1980s "as the key player in initiating and directing democratic transformation" (Vodovnik 2017, 2). After some NSMs institutionally connected with the League of Socialist Youth of Slovenia (LSYS) in order to avoid repressive actions from the state or when other movements assimilated intellectuals with a different ideological stance, political visions and conceptions of political action, a "new" or "bourgeois" civil society consolidated

---

61 "Population by ethnicity, 1971/2011 censuses". Data published by the Croatian Bureau of Statistics, available online at: https://www.dzs.hr/Eng/censuses/census2011/results/htm/usp_03_EN.htm. Last accessed on May 24, 2018.
62 "227. Slovenia since 1990". Report by Sabrina P. Ramet. *Wilson Center*, July 7, 2011. Retrieved on February 5, 2019, from: https://www.wilsoncenter.org/publication/227-slovenia-1990.

itself. This led to a gradual merger of the political pluralism issue with the Slovenian national question (Vodovnik 2017, 3). In this way the NSMs and their ideas, including democracy as an inclusive political community, were marginalized in favor of an ethnocracy (16). In other words, the successful economic transition and state-building were not necessarily accompanied by a democratization of society, leading to what Vodovnik calls the "democratic paradox" or the "schizophrenic nature" of the Slovenian democratization process (17). Following the first pluralist political elections in April 1990, a coalition government was formed by center-right parties that stayed in power until 1992. In the same year, Janez Drnovšek became Prime Minister and retained the post for almost a decade (with the exception of six months he spent in the opposition in 2000). His Liberal Democracy of Slovenia *(Liberalna demokracija Slovenije*, LDS) party, the legal successor of the Association of Socialist Youth of Slovenia *(Zveza socialistične mladine Slovenije)*, ruled the country with its coalition partners during most of the transition period (1992–2004, 2008–2012). In Croatia, the Croatian Democratic Union *(Hrvatska demokratska zajednica*, HDZ) has been holding the reins of power for most of the country's independent history. Formerly a nationalist, right-wing party, the HDZ reformed itself in the early 2000s, becoming a pro-European center-right party occasionally flirting with far-right ideas. Around the same time the main goal of Croatian foreign policy became Euro-Atlantic integration, and all segments of society converged towards it, visibly reducing the gap between political and societal discourse. Until Franjo Tuđman's death in 1999, Croatia lived in relative political isolation. The year 2000 and the new millennium brought the needed democratic changes and a break with governmentally induced revisionism in the name of Europeanization, as Europe was considered Croatia's political and cultural home (Subotić 2011, 311). A decade later, Tuđman's successor in the presidency of the Croatian Democratic Union (HDZ), Ivo Sanader, distanced himself from the purely revisionist rhetoric by reaffirming Croatia's role as a victim in the Homeland War, a victim of Serbian fascism. Sanader and his collaborators condemned and equated Ustasha-Nazi and communist crimes, an EU-driven (bottom-up and top-down) process common to almost all postsocialist states (Radonić 2012). In Slovenia, the politics of national reconciliation aimed at creating equilibrium between the two sides that fought in World War II, the Domobranci and the Partisans, has its problems on the level of statehood (Zajc 2015). Slovenia as a state was created during the Partisan struggle, which means that leaving the Partisans out of the Slovenian historical narratives is equivalent to undermining the basis of Slovenian statehood. The Center and the Right are, according to Zajc, treating the issue differently. While

> "the Right denies any Partisan contribution and tries to invent an alternative historical narrative, the Center only embraces the 'good stuff' (liberation, the establishment of the Slovenian state, a new border in the West, etc.) and conceals the unlikeable parts of the 'Liberation War'" (Zajc 2015, n.p.).

The revolutionary emancipatory potential of the Partisan struggle is dismissed by both sides.

EU conditionality failed to bring about a large-scale transformation in Croatia and was instead reduced to legalistic compliance (Baker 2015, 108), which became visible even before the country's EU accession in 2013. Slovenia, on the other hand, was among the ten Central-Eastern European (CEE) countries that entered the EU in 2004 and in 2007 became the first former socialist country to adopt the common European currency, the euro. Economic transition to a market economy, and one of the most intriguing aspects thereof, privatization, was handled differently in the two countries. In Croatia it unfolded by transferring the control of the economy to a new political elite, while in Slovenia an approach combining a gradual, decentralized and commercial privatization was chosen (Mencinger n.d., 4–5).

1.3. "Europe Now!"

I recently read an interesting definition of Slovenia as a country that is geographically Mediterranean, culturally Central European, and, due to its ties with Yugoslavia, *was* politically Eastern European (Ambrožič and Žumer 2015, 742, my emphasis). This sentence is interesting because it points out a common occurrence in *former*

Eastern European[63] countries: the wish to distance themselves as much as possible from Eastern Europe, identified with backwardness and communism. The borders of Europe are relative, anyway — as far as I am aware, six places in Belarus, Estonia, Hungary, Lithuania, Slovakia and Ukraine are currently claiming to be the geographical center of Europe. Another example would be the article celebrating the fact that an American geography textbook classified Czech Republic as a Western country belonging to the core of Europe, while neighboring Slovakia was left outside of both.[64] And this leads us to another important point: the "othering" of the neighbor. In former Yugoslav countries the "bogeyman" is the Balkans. The essentialization of identities within the civilized/uncivilized, Europe/Balkans, Christian/Muslim dichotomy, as well as the progressive transfer of negative attributes to those further East (or South) in former Yugoslavia, has already been researched and was given the name of "nesting orientalisms" (Bakić-Hayden 1995). In the symbolic geography of Yugoslavia, Bakić-Hayden writes, being "North" and "West" carried positive associations, which could not be said of the "South" and "East" (Bakić-Hayden 1995, 924). Once the neutralizing framework that Yugoslavia provided to the valorization of the abovementioned categories was gone, a struggle for the redefinition of the "self" and the "other" led to a rediscovery of the pre-Yugoslav past, often completely devoid of any diachronic consideration (922). According to this logic of "nesting orientalisms", the "northern republics" (Slovenia and Croatia), which were under Habsburg rule for centuries, qualify to "join Europe", while "those Yugoslavs who have not scored high on the hegemonic western scale find their own 'others', whom they perceive as even lower" (924). As Bakić-Hayden reports, there were even attempts at

---

63 A way to repudiate Eastern Europe as a political concept without having to use "former" would be to stop capitalizing the "E" in Eastern and treat it as a geographic category. In any case, in this text I will stick to the capitalized version.

64 "Confirmed: Czech Republic is in Western Europe, says US textbook". *Expats.cz*, February 4, 2019. Retrieved on February 5, 2019, from: https://news.expats.cz/weekly-czech-news/confirmed-czech-republic-is-in-western-europe-says-us-textbook/.

institutionalizing this "narcissism of minor differences"[65], when ten Slovenian Members of Parliament representing eight political parties proposed a "Resolution about the Central European Character of Slovenia", which was intended to separate it from the Balkans (924). The "nesting orientalisms" is both an internal and an external phenomenon: suffice it to think about the designation introduced by the European Union for aspiring members in the countries of former Yugoslavia, including Albania, the "Western Balkans". Once the country joins the EU it is no longer "Western Balkan". Once and if all these countries become members, will the (Western) Balkans as a whole cease to exist? In any case, in the perceived "geographical hierarchy", the West and the North (the Republic of Macedonia recently "upgraded" from former to North Macedonia) do enjoy a better reputation than the East or the South. As Maria Todorova argues in her best-known book, Imagining the Balkans, "'Europe' ends where politicians want it to end" (Todorova 2009, 139).

The politicians of the Slovenian League of Communists *(Zveza komunistov Slovenije ZKS)*, which in 1990 would become the Party of Democratic Reform *(Stranka demokratične prenove SDP)* wanted "Europe now!" when they presented their new slogan and party program in late 1989. Similarly, Tuđman ran his election campaign in 1997 under the motto "Tuđman, not the Balkans!". Following the proclamation of independence in June 1991, politicians in both Croatia and Slovenia engaged in a campaign to affirm their countries' belonging to Europe, while at the same time emphasizing their distance from the Balkans and from Yugoslavia (the state union between Serbia and Montenegro was called Federal Republic of Yugoslavia FRY until 2003). In this way, Europeanness was coupled with Slovenianness and Croatianness, respectively, to form the

---

65 In his book *The Warrior's Honor: Ethnic War and the Modern Conscience* (1998), Michael Ignatieff uses the Freudian concept to explain the violence and brutality during the war in Bosnia. On the applicability of the concept in the context of ethnic conflict see Pål Kolstø's article "The 'Narcissism of Minor Differences'-Theory. Can it explain Genocide and Ethnic Conflict?" (2007). The author discusses Ignatieff's usage of the term on pages 10–12: https://www.duo.uio.no/bitstream/handle/10852/25227/86810_kolstoe.pdf?sequence=1. Last accessed on March 23, 2019.

pillars of identity in the two former Yugoslav republics. The idea of a "return to Europe" was expressed not only through slogans, but also in the statements of politicians, resolutions and diplomatic moves.[66] For instance, one of the five strategic points outlined by the Slovenian Ministry of Foreign Affairs in 1992 foresaw

> "a final exit from the Balkans and adaptation to the new political role (and thus to new challenges and tasks) within the framework of the Southeast European countries, particularly those emerging from the ashes of the former Yugoslavia",

while the Croatian president Tuđman spoke of Croatia joining Europe, "where it historically belongs" (Lindstrom 2003, 317, 321). Sometime later both countries hesitated to join the Southeast European Cooperative Initiative (SECI), which in Croatia resulted in a constitutional amendment in 1997 stating that

> "It is prohibited to initiate any procedure for the association of the Republic of Croatia into alliances with other states if such association leads, or might lead, to a renewal of a South Slav state community or to any Balkan state form of any kind" (art. 135, NN 8/1998).

The same exclusionism did not apply to other regional associations including Mediterranean, Danubian and/or Alpine countries, which both countries readily joined. Identification with Central Europe as opposed to the Balkans is equally strong: this is emphasized in the Declaration of Foreign Policy issued by the Slovenian Parliament in 2000:

> "The Republic of Slovenia is a Central European Country [...][which] finds cooperation and linking with the countries of Central Europe, in particular in the economic and cultural fields [...] It is further linked with numerous Central European countries through the preparations for full EU membership" (Lindstrom 2003, 324).

Also, Tuđman in an address in 1997 highlighted that "by its geopolitical position, by all of its fourteen-century history, by its civilization and culture, Croatia belongs to the Central European and Mediterranean circles of Europe. Our political links with the Balkans between 1918 and 1990 were just a short episode in Croatian history

---

66 For a more detailed analysis see Lindstrom (2003).

and we are determined not to repeat that episode again" (325). In the second half of the 1990s the Slovenian establishment declared itself ready for cooperation with Southeast European countries, this time as a "bridge" between the international community (Europe) and the Balkans (322).

A strictly anti-Yugoslav rhetoric was more characteristic of Croatia in the 1990s than of Slovenia, not least because of the 1991–1995 war and the identification of Yugoslavia predominantly with Serbia, with which Croatia has deeper cultural and linguistic ties than Slovenia. In fact, language as an important component of identity was the object of political instrumentalization and became an important tool for the measurement of the distance between Croatia and Serbia. First the anti-Yugoslav rhetoric will be briefly examined, followed by a section on language policies.

1.4. A Spectre is Haunting Croatia – The Spectre of Yugoslavia[67]

The demonization of Yugoslavia was particularly strong in the Tuđman era, becoming less accentuated after the democratic changes in 2000, but it still occasionally resurfaces, as it did in 2014–2015 during the protest of war veterans. Rather than being directed at a particular state formation, such as the Kingdom of Yugoslavia (1929–1941)[68], the Socialist Federal Republic (1945–1992)[69], or the State Union of Serbia and Montenegro (1992–2003)[70], the negative

---

67 Minor parts of this and subchapter 1.6 have previously appeared in Komnenović (2018).
68 The kingdom of Serbs, Croats and Slovenes (*Kraljevina Srba, Hrvata i Slovenaca / Kraljevina SHS*) was founded in 1918 and its name was officially changed into Kingdom of Yugoslavia (*Kraljevina Jugoslavija*) in 1929.
69 The Anti-Fascist Council for the National Liberation of Yugoslavia (*Antifašističko vijeće narodnog oslobođenja Jugoslavije* AVNOJ) announced the creation of Democratic Federal Yugoslavia (*Demokratska federativna Jugoslavija*) on November 29, 1943. Two years later The Federal People's Republic of Yugoslavia (*Federativna narodna republika Jugoslavija* FNRJ) was proclaimed after the deposition of the Monarch, King Peter II. In 1963 the name Socialist Federal Republic of Yugoslavia (*Socijalistička federativna republika Jugoslavija* SFRJ) was introduced.
70 In 1992, after both Macedonia (September 1991) and Bosnia and Herzegovina (March 1992) had declared independence, Serbia and Montenegro established a Federation, the Federal Republic Yugoslavia (*Savezna republika Jugoslavija* SRJ).

discourse takes aim predominantly at the idea of "a political link with the Balkans", as mentioned above. "Yugoslavia" is thus stripped of its historical content, and it becomes apologetic or ideological (Jacoby 1975, 5).

> "The first task of a free and independent Croatia, following the liberation from foreign occupiers, was to work on societal and spiritual renewal. It was necessary to free our Croatian man from Communist totalitarianism, from the illusion of Yugoslavism, from the practice of Serbian theft, bribes and corruption, from the inherited Ottoman 'mañana'[71,] and from the newly established slavery to Western European mammonism" (Baković 1992, 5).

These sentences, together with the title of the volume they were taken from, *Duhovna obnova Hrvatske* (Spiritual Renewal of Croatia), perfectly capture the *Zeigeist* of the early 1990s in Croatia. The volume collects the proceedings of a two-day conference of the same name held in Zagreb in June 1992, the year of Croatia's international recognition and admittance to the United Nations. The conference, organized by Rev. Anto Baković under the aegis of the Ministry of Reconstruction *(Ministarstvo obnove)*[72], gathered approximately 70 speakers, including academics, economists, ministers, religious and other prominent (public) figures. The conference proceedings, edited by Baković and sponsored by the Ministry of Science *(Ministarstvo znanosti)*, are divided into five sections dealing with the various dimensions of spiritual renewal: societal and moral, cultural, political, economic, and purely spiritual. The volume abounds with

---

Between 2003–2006 the country was known as Serbia and Montenegro. After a second referendum for independence (the results of the 1992 referendum favored the state union with Serbia) Montenegro declared independence in June 2006. Finally, in February 2008 Kosovo declared independence from Serbia, which increased the number of states formed after the breakup of Tito's Yugoslavia to seven.

71 I replaced Baković's expression "'lahko' ćemo-sutra ćemo" (we will do it easily-tomorrow) with what seems to be a more appropriate term in the English language.

72 The Ministry of Reconstruction was instituted during the Government of National Unity (*Vlada nacionalnog jedinstva*) led by Franjo Gregorić from July 1991 to August 1992. Slavko Degoricija was named Minister on December 31, 1991, and held the post until August 1992. The Ministry consisted of seven committees, one of which was the Committee for Demographic and Spiritual Renewal (*Odjel za demografsku i duhovnu obnovu*), led by the priest Anto Baković.

derogatory terms directed at Yugoslavia, socialism and the Serbs ("Yugo-hell", "Serbian theft" p. 5, "monstrous mixture" p. 11, "distorted negative perspective" p. 87, "political and spiritual terror" p. 122), but it also raises significant questions about the direction the newly independent Croatia should take. Most importantly, one of the speakers confronted the audience with the choice between continuity and discontinuity with the country's (socialist) legacy

> ("Whether we want it or not, like it or not, a smart young state first needs to take care of continuity, albeit momentarily and in organizational forms that principally do not seem appropriate, but they are here and are producing an instantaneous result. Not to destroy the remains of buildings that are still not that unstable to be torn down, but, conversely, to repair them and expand them", 100–101).

Nevertheless, in the years that followed, the idea of spiritual renewal did not figure as prominently in the governmental agenda and was relegated to church activities.[73]

More than twenty years later, right-wing politicians and their supporters are still occasionally fighting against the spectre of Yugoslavia in a country with high levels of citizen loyalty to the state[74], formally allied to NATO, where the Constitution prohibits any other alliance which might lead to the creation of a South Slav state ... Why? To divert the citizens' attention from *real* problems, to further polarize society by producing imaginary enemies and thus creating a source of legitimacy for their rhetoric without even needing to have a program.

Interestingly, the necessity to engage in battles against Yugoslavia becomes stronger whenever the biggest center-right party, Croatian Democratic Union *(Hrvatska demokratska zajednica – HDZ)*, finds itself in the opposition. The party's backing of the protest of war veterans (known in Croatia as defenders—*branitelji)* between October 2014 and April 2016 is a case in point. The sit-in outside the

---

73 For a more detailed analysis of the counselling and the edited volume, see Lešaja 2012, 504–528.
74 Based on the results of the major opinion poll conducted in six former Yugoslav states and Albania in the framework of international research project "Symbolic Nation-Building in West Balkan States: Intents and Results" led by Pål Kolstø between 2011–2014. See Kolstø (ed.) (2014).

Ministry of Defence was launched by disabled war veterans asking for improved and constitutionally guaranteed rights and the dismissal of Minister Predrag "Fred" Matić (from the Social Democratic Party *Socijaldemokratska partija Hrvatske* — SDP) and his assistants. Two of the banners displayed in front of the protesters' tent read "1991: Against Yugoslavia, 2014: Against Yugoslavs", and "1991. They both fell. 2015. They both will fall". This was apparently a reference to the widely known exclamation by a soldier who witnessed the downing of two Yugoslav People's Army (YPA) planes in 1991. In 2015 the exclamation was supposed to symbolize the fall of President Ivo Josipović, defeated by Kolinda Grabar-Kitarović (HDZ) in the 2014–2015 presidential elections and PM Milanović (SDP), ousted from power by the HDZ in 2015. Grabar-Kitarović visited the protesting veterans on the first day of her mandate (as she did during the campaign), and one of her first action as President was to remove the bust of Josip Broz Tito and other works of art and artefacts belonging to the legacy of Josip and Jovanka Broz from the Presidential Office (originally built for Tito as Vila Zagorje). The objects were handed over to the Museums of Croatian Zagorje *(Muzeji Hrvatskog zagorja)*, an institution consisting of five units including the "Old village" museum *(Muzej Staro selo)* where Tito's birthplace is.

On the banners of the protesters the present was compared to 1991, and the military vocabulary implied that the war was not over (yet). In April 2016 the tent was removed, and some of the protesters were given positions in the government and the presidency. Both on the banners and in the discourse of right-wingers in general, the year 1991 is of crucial importance. It not only marks the birth of independent Croatia, but it is also a source of identification and measure of one's adhesion to the Croatian state and nation. As Boris Dežulović wrote in an article,[75] "Where were you in 1991?" has become the (rhetorical) question number one in Croatia, regardless of the interrogator and the respondent. For instance, at the

---

75 Dežulović, B. "Gdje ste bili devedeset prve?" (Where were you in 1991?). *Globus*, September 24, 2014. Retrieved from http://www.6yka.com on November 25, 2014.

Yugoslavia, Europe and the World After 1989   63

commemoration of the 19th anniversary of Operation "Storm" in 2014 in Knin, a war veteran managed to bypass security and to verbally assault the then President of the Republic and the Prime Minister by repeatedly asking the same question. As a result, the same query was directed to (or better, shouted at) him by some people from the audience, which created further havoc.[76] A month later, another such incident was reported in the press: this time a visibly drunk guest attacked (verbally and physically) a 19-year-old waitress in a bar in Ploče, when she refused to serve him more alcohol.[77] Apparently the question has gone viral and it even inspired a simply downloadable Smartphone application, which calculates where the user (or any other person) was in 1991.

Unless it is used in a derogatory sense, the name Yugoslavia hardly ever appears in the Croatian public discourse and space. The figure of Josip Broz Tito, the communist leader of the National Liberation Struggle and life-long president of Yugoslavia, is highly disputed in Croatia and in the region: in 2017 two squares bearing his name in Zagreb and Karlovac were renamed into Republic of Croatia Square *(Trg republike Hrvatske)* and Croatian Defenders Square *(Trg hrvatskih branitelja)* respectively, while in 2018 a statue of Tito was erected in Podgorica, the capital of Montenegro. A couple of months earlier the flower bed of a traffic island in Vodice, Croatia, had to be removed because a number of veterans saw in it the shape of a five-pointed star, even if the representatives of the municipality explained it was a red flower, the logo of the local tourist organization.[78]

---

76 "Verbalno napao Josipovića: Stidite se i vi i Milanović! Gdje ste vi bili '91.?" (Verbally assaults Josipović: Shame on you and Milanović! Where were you in 1991?). *Večernji list*, August 5, 2014: http://www.vecernji.hr/hrvatska/verbalno-napao-josipovica-stidite-se-i-vi-i-milanovic-gdje-ste-vi-bili-91-954182. Last retrieved on November 27, 2015.
77 "Pijani 50-godišnjak pretukao 19-godišnju konobaricu: Gdje si bila '91.?" (Drunken 50-year-old beats up 19-year-old waitress: Where were you in 1991?). *Slobodna Dalmacija*, September 20, 2014. Retrieved on November 25, 2014, from: https://slobodnadalmacija.hr/dalmacija/dubrovnik/clanak/id/247302/pijani-50-godisnjak-pretukao-19-godisnju-konobaricu-gdje-si-bila-91.
78 Ante Talijaš. "Umjesto cvijeta vidjeli petokraku" (Instead of a flower, they saw a five-pointed star). *Jutarnji list*, April 26, 2018. The article also mentions that

It is my impression that the picture below exemplifies the predominant attitude towards Yugoslavia in today's Croatia.

Figure 1. Somewhere in Rijeka, 2016. Photo by Dora Komnenović

Whatever the reasons for the removal of the letter "J" from this container are, Jugolinija, one of the biggest liner shipping companies in the world, was founded in 1947 in Rijeka and followed the destiny of the country, the name of which it (partially) bore. Renamed into Croatia Line in 1992, it kept accumulating debts until it declared bankruptcy in mid-2000.[79] Neither the name *Jugoslavija* nor the prefix "Jugo" (unless it refers to the word *jug*, which means south) are anywhere to be seen in public; the most widely used expression to denote socialist Yugoslavia is rather "former state" *(bivša država)*. Some of the other "purged" words will be mentioned in the next section.

---

allegedly the flowers had to be removed because they had been run over by a car. Last accessed on April 20, 2019.

79 A condensed history of the company can be found in Žuvić (2016 Interestingly, when talking about the postsocialist restructuring of the company, the author uses the word "cleaning" (81). The article is available online at: https://www.toms.com.hr/index.php/toms/article/view/143. Last accessed on April 24, 2018.

1.5. A for Another, B for Balkanization: Language in (Post-)Yugoslavia

Language is an important source of cultural and national identity all around the world, not least in former Yugoslavia. The review of library stock and ensuing discarding after the breakup of Yugoslavia can hardly be disentangled from the language policies implemented in the same period, which, on the other hand, can only be grasped in the context of the complex language situation in Yugoslavia. There were three state languages in socialist Yugoslavia: Serbo-Croatian (or Croato-Serbian), Macedonian and Slovenian. While Serbo-Croatian was the official language in the Socialist Republics of Bosnia and Herzegovina, Croatia, Montenegro and Serbia, Macedonian was spoken in the Republic of Macedonia and Slovenian in the Republic of Slovenia. A narrative that was widely spread during Yugoslav times in Slovenia is that Serbo-Croatian was in a privileged position, which is why it was important to preserve the linguistic individuality of the Slovenian language. In fact, the military trial of Janez Janša, Ivan Borštner, David Tasić and Franci Zavrl (also known as the Ljubljana trial, JBTZ Affair or the Trial against the Four), held in Ljubljana (Slovenia's capital) in 1988 in Serbo-Croatian, is perceived as a catalyst that crystallized public opinion around the view that the preservation of linguistic individuality is no longer possible within Yugoslavia (Dular 2001, np). Three "Mladina" journalists and a Sergeant-Major of the Yugoslav People's Army were charged with possession of a secret YPA document, which included military plans for containing civil disorder in Slovenia, with the intent to publish it. The apparent unconstitutionality of the trial (it was held in Ljubljana in Serbo-Croatian and not Slovenian) galvanized the public and led to the establishment of the Committee for the Defence of Human Rights. As Gow and Carmichael argue, quoting Dimitrij Rupel, "for the Slovene leadership and the Slovene people the trial had been an attack on them and their land", which unified Slovenian politics in a period marked by fear of a potential Army takeover and the push for further liberalization (2000, 154).

The unified Serbo-Croatian language as a cohesive factor was the result of language planning dating back to the mid-19th century. The Serbo-Croatian standard was created with the signing of the Novi Sad Agreement *(Novosadski dogovor)* in 1954. It caused dissatisfaction among a group of scholars, which was expressed in the "Declaration on the Name and Status of the Croatian Literary Language" *(Deklaracija o nazivu i položaju hrvatskog književnog jezika)* published in March 1967. The Declaration argued for the equal status of four languages in Yugoslavia (Croatian, Serbian, Slovenian and Macedonian). Its demands were integrated into the 1974 Federal Constitution. With the breakup of Yugoslavia, the Serbo-Croatian language ceased to exist, at least politically, and it is now called Bosnian-Croatian-Serbian-Montenegrin.[80] The Cyrillic script is in use in the Serbian and Montenegrin variants. The term Serbo-Croatian is no longer considered politically correct, even if it still sometimes used for the sake of simplicity, or better, convenience. Internationally, Serbo-Croatian was separated only in 2008 when the International Organization for Standardization approved the usage of two separate linguistic codes *(hrv and srp)* for Croatian and Serbian, respectively, in library and terminological classifications (Stolac 2014, 110). Linguists like Mate Kapović suggest the usage of the ethnically neutral and scientifically founded term "Štokavian" (Kapović 2011, 54–55). Whatever these languages (?) are called, they are mutually intelligible, which is why distinguished linguists like Ranko Bugarski or Snježana Kordić (e.g., Bugarski 2002, 2005, 2010, 2012; Kordić 2010) argue that they are one polycentric language that politically equals the four languages. Together with two other linguists, Hanka Vajzović and Božena Jelušić, Bugarski and Kordić formed a working group and, in cooperation with organizations from Bosnia and Herzegovina, Croatia, Montenegro and Serbia, started the project *Jezik i nacionalizmi* (Language and Nationalisms). In 2017 they presented the "Declaration on the common language" *(Deklaracija o zajedničkom jeziku)*, available for signing to anyone subscribing to the idea that Bosnian, Croatian, Serbian and Montenegrin are a polycentric language comprising several easily

---

80   On the demise of Serbo-Croatian see Greenberg (2004).

Yugoslavia, Europe and the World After 1989 67

recognizable variants in the same way as English, German, Spanish, or any of a number of other languages. As can be read on the project's website, it is an attempt at countering the rigorous separation of these languages and the negative consequences such separation entails: the segregation of children in multi-ethnic communities, the overblowing of differences where there are none, unnecessary translations in bureaucracy and the media, the imposition of language as a sign of ethno-national belonging and a tool of showing political loyalty.[81]

In spring 1990 the first multi-party elections in Croatia saw the victory of the nationalist Croatian Democratic Union *(Hrvatska demokratska zajednica* HDZ). The new government started to revive old national symbols, to change street names and to establish Croatian national institutions that were competing with the federal ones (Langston and Peti-Stantić 2014, 3). Among the changes brought by the new Constitution (the so-called Christmas Constitution NN56/1990), promulgated in December 1990, were the removal of the adjective "socialist" from the official name of the republic and the declaration of Croatian as the official language (art. 12) (4). Croatian as a distinct language, separate from Serbian, was thus seen as a crucial instrument of identity and national self-determination (4). In practical terms, this translated into attempts at "purifying"[82] the language from Serbian loanwords while simultaneously augmenting the distance between the two standards under the motto that Croatian was overshadowed by Serbian in Yugoslavia. This is not to say that purism is an exclusive characteristic of the Croatian language and a product solely of the sociocultural context in the 1990s. On the contrary, purism is closely connected to the process of language standardization and is a common attribute of standard languages. As Turk and Opašić (2008) argue, it bears negative connotations and is often associated with exclusionism and intolerance since it aims at "protecting" the standard language as "symbol of national identity" from foreign influence (80). One of the proposals

---

81 *Deklaracija o zajedničkom jeziku*. Retrieved from: http://jezicinacionalizmi.com/. Last accessed on March 18, 2019.
82 I wish to thank Ivan Miškulin for encouraging me to emphasize this point and for the reference.

on how to implement purism was put forward by the nationalist politician Vice Vukojević in 1995, which clearly shows that language planning is almost never an exclusive prerogative of linguists. With the Proposal for a Language Act (*Priedlog zakona o hrvatskom jeziku*) and the Proposal on the Establishment of a State Language Office (*Priedlog zakona o osnivanju državnog ureda za jezik*) he promoted the readoption of the etymological writing system (*korienski pravopis*) dear to the Ustasha and the elimination of loan words. The act called, among other provisions, for the introduction of a fine and prison sentence of up to six months for not speaking and writing in Croatian. The draft, however, never entered the Parliamentary procedure, also meeting with rejection by linguists on the pages of the weekly *Feral Tribune*, where the text was published (Vlašić 2010, 185–187). The most indicative signal of the desire to separate Croatian from Serbian was probably the distribution of the first Serbian film after the disintegration of Yugoslavia, *Rane* (Wounds, 1998, directed by Srđan Dragojević), with subtitles (the title in Croatia was *Ozljede*).[83] At this point I wish to mention another case involving a Serbian film and the request to add subtitles to it: first of all, because it happened in 2012, which shows that such tendencies are not an exclusive characteristic of the 1990s; secondly, because it is a demonstration of the selectivity with which laws are implemented in Croatia; and finally, because it confirms that state officials can issue not only inflammatory, but also conciliatory statements. Following the complaint of a viewer "who does not understand Serbian", the Electronic Media Council *(Vijeće za elektroničke medije)* issued a warning to RTL television against showing the film *Žikina dinastija* (Žika's Dynasty, 1985, directed by Zoran Čalić) without subtitles. Namely, pursuant to art. 4 of the Electronic Media Act (*Zakon o elektroničkim medijima*, NN 153/2009) "media service providers are obliged to broadcast programs in the Croatian language and the Latin script or translated into Croatian, in accordance with the provisions of this Act". A polemic ensued, and the then-Minister of culture Andrea Zlatar (Croatian People's Party – Liberal Democrats; *Hrvatska narodna stranka – Liberalni demokrati*,

---

83 For a detailed scrutiny see Žanić (2009).

Yugoslavia, Europe and the World After 1989   69

HNS—LD) stated that there are no reasons to translate Serbian films and literary works: "this is a language for which we require no translation. The practice should be oriented towards practical solutions. Serbian is a foreign language, but we understand it. This is a matter of common sense."[84]

Another singular "language" episode created by the desire to implement the law — in this case, on behalf of the government — are the so-called Anti-Cyrillic protests in Vukovar, a city that was besieged during the War of Independence, of which it became a symbol. Art. 12 (1) of the Constitutional Act on the Rights of National Minorities (*Ustavni zakon o pravima nacionalnih manjina*, NN 155/2002) provides that "equality in the official use of a minority language and script shall be exercised in the territory of a self-governing unit where the members of a national minority make up at least one third of the population". This implies the introduction of bilingual and/or biscriptual street signs in Vukovar, where more than one third of the population is Serbian. When the signs were put up in 2013, a wave of protests and smashing of the signs led by War veterans started. In the same year, the Headquarters for the Defense of Croatian Vukovar *(Stožer za obranu hrvatskog Vukovara)*, a committee formed in opposition to the erection of bilingual signs in Vukovar, gathered 650,000 signatures, asking for a referendum amending the existing Law on National Minorities Rights. The referendum was, however, declared unconstitutional by the Constitutional Court in August 2014. A year later the City Council of Vukovar changed the Statute of the City in order to circumvent the provision by subjecting the introduction of such street signs to the prior fulfillment of other criteria. Some of these amandements were repealed by the Constitutional Court in the summer of 2019.

The purist tendencies in language planning produced mixed results: some terms, such as *putovnica* (passport) and *izbornik* (football coach), managed to replace the previously used *pasoš* (which is

---

84   I am quoting the statement as reported on the news portal net.hr: "Cirkus u Otvorenom zbog prijevoda srpskih filmova" (Circus in *Otvoreno* because of the translation of Serbian films). Net.hr, January 25, 2012: https://net.hr/danas/hrvatska/cirkus-u-zbog-prijevoda-srpskih-filmova/. Last accessed on March 28, 2019.

still used colloquially) and *selektor*, but the "inverted 'logic' that all that is unusual is 'real Croatian' due to the post-1990 're-Croatization' of Croatian" has led to "undesired effects" such as the usage of the Russian loanword *izvješće* (report) instead of *izvještaj*, "of 'pure Croatian'" origin (Kapović 2011, 49). Croatian speakers have reacted to the "puromania" principally in two ways: by ridiculing it and/or by being afraid of speaking publicly in order "not to make a mistake" (49). What is perhaps more interesting for the purpose of this text is that all libraries in Croatia that officially carried the name *biblioteka* (library) progressively adopted the designation of *knjižnica* (library). The two synonyms appeared almost equally in everyday language, but the discussions among professionals in the 1960s privileged Latin and Greek terminology to denote "the prestigious, scientific, higher cultural meaning and function of these institutions". Conversely, the term *knjižnica* indicated the idea of national awakening while Croatia was under foreign rule (Mesić 1991, 146). Is the official re-introduction of the word *knjižnica* to be interpreted as a tribute to the (pan-Slavic) Croatian national revival, an attempt at bringing libraries closer to their patrons by using a "popular" rather than a scientific term or simply as an act of "purifying" the language by replacing a word that is more commonly used in Serbian? On the other hand, the term *narodna* (meaning popular or the people, but carrying the additional meaning of national) continues to be used for public libraries. Or it was until the new Act on Librarianship was published in the *Official Gazette* (NN 17/2019) in February 2019, in which the word that is used is *javna* (public) instead of *narodna*. Is it a literal translation from English, as some librarians argue; an attempt at distinguishing public from private libraries, which are mentioned for the first time in the Act; the replacement of an outdated term that no longer reflects the function of public libraries; or something else? The term *narodna* (or *pučka*) appeared at the turn of the century and it emphasized the romantic function and the target group of public libraries: institutions open to everyone for free (or subject to the payment of symbolic fees) with the task of educating "simple people": workers, peasants, the poor. The other terms suggested as alternatives after 1945 included mass *(masovna)* and *za narod* (for the people) or popular *(popularna)*.

Mesić, for instance, supports the terms *javna* (public) and *opća* (general), which refer to the type of content that is found in the collections of public libraries (Mesić 1991, 150–153). This is the case with the Slovenian term used for public libraries, *splošnoizobraževalne* (general education). Linguistic and terminological issues are, however, not the primary concern of this book, and a deeper discussion of these issues goes beyond its scope.

In the previously mentioned volume devoted to "Spiritual Renewal", one could hear, among other things, that "only an expert who possesses Croatian national identity can write history textbooks" (Baković 1992, 121). Standing as corollaries to this policy of purist language were a couple of statements and ministerial directions aimed at school and public libraries, which will be examined in the next section.

1.6. The "Spirit of Renewal" is Sweeping Libraries

The official opening of the new building of the National and University Library in Zagreb took place on the 28th of May 1995[85] in the presence of President Tuđman and the Minister of culture Ljilja Vokić. This ceremony, part of the celebration of the 5th Croatian Statehood Day *(Dan državnosti)*, emphasized the inextricable link between statehood and national culture as symbolized by the biggest and most important library in the country. Although some sources[86] report that on that occasion the official name of the institution was changed from *Nacionalna i sveučilišna biblioteka* to *Nacionalna i sveučilišna knjižnica*, the renaming was entered into the register of the Commercial Court in Zagreb on the 16th of January 1997.[87]

---

[85] Until 2002 Statehood Day was celebrated in Croatia on the 30th of May, when the first multi-party Parliament was constituted in 1990. It is now celebrated on the 25th of June, when Croatia declared independence from Yugoslavia in 1991.

[86] "Otvorena nova zgrada NSK u Zagrebu" (New building of the NSK opens). Retrieved from: https://povijest.hr/nadanasnjidan/otvorena-nova-zgrada-n sk-u-zagrebu-1995/. The text was also taken over by the portal Zagreb Info: https://www.zagreb.info/ritam-grad/nadanasnjidan/otvorena-nova-zgrada -nacionalne-sveucilisne-knjiznice-zagrebu-1995/129960. Last accessed on March 28, 2019.

[87] I wish to thank Ante Lešaja for forwarding the Decision of the Commercial Court in Zagreb (Tt-97/84-2) to me. It is still unclear who and when took the

The building, whose cornerstone was laid in 1988 by the academics Ivan Jurković and Andre Mohorovičić, thus became "the second building that the Croats built for their National Library in one century".[88] While it is incumbent upon the National and University Library to "assemble and organize the Croatian national collection of library materials", by no means is this a task normally expected of school libraries, which primarily serve educational institutions. Nevertheless, two controversial documents insisting on the Croatian nationality of the authors whose works can and should be found in school library collections were produced in mid-1992. Created around the same time that the "Spiritual Renewal" consultation was taking place, the two memoranda are couched in wording similar to that displayed at the conference. The first is a document for "internal use",[89] the Instruction on the Procedure for Elementary School Libraries *(Naputak za rad sa knjižnicama osnovnih škola)*, signed by Veronika Čelić-Tica on behalf of a working group sponsored by the Institute of Education of the Ministry of Education, Culture and Sport *(Zavod za školstvo Ministarstva prosvjete, kulture i športa)*, the Development Service of the National and University Library *(Razvojna služba nacionalne i sveučilišne knjižnice)*, and the Central Commission of Zagreb Libraries *(Matična služba Knjižnica grada Zagreba)*. The Instruction, for example, asserted that school library collections need to include books "exclusively by Croatian authors or translators, written in the Croatian standard language and Latin script (exceptionally, authors of other nationalities if their works are to be found in the list of suggested readings)". Besides volumes that are included in the suggested reading lists, libraries should "only contain a selection of authors of Croatian nationality, respecting the principles and the criterion of quality". Moreover, school library inventories must not contain "ideologically tainted

---

decision, which in any case was subject to the approval of the founder, the Republic of Croatia.
88 As stated by Tihomil Maštrović, the Director of the Library between 2007–2011, in an interview with Zlatko Vidačković in *Vijenac* 359 (2007).
89 Lešaja in fact writes that the text was not published in Croatia until 2000, in an article by Rade Dragojević, "Disanje latinicom" (Breathing in Latin Script), *Feral Tribune*, April 22, 2000. It had, however, been published in Slovenia in August 1992 in *Knjižničarske novice* 2 (8) (1992) (Lešaja 2012, 106–107).

Yugoslavia, Europe and the World After 1989 73

literature" and "unsuitable and ideologically tainted textbooks" *(Prosvjeta* vol. 12 (37) n. 71 (681), 2005, 4–5, 8, 24, 28–29; Lešaja 2012, 106–116). While public libraries fall under the jurisdiction of the Ministry of Culture, school and scientific libraries are a responsibility of the Ministry of Science and Education *(Ministarstvo znanosti i obrazovanja)*[90] (Strićević and Pehar 2015, 679). The memorandum was followed by the "Binding Instruction on the Usage of School Library Book Inventories" *(Obvezatni naputak o korištenju knjižnog fonda u školskim bibliotekama)*[91], signed by the Minister of Education, Culture and Sport, Vesna Girardi-Jurkić.

The Binding Instruction required the introduction of "literature for the needs of religious culture and religious instruction in schools" and advised that

> "ideological literature from the past system that provides its own interpretation of the historical truth may, in an adequate number of copies, form a special collection as a testimony to a specific period, while the remainder, in compliance with library regulations, should be offered to an appropriate library that preserves such collections or similar" (679).

Considering that the inventories of school libraries mostly consist of volumes which are suggested readings defined by the curricula, it is interesting to observe what happened with those in the same period. Marijana Hameršak argues that the reading lists outlined in school curricula do not always reflect ideological and political changes so much as they do the developments in the publishing industry (Hameršak 2006, 104–105). For instance, in the curriculum for the years 1991–1993, the list for elementary schools included for the first time books with a religious background[92], and it excluded literary works that thematized the World War II partisan struggle

---

[90] Between 1990 and 1995 culture and education pertained to the same Ministry, the Ministry of Culture and Education *(Ministarstvo kulture i prosvjete)*, between 1990–1993 named the Ministry of Education, Culture and Sport *(Ministarstvo prosvjete, kulture i športa)*.
[91] It was published in the June 23, 1992, gazette of the Ministry of Education, Culture and Sport 2 (5): 15–16.
[92] The author quotes two titles: *Dijete je rođeno* by Jindra Čapek and *Bor koji je ostao neokićen* by Ruth Hagen-Torn (104).

or the socialist experience.[93] Nevertheless, it still included works that are part of the national corpuses of the other (former) Yugoslav republics.[94] On the other hand, these titles have not been reprinted or republished in the given period, which indicates that they have not been used in practice (104–105). Another important insight I gained when comparing actual reading lists with media writings about them is that they do not change as often as it might seem. In fact, it can happen that discussions, which do not lead to a change of the reading lists (usually in the framework of the debate on the national school program) receive extensive media coverage, creating the opposite perception. This issue will be examined more extensively in subchapter 3.1.

Almost a decade later, Girardi-Jurkić stated that, in the political context of the time, the Binding Instructions were "the 'mildest' one could sign, considering the amount of pressure she was exposed to" (Lasić 2015, np). It is hard to determine, however, whether there were other, similar, internal or even oral instructions that were less "mild", as some people who worked in the fields of education and culture in the given period claim.[95] One example from Korčula seems to suggest that librarians were occasionally pressured with regard to the books they were displaying: In 1994 the President of the Steering Committee of the "Ivan Vidali" library in Korčula, Alena Fazinić, sent a letter (published in facsimile in Ante Lešaja's book) to the Head of the Library, Tajana Grbin, demanding the removal of the "shameful" book by Vladimir Dedijer,

---

[93] Compared to the 1989 Curriculum, the following works did not figure in the period 1991-1993: Ja sam pionir by Emil Paravina and Josip Bifel, France Bevk's Priče o Titu, Priče partizanke by Branko Ćopić, Kurir s Psunja written by Gabrovidović and, finally, Pirgo and Mali konjovodac by Anđelka Martić (Hameršak 2006, 105).

[94] Ježeva kućica by Branko Ćopić, Tko je Videku napravio košuljicu by Fran Levstik, Ledena gora by Ahmet Hromadžić, Vehbi Kikaj's Iz priče u priču, Bijeli dvori, Bijelo cigance by Vidoe Podgorec, Družina Sinjega galeba by Tone Seliškar, Orlovi rano lete by Branko Ćopić, Plavi čuperak by Miroslav Antić, Branislav Nušić's Autobiografija and a poetry selection from South Slavic literatures Svjetiljka snova (Hameršak 2006, 104-105).

[95] Informal conversation with schoolteachers and acquaintances. In a phone interview with me, the journalist VI also mentioned that there may have been other, "secret" instructions.

Vatikan i Jasenovac (published in English as *The Yugoslav Auschwitz and the Vatican: The Croatian Massacre of the Serbs During World War II*) to storage. Fazinić writes

> "that it is commonly known what kind of 'truths' and 'documents' are presented in it. Because of that, this book and numerous similar works written on the topic of the 'genocidal inclination' of the Croats and the Church in Croatia were published in the former system in Yugoslavia and widely distributed".

The genocide of the Serbs perpetrated by the Ustasha during World War II resurfaced in the debates among historians after Tito's death in the 1980s and these were transmitted into mass politics through Croatian and Serbian nationalist ideologies (Denich 1994, 369). One of the most prominent participants in the debate was the historian and YPA general and later President of Croatia, Franjo Tuđman. In his book *Wastelands of Historical Reality* (1989), Tudman relativized the crimes of the Ustasha and argued that "genocidal inclinations" cannot be ascribed only to certain nations.[96] Interestingly, Stipe Šuvar writes that, like Dedijer's book, even Tuđman's works celebrating Tito, the socialist revolution and the National Liberation Struggle were a thorn in the eye that needed to be removed from public libraries in order to erase this part of his past (Šuvar 2003, 130).[97] Librarians were, however, pressured not only by those above them, but also by the library's patrons: Lešaja, for instance, writes of librarians who would "hide" Belgrade editions of books in order to avoid unpleasant incidents, as happened with the father of a boy who was given a copy of *The Praise of Folly* by Erasmus in ekavian.

---

96 On the symbolic revival of genocide and the disintegration of Yugoslavia see Denich (1994).
97 Franjo Tuđman (1922-1999) acted as a political commissar during the National Liberation War and became the youngest general of the Yugoslav People's Army in 1959. After leaving the Army in 1961 he moved to Zagreb to become the Director of the Institute for the History of the Worker's Movement. His views gradually turned more nationalist, for which he was expelled from the League of Communists of Croatia and lived the next 23 years as a dissident. Stipe Šuvar (1936-2004) was a Communist official that unlike many of his colleagues did not dismiss his socialist beliefs. His name is most commonly associated with the controversial education reform introduced in the 1970s when he was the Croatian Minister of Education.

Another public statement worth mentioning refers to public libraries and could be read as an indirect invitation to a "cleansing" of libraries. This statement came from a high-ranking politician, the Minister of Finance Borislav Škegro. As *Novi list* reported[98], during a parliamentary session in which the budget for the upcoming year 1998 was being discussed, the MP Marija Bajt (HDZ, a librarian by profession) asked Škegro whether the newly introduced Value Added Tax (VAT) would apply to books as well. His answer was affirmative, but he also mentioned that the government would be implementing other measures to support publishers:

> "the government will introduce measures for galvanizing the publishing that the Croatian state needs. For instance, public libraries will be financed to remove books in Serbian and similar languages, or those with inappropriate and obsolete translations" (*Novi list*, November 27, 1997).[99]

I interviewed a journalist who closely followed the case, and here is what he said:

> "he [Škegro] very simply combined the economic cycle with the ideological endeavor of cleansing. In a way, his statement articulates what has happened before and in a novel way institutionalizes what is still happening today. It is about taking control of the cultural milieu from economic positions, to introduce a new order" (IL, journalist, personal interview, Zagreb, October 7, 2015).

"The book business is where culture and economics meet in any society", write Rüdiger Wischenbart and Nenad Popović (2000, np). The Finance Minister's statement touches upon the publishing industry and the acquisitions of new volumes in public libraries, which is the greatest point of contact between these two important but fundamentally different (primarily because of their private and

---

98   On page 221 of his book Lešaja writes that the same sentence was left out from the Parliamentary report on that session about the government budget (*Izvješća Hrvatskog Sabora* n. 204, dated December 8, 1997).
99   The statement, however, is not recorded in the official parliamentary reports (*Izvješća Hrvatskog Sabora*) about the debate on the VAT (n. 204, December 8, 1997, p. 5), but was reported in *Novi list* (Lešaja 2012, 221). Another statement that is often cited as indicative of the anti-intellectualism of the 1990s is "How much for a kilo of brain? 2.5 DM for a kilo", issued by the Keeper of the State Seal, Ivan Milas. In Zlatar, A. (2001). "Kultura u tranzicijskom periodu u Hrvatskoj." *Reč* 61 (7): 59–74, at 66.

public nature) components of a nation's book policy. For this reason, I will now briefly outline the changes the publishing sector in Croatia and Slovenia underwent after 1991. Before I do that, a brief elucidation of the process of book acquisition in Croatian libraries will serve to contextualize Škegro's sentence.

Public libraries commonly acquire new books in four ways: through purchase (with the library's funds stemming from its founder, i.e., state and local authorities), donation, exchange and legal deposit. State purchase became established as a common practice in the 1980s in Croatia. This method of acquisition supports local publishers and, for libraries with limited funds, is actually the only way of building a collection, as is the legal deposit for some others. State purchase often led to the acquisition of works of highly debatable quality, but works that were in line with "what the Croatian state needs".[100] This practice was severely criticized by librarians since they did not have any influence over the selection of books. Their critique eventually resulted in a bigger inclusion of librarians in the process. As it will be shown in Chapter Two, using the example of public libraries in the Croatian capital, the volume of acquisition was much lower in the period 1991–1998 than in the last years of Yugoslavia. What is more, in 1993–1994 more volumes were discarded than acquired. Among the books that found their way onto the shelves in the early 1990s were those that were kept in "closed funds" during socialist Yugoslavia. As Željko Vegh writes, the following categories of volumes were kept in closed stacks, generally unavailable to library users: books not in line with communist ideology; those representing the USSR in a bad light; those by authors who were writing against leftists; books by the Ustasha, Chetniks and other enemies; and books dealing with religious topics (Vegh 2015, 28). Quoting Stipčević, he stresses that the removal of books during socialist Yugoslavia was done at the discretion of each librarian and local authorities. For example, in the Zagreb City Library, 2800 titles were relegated to the closed stacks (27). Similarly, in the National and University Library, émigré literature was kept in the so-called D-fund (the Director's Fund),

---

100 For a more detailed review of the problem see Nebesny (nd).

available only to researchers upon request. The collection was shown to the public for the first time in 1989 in an exhibition; it is today part of the Foreign Croatica Collection *(inozemna Croatica)* and available to the public in its entirety. A considerable part of the collection was donated to the NSK by Croatian émigrés, including Vinko Nikolić, a former Ustasha-official in the Nazi-puppet Independent State of Croatia (1941–1945), who, like many others, returned to Croatia in the early 1990s and occupied important (governmental) positions.

The entire cultural infrastructure, including libraries, publishing companies, sales and distribution, was badly affected by the disintegration of the intellectual community, of the shared Serbo-Croatian linguistic culture, and of the common economic area caused by the dissolution of Yugoslavia. As Rüdiger Wischenbart and Nenad Popović write, "traffic in ideas is a first casualty in war". The publishing industry was severely affected by the war, with the exception of Slovenia. Had it not been for the war, former Yugoslav republics "could have become shining examples of the conversion of state-controlled to free-enterprise publishing" (Wischenbart and Popović 2000, np). The industry was responsive to readers' demands, moral censorship was almost absent, while political control was minimized, informal and mostly directed at direct "enemies" of the party, such as Milovan Đilas (Booher 1975, 129). Edward Booher ends his 1975 article on publishing in the USSR and Yugoslavia with the following sentences:

> "The right to read, and hence the right to know, is a concept accepted by Yugoslavs. These rights are observed more openly and with greater respect than in other parts of Eastern Europe. Whether this policy will continue after Tito's rule ends is a question I am frequently asked. I believe it will."

The author concludes that Yugoslavia's publishing system contributes to the development of "an open society that could lead to economic and political democracy" (118). Each of the republics had its own educational publishing companies, the national academies were also actively publishing, and all languages benefited from a flourishing translation industry (a quarter of the total output, mostly from USA, GB, France, USSR and Germany). Publishing houses operated like the ones in the West, with the exception that the initial capital was provided by the State and that employees participated in management and profits (126). Out of the 1666 foreign titles published in 1967, 408 were from Anglophone publishers and 226 from the USSR, despite the fact that Soviet authors could be published free of license fee (Booher 1975, 127). Not only contemporary literature, but also history and political writings were translated. Interestingly, of some 68 million books produced in 1968, 22 million were literary works, half of which were translations. In the same year, 186,000 "Marxist-Leninist works" were produced, as well as 6.5 million books belonging to the categories "Economics", "Applied Economics" and "Business Organization" (Booher, 1975, 129).

Slovenian publishing was unique insofar as the use of the Slovenian language ended at the county's borders. The four Serbo-Croatian speaking republics could count on a larger market outside the borders of the respective states. Slovenian identity was mostly defined through language, and maintaining a flourishing publishing industry in the language was a way of perpetuating that identity. In the late 1980s a number of small privately-owned publishing houses started operating, many of which failed. Michael Biggins identifies the potential causes of their failure in "the retention of all established bookstores in the hands of the three largest publishers"; the budgetary neglect of public and school libraries by the Ministry of Culture; the decrease in governmental subsidies; a drop in demand; rising retail book prices; and literature's loss of social status due to the imperative to survive in market conditions by searching for business opportunities (Biggins 2000, 12). The three main publishing houses established in the Yugoslav period—"Državna Založba Slovenije" (State Publishing House of Slovenia), "Mladinska knjiga" (Youth Books), and "Cankarjeva Založba" (Cankar Publishing House)—continued operating in the 1990s, unlike their counterparts in other Eastern European countries, thanks to their adaptation to market standards several decades before. An exception was "Komunist", the publishing house of the League of Communists, which was a casualty of the economic transition (11).

Generally speaking, culture was not immune to the changes brought by a transition to market economy, which is best illustrated by budget cuts: culture's percentage share of the government budget in Slovenia was 1.02 in 1990, a figure which dropped to 0.79 in 1991 and to a further 0.53 in 1993 (UNESCO recommends a minimum of 1.5) (Biggins 2000, 13). While state subsidies decreased, the number of published volumes rose, albeit with lower press runs. For instance, while the number of published volumes in Slovenia rose from 1932 in 1989 to 3647 in 1997, state subsidies decreased from 5,000,000 DM in 1990 to 1,017,000 DM in 1995 (Biggins 2000, 14). Biggins writes that in the mid-1990s the press run in Slovenia was between 200–1000 copies, where 500 was considered good (Biggins 2000, 13). In fact, the pre-1990 press runs of 2000–3000 copies were exaggerated and often remained unsold. The introduction of a sales tax in 1992, which was later replaced by the value added tax, further augmented the price of books, which became a taxable commodity. Publishers protested the introduction of VAT on their stock at the time of production rather than sale, since it takes an average of two years to sell the usual Slovene press run. The tax issue may be affected by lobbying efforts. For instance, Croatian publishers were able to reduce the 22 percent tax to zero less than two years after it was introduced in 1998. Today the VAT on books in Croatia is 5 percent, while in Slovenia it is 9.5 percent.

In Croatia, research about the production and distribution of books, as well as reading habits, is not being carried out as systematically as in Slovenia. The shrinking of the book market after 1991, the war, and questionable privatization endeavors led to a decrease in the number of bookstores from 200 to 70 by the year 2000 (Wischenbart and Popović 2000, np). For instance, "Mladost", once Yugoslavia's biggest book company, was closed and its assets sold or destroyed. On the other hand, publishing houses were springing up in massive numbers in the 1990s: In 1993 there were 353 registered publishing houses, and by 2004 the number rose to 5164.[101] During the war 1500 publishing houses were established, many of which published only one book (Jelušić 2004, 94). It is common for

---

101 "Nakladništvo" (publishing). Retrieved on March 30, 2019, from: http://www.enciklopedija.hr/natuknica.aspx?id=42840.

Yugoslavia, Europe and the World After 1989   81

publishers to own bookstores, which can lead to a conflict of interest. The publishing sector is heavily dependent on state support in the form of subsidies for the publication or purchase of the finished product.

The aim of this chapter was to describe the general context within which individuals and institutions found themselves operating immediately after the dissolution of Yugoslavia. In doing so, I emphasized what I think are the most important officially promoted and unofficially supported state policies which should be taken into consideration when examining the discarding of books from public libraries. Chapter Two will deal extensively with the latter and the interpretations thereof.

2. The Discarding of Books in the 1990s: A Fact, a Perception, a Metaphor ...

In the previous chapter I examined those aspects of the transition period in Eastern Europe, former Yugoslavia and more specifically, Croatia and Slovenia, which I consider relevant for studying the discarding of books from public libraries in the aftermath of the Yugoslav breakup. The examined developments range from the general characteristics of the postsocialist condition to the very specific circumstances in the two countries I am predominantly focusing on. This examination contributes to a better and more nuanced understanding of the context conducive to a massive discarding of books after 1989. What makes the Croatian case stand out, however, is that the discarding involved not only so-called "red literature", but also books in Serbian and Cyrillic. Even though the "cleansing" of Croatian libraries was not enforced with a particular act or decree, it was openly encouraged by the upper echelons of power. Internal documents such as the previously mentioned Instruction on the Procedure for Elementary School Libraries; incautious public statements by politicians; purist tendencies in language planning bordering on the absurd; and the general cultural climate created by state-building *(državotvorni)* media – all of these point to the fact that the practice was tacitly supported by the state. However, public libraries are only loosely coordinated heterogeneous units where many decisions are taken independently from local and national authorities. In other words, the framework conditions for a politicization of library practices were there, but this did not affect each library equally. When cases of inappropriate, politically motivated discarding became known, the state and professional bodies in most cases failed to react by sanctioning those responsible, or by condemning the occurrence more resolutely. These omissions, together with the more proactive measures mentioned above, are yet another proof of the inadequate protection accorded to books, "an integral part of the cultural life of a nation" (Živković 2008, np), by state institutions. In this chapter I will outline my approach to the topic and briefly dwell upon the practice of weeding and discarding, since this practice, like books, does not have the same meaning for librarians and non-librarians. In fact, most intellectuals and book-loving people will not spare words to condemn the disposal of books, let alone bigger acts of violence towards them. Yet, librarians must discard books as a part of their job. I will then review Ante Lešaja's book *Libricide. The Destruction of Books in Croatia in the 1990s*, which was an invaluable source of information and the starting point for my research, together with some less comprehensive writings on the topic. Subsequently, the debate in the media about "libricide" will be reconstructed and analyzed and compared with the findings from Slovenia.

2.1. My Approach to the Topic

In her recent monograph on the Yugoslav wars of the 1990s, Catherine Baker argues that microhistorical approaches might shed some light on the dynamics of the conflict and on the 1990s as a whole (Baker 2015, 19). Although Baker primarily refers to organized crime and everyday life on the battlefield, by extension the same applies to "battles" fought on the cultural front. By looking at everyday practices of institutions and services operating primarily on the local level, one might be able to better discern how certain processes unfold on a larger, societal level. In other words, could the increased reviews of public library collections in the 1990s reveal something about the mechanisms underlying the formation of an increasingly nationalist culture? To what extent was the practice of discarding influenced by primarily political, but also social and economic, changes after the breakup of Yugoslavia? By retaining some books and discarding others, do libraries perhaps have a bigger say in the availability of information and the construction of the national narrative than one might think? In an attempt to answer these and other questions, this study starts from an examination of discarding in public libraries in Slovenia. The scarcity of material on this subject stands opposed to the vast amount of material that Ante Lešaja has gathered over the years about Croatia. In his encyclopaedic *Libricide. The Destruction of Books in Croatia in the 1990s*, Lešaja presents all the relevant official documents, data (when available), and newspaper articles related to the fate of "unsuitable" books in the 1990s. The author often reports articles and documents in their entirety and "lets them speak" by limiting his own interventions to a minimum. The book comes with a CD on which there are numerous official papers related to the legal proceedings in the "Korčula case" and more than a hundred newspaper articles related to the topic of book destruction that Lešaja has meticulously collected over a period of twenty years. This author's work was thus a starting point for my research, during which I maintained an ongoing e-mail correspondence with him. The attentive scrutiny of the book and sources included in it revealed inconsistencies, exaggerations, and terminological inaccuracies in the newspaper accounts on the topic of "bibliocide". For that reason, I interviewed or had informal conversations, in person or by phone, with the journalists that closely followed or had some first-hand experience with the topic: Igor Lasić, Viktor Ivančić, Rade Dragojević, Srećko Pulig, Igor Ružić and Filip Švarm. What most of these journalists have in common is that they wrote for anti-establishment newspapers such as the political weekly *Feral Tribune*, the cultural biweekly *Zarez*, the daily *Novi list*, and the outlets of the Serbian National Council such as *Prosvjeta* and *Novosti*. Rade Dragojević edited the special issue of *Prosvjeta* titled "Bibliocide—Culturecide: Where one burns books, one will soon burn people" in Serbo-Croatian (2003) and English language (2005) editions. Viktor Ivančić, one of the founders of *Feral Tribune*, devoted a chapter to "libricide" under the title "Culture of Death" in his book *Dot on the U. The Šakić Case: Anatomy of a Scandal* (2000). Igor Ružić is a theatre critic who found discarded books in a trash container and years later brought them for scanning to the exhibition action "Discarded. On the Occasion of the 20th Anniversary of Operation Storm", which will be analyzed in Chapter Three. Finally, Filip Švarm (the pseudonym of Damir Kalember) is the managing editor of the Serbian weekly *Vreme*, one of the few independent media outlets in Serbia. When I started my research, cases of "murky" discarding were (well) known in Croatia, while no such cases were systematically documented in other former Yugoslav republics, with the exception of war-related damage, hearsay stories and sporadic writings about sloppy discarding, some of which will be briefly mentioned. It has already been mentioned in the introduction that a simple web search reveals a certain terminological confusion on what "libricide"/"bookicide" is, whether destruction refers to the violent damaging of monuments and books in conflict-ridden areas or outside the war zone, and whether books were actually burned or if the expression was used metaphorically. One of my initial priorities was thus to clearly delineate and define the phenomenon in question: to redefine the term "destruction" by separating war-related destruction from the removal of books of libraries which may or may not have ended up in the garbage, and by separating actual burning from "burning" as a metaphor. I then tried to find out whether something similar to the events in Croatia occurred in Slovenia, considering that in many of the occasional conversations with intellectuals who actively followed the sociopolitical situation in the 1990s this was not explicitly excluded, but on the contrary convincingly assumed. This led me to the Centre for Library Development at the National and University Library in Ljubljana, which monitors the activities of all publicly funded libraries in Slovenia. It collects and analyzes (statistical) data about libraries and participates in the planning of the activities of the regional central libraries. Looking for newspaper articles on the topic, I conducted research in the archive of the Institute of Contemporary History *(Inštitut za novejšo zgodovino)* in the Slovenian capital where I searched for newspaper articles about discarding in the two leading newspapers *Delo* and *Dnevnik*. In parallel, I conducted semi-structured interviews with several librarians at the National and University Library, the largest branch of the Ljubljana City Library, the Oton Župančič Library, as well as with two librarians at my host institution, the Faculty of Social Sciences at the University of Ljubljana. I also interviewed three used book dealers, one of whom was a publisher in the late 1980s. Moreover, I met the members of a Serbian cultural institute operating in Ljubljana and a former employee of a paper-recycling center. The interviewees were selected through snowball sampling, i.e., my interlocutors referred me to potential conversational partners. Most of the interviews were recorded by using a digital voice recorder or a phone; some were not taped at the explicit request of the interviewees, while others were

The Discarding of Books in the 1990s 87

not due to the modest amount of information the interviewee was able to provide or due to the spontaneous and informal nature of the interview. I thus prefer labelling the latter as informal conversations, while I define as occasional conversations the talks, I had with people who would freely share their opinions or knowledge with me. This would often happen during conferences or workshops where I would present my work, but not exclusively. In some cases, these occasional encounters turned into examples of successful collaboration: for instance, with Ana Bilankov. I met her several times to discuss her film *In War and Revolution*, and in May 2015, in cooperation with the International Graduate Centre for Culture, we organized a screening, followed by a talk with the artist in Gießen. In total, I conducted fourteen personal, two phone/Skype and five e-mail interviews, together with countless less formal conversations. The recorded interviews were all transcribed and can be found in my personal archive, together with the e-mail interviews, my notes, and research diary. With some of my interviewees I communicated chiefly via e-mail, as was the case with one publisher and with the artists who contributed to the exhibition "Discarded. On the Occasion of the 20th Anniversary of Operation Storm" and who kindly agreed to answer my questions in writing and shared the photos of their performances. The interview with one of the two organizers of the abovementioned exhibition took place via Skype. To these should be added the phone conversations and e-mails to which I resorted when I had questions for librarians at the National and University Library in Zagreb and the National Library in Serbia. Most addressees were cooperative and only a minor part of e-mails remained unanswered. All the previously mentioned interviews, archival work, informal and occasional conversations took place in the period between 2014 and 2018.

In the preliminary research phase I spoke with historians dealing with the contemporary history of former Yugoslavia, people involved in the book business, and frequent library users. While it soon became clear that research involving the entire former Yugoslavia would require more time and financial resources than what I had at my disposal, these conversations confirmed that a comparison between Croatia and Slovenia might yield more fruitful results. Even if at first sight the nationalist discourse propagated in Croatia in the 1990s can find a counterpart only in Serbia, it is Croatia and Slovenia that parallelly inaugurated a distancing process from Yugoslavia, which found its expression, among others, in cultural policies. Also, a couple of newspaper articles that I will analyze in this chapter testified to the fact that the "cleansing of libraries" in Croatia did not pass unobserved in Slovenia, where apparently the same was happening, "but was not political". In general, the similarities and differences between the two countries appeared as a good background against which to test the various claims about "library cleansing". Once the economic "motor" of Yugoslavia, Croatia and Slovenia share most of their pre-Yugoslav past, but were not equally affected by the wars of Yugoslav succession. On the one hand, the war fought between 1991 and 1995 is inseparable from the Croatian context, but on the other it risks being used as a justification for certain preposterous actions. The comparison between the two countries was thus aimed at disentangling from the war context and from the specific position the Croatian language planners found themselves in, that is, wanting to differentiate the Croatian standard from the Bosnian and Serbian. Slovenian is and was a separate language even before the breakup of Yugoslavia, while, Bosnian, Croatian and Serbian were known under the syntagm Serbo-Croatian (which does not mean that there were no disagreements among linguists on that matter even prior to the 1990s), a language that was taught in Slovenian schools as well. Nonetheless, language is a crucial identity marker in both cases, as is the conviction, the desire and now the fact of formally belonging to Europe.

2.2. The Theory and Practice of Weeding and Discarding in Public Libraries

Since public libraries are technically accessible to everyone and their collections are the most varied — insofar as they lack the thematic specialization which may characterize a special (in the form of professional literature) or a school library (in the form of books that appear on the suggested reading lists) — I decided to examine those institutions (*narodne knjižnice* in Croatian or *splošnoizobraževalne* or *splošne knjižnice* in Slovenian). The *IFLA/UNESCO Public Libraries Manifesto 1994* defines public libraries as "local centre[s] of information, making all kinds of knowledge and information readily available to its users" where the "material must reflect current trends and the evolution of society, as well as the memory of human endeavour and imagination". Most importantly, "the collections and services [of the libraries] should not be subject to any form of ideological, political or religious censorship, nor commercial pressure".[102] Even if libraries might not be the primary source of information for many in today's digital environment, they do have a role to play through the various programs and formats they offer that go well beyond the borrowing of (physical) books. In fact, in the past decades the function of libraries has changed from a transactional to a pronouncedly relational one, as they have redefined themselves to become places of encounter and long-life-learning, other than facilities where books can be borrowed. The steady number of library users seems to be suggesting that the "rebranding" has served its purpose.

In Croatia and Slovenia, the public library network consists of more than 250 (269 in 2012 in Croatia, 265 in Slovenia in the same year) [103] public libraries, which are generally subject to the control of central libraries (usually the biggest library in a county or region) that are answerable to the National and University Library which, in turn, is under the supervision of the Ministry of Culture and the Ministry of Education. The latter is also responsible for elementary and high-school libraries. The central libraries are the National and University Library *(Nacionalna i sveučilišna knjižnica – NSK)* in Zagreb and the National and University Library *(Nacionalna in*

---

102 *IFLA/UNESCO Public Library Manifesto 1994*, available online at https://repository.ifla.org/bitstream/123456789/168/1/pl-manifesto-en.pdf. Last accessed on April 5, 2019.
103 These are the numbers reported in the 2016 "Croatia in figures" publication by the Croatian Bureau of Statistics (33) and Ambrožič and Žumer (2015, 733) respectively. It is nevertheless hard to establish the exact number of libraries since some operate within other institutions, such as public libraries operating within cultural centers or school libraries operating within rehabilitation centers (Stričević and Pehar 2015, 679).

univerzitetna knjižnica – NUK) in Ljubljana, which are both the central libraries of the largest university in the country (Zagreb and Ljubljana) and the central library of the national library system. The National and University Library often assumes the role of archive, since it is obliged to keep at least one copy of each book that has been printed in the language of the corpus *(Slovenica* in Slovenia, *Croatica* in Croatia) which it is guarding (the so-called legal deposit). Even if National and University Libraries no longer receive the legal deposit copy from other former Yugoslav states, they acquire some of these volumes through exchange with the other national libraries, through donations, and through purchase. Among former Yugoslav national libraries, the cooperation between the National and University Library in Ljubljana and the Croatian National and University Library is the most fruitful, partly because of the proximity of these two countries (Poličnik-Čermelj and Sešek 2006, 79). In Slovenia, libraries did not undergo dramatic changes after the dissolution of Yugoslavia (Ambrožič and Žumer 2015, 743). Since 1990 the number of public and school libraries increased, as well as membership. In 2012 there were 265 public libraries, 966 school and 115 special libraries (733). In 2012, there were 1185 library staff members, of whom 930 were qualified librarians (739).

On the other hand, Strićević and Pehar (2015) argue that a number of factors influenced the post-Yugoslav developments in Croatian libraries, some of which were country-specific, others global: the proclamation of independence and the transition from socialist (self-managed) to market economy, war-related destruction and subsequent reconstruction, technological advancements in the IT sector and the global economic crisis (Strićević and Pehar 2015, 675). The war (1991–1995) left a direct (through the partial or complete destruction of 200 libraries and their funds) and indirect (lack of funding, inadequate infrastructure) mark on library operations in general. Nevertheless, during the war and in the immediate postwar period, public libraries registered a rise in membership. In fact, even when schools were temporarily closed, libraries were opened, people were encouraged to take a book with them to the shelter, and a large number of refugees coming from Bosnia-Herzegovina and war-torn parts of Croatia went to inhabit areas less

The Discarding of Books in the 1990s   91

affected by the conflict (678). Also, bibliotherapy programs were put in place to help people forget the horrors of their wartime everyday life and/or deal with it through discussions.

Libraries are public institutions with the primary task of informing the public. They are founded and funded by the state and its local organs in order to ensure an indiscriminate access to information to all citizens. Contrary to what the public perception on the function of libraries might be, public libraries are not archives, and their collection is there to be borrowed. What they are supposed to store permanently are, however, local studies volumes (Kernel 1999, 25). Libraries must periodically remove items from their collections by weeding or discarding them. As it was already mentioned in the introduction, weeding and discarding are often used as synonyms although they are technically not the same procedure. Translated into everyday domestic life, weeding would be like moving a household item to the basement, while discarding, as the word itself suggests, means giving the item away so it is no longer in your possession, be it to a friend or a waste management company.

According to the internationally accepted guide for small libraries issued by the American Library Association[104], weeding is an important factor in the development of a library collection and as such it complements the acquisition policy (Doll and Barron 2002, 59). There are many reasons for weeding, ranging from a lack of storage space and the existence of duplicate copies to inaccuracy of information contained in the book. What public libraries are usually advised to weed is materials or books of poor appearance or poor content, unused materials (which have not circulated in the past 3–5 years), and material that loses its importance due to demographic or other changes; local history volumes should be retained except when shabby and beyond repair (Larson 2012, 20). The most commonly cited weeding criteria are based on the MUSTIE

---

[104] I am quoting two American manuals because these guidelines are internationally accepted and even if it is common for individual libraries to issue their own guidelines, this is always done by respecting national and international standards.

guidelines.[105] Ideally, the librarian responsible for the development of the collection in a given disciplinary area decides about weeding in that particular field, but the final verdict is sometimes in the hands of the library director or a board. Regardless of the decision-making body, weeding is a highly discretionary, even subjective procedure that heavily depends on the professional skills, experience and ideological convictions of the individual or board in charge of it. As suggested in the CREW *Weeding Manual for Modern Libraries*, "weeding library materials that are no longer of use is no more 'irresponsible' than discarding broken equipment from the recreation center or repaving a road that has become worn from use" (89). It should be carried out periodically, depending on the size of the library, but it can be also executed continually. In fact, the CREW (Continuous Review, Evaluation and Weeding) method argues for a continual review of the collection, which makes it a kind of SWOT (Strength, Weaknesses, Opportunities and Threats) analysis of the library.

The purpose of weeding is to adapt the collection to the needs of the patrons by developing it and renewing it. "In too many libraries, collection development is based on the book as an object. Public libraries should not be in the business of accumulating physical objects", argues Janet Larson, the author of the CREW *Weeding Manual* (11). In other words, for the librarian it is the collection as a whole that matters, an approach which should be equally taken into account when acquiring and discarding volumes. In the latter case, some factors "exogenous" to the library also play a role. One such factor is whether the volume can be obtained in another library. This is the reason why in Croatia and Slovenia lists of volumes that are suggested for discarding are sent to the respective Central libraries and to the National and University Library, which should prevent the loss of rare books. A second factor is whether there are available funds to purchase a more satisfactory item. Weeding complements the acquisition policy, and if there is no money available

---

105 M: misleading; U: ugly, S: superseded; T: trivial; I: irrelevant; E: may be obtained elsewhere. https://olcsmalllibraries.wordpress.com/2009/05/04/weeding-library-collections/ Retrieved on April 7, 2015.

to purchase new items, it makes little sense to weed unless the volumes are damaged beyond repair. A third factor is whether more accurate information is to be found on the Internet.

The rule of thumb, according to Larson, is to weed 5 percent of the collection every year, a policy which allows the turnover of the collection every 20 years (17). What to do with discarded materials that neither the Central nor the National and University Library wish to take? The options are selling, giving away, exchanging, recycling, and destroying by incinerating or throwing into the trash. The CREW *Manual* advises giving away books because it "allows the library to avoid public relations issues that may arise if the community perceives the library as 'throwing away perfectly good books'" (84). Destruction is only the last resort and only for severely damaged volumes beyond repair that cannot be recycled or sold for pulp. "If [this] method is used, be sure the books won't be seen by someone passing by. Citizens might misunderstand the reasons for destroying 'valuable' books" (83). Moreover, "book burning" evokes unpleasant associations (86).

I have quoted from two international manuals, whose guidelines, however, are "not intended to act as a substitute for professional judgment calls and common sense" (22; in bold in the original) to give the reader a sense of the collection development and pruning standards that are generally accepted by librarians all over the world. Nevertheless, what occurs on the ground is often miles away from the best practices outlined in manuals. Libraries often do not have a collection development policy reflecting their mission statement, which is sometimes also lacking. In less affluent countries they cannot count on sufficient funds to replace damaged items, which is why it is common to "artificially" protract the useful life of an item by repairing it *ad infinitum*. Continual reviews are rare; long intervals between major weeding efforts are a more common occurrence. In practice, libraries do not even weed enough, as my research in Slovenia confirmed. What is more, smaller libraries in peripheral towns frequently do not employ professional librarians, even if the law requires it. To summarize, despite all the manuals and professional declarations and domestic law modeled on internationally accepted standards, the implementation thereof is lagging behind.

Probably the most authoritative among international organizations of the library profession is the International Federation of Library Associations (IFLA). It presents itself as "the global voice of the library and information profession" and counts among its members more than 1400 libraries worldwide. In 2001 the Freedom of Access to Information and Freedom of Expression (FAIFE) Advisory Committee operating within IFLA issued a report on libraries and intellectual freedom. Within the project more than 140 countries were contacted and 46 submitted their reports; among them were Croatia and Slovenia. The two reports give a short overview of the most important challenges the libraries in these two countries were facing in terms of the access to information at the end of the first decade as independent states. The one-page report about Slovenia concludes that the main obstacles to the free access to information for all users are of a financial nature, that is, the charging of membership fees and extra library services and the "deficient knowledge of librarians as regards their professional role". Another critical issue raised in the report is the uneven catering to the needs of national minorities: only the status of autochthonous groups, namely, the Italian and Hungarian minorities, is defined in the Constitution and in the Librarianship Act (art. 13), but not that of other minorities. The same applies to users with special needs. Finally, two cases are mentioned that could have been interpreted as hindrances to the free access to information: first, the ban on the distribution of a book about free masonry by Andrej Dvoršak, which was lifted after the court proceedings were concluded; and second, a proposal "that could have led to ideologically founded reshaping of library collections". This was the proposal of a Ljubljana City Council member from the Christian Democratic Party *(Slovenski krščanski demokrati* — SKD) to have library collections surveyed for "their ideological equilibrium and political spectre".[106] On this

---

106 The whole report "IFLA/FAIFE World Report: Libraries and Intellectual Freedom. Slovenia" is accessible on the IFLA website: https://www.ifla.org/fil es/assets/faife/pub-lications/ifla-world-report/slovenia.pdf. Last accessed on March 18, 2019.

point, the report cites a short article published in *Delo* on June 8, 1999, "Slovanski knjižnici ostaja staro ime" (Slovanska library keeps its old name). The article gives a very concise summary of a meeting of the Ljubljana City Council during which Drago Čepar (SKD) presented his proposal for an ideological survey. The latter was followed by an "ideological discussion", which was interrupted because it was late.[107]

The three-page report on Croatia cites several obstacles to the access to information, including the negligible role of librarians in the collection building process (which has been mentioned in subchapter 1.6); the instability of the publishing industry and its dependence on state subsidies; inadequate funding, equipment, and space; and the hiring of non-professionals for lack of qualified staff, particularly in smaller libraries. The selection and acquisition of library materials are not an exclusive prerogative of professional librarians: between 10 and 30 percent of the annual acquisition for public libraries (it is even higher for school libraries) is purchased by the state and/or local authorities within the national scheme of subsidies for publishers. In fact, publishing is subsidized by the state and subject to the approval of committees appointed by various ministries. Smaller libraries are particularly dependent on state purchase of new titles, while larger libraries have their own acquisition fund and there is no coordination of the acquisitions performed by the state and libraries. Smaller libraries are often understaffed and have to employ non-professionals who are expected to earn a professional degree, but since there is no funding provided for this purpose, it is unclear how this requirement of the Librarianship Act can be realized.

When it comes to weeding, the report on Croatia mentions that with the introduction of the new educational program in the early 1990s, "school libraries performed radical weeding of their collections" to acquire the new books listed as recommended readings. There is a paragraph on media reports about "several cases of discarding of books done by librarians". Inflammatory press reports about a librarian in Korčula alleged to have thrown away

---

107 I wish to thank Igor Zemljič for sending me a copy of the article.

Serbian-language books or books by Serbian authors were determined after further investigation to have been based on an "incorrect" assumption. The Croatian Library Association (CLA) was informed about this 1997 event but did not react in public. However, in response to "the incidents reported in the media," the CLA established its Committee on the Freedom of Expression and Free Access to Information in 1998.

It is then mentioned that

> "the then Dean of [the] Faculty of Philosophy in Zagreb ordered an undetermined number of books and periodicals written in German, Macedonian, Bulgarian, Croatian (and perhaps some other languages) to be taken away from the storage room of the Faculty and sold as used paper. [...] Although political reasons obviously were not the primary cause to discard these books, the Dean's decision reflects the decision of the Faculty administration towards the library collections in the institution".

The public image of librarians was damaged

> "due to a number of articles published in the last few years describing librarians as persons responsible for extensive book purges in the war and post-war years. Apart from the articles where individual librarians accused of book cleansing have been named, there is a number of articles in which the library profession as a whole has been qualified as guilty of book cleansing, burning and purging".

The interview that overseas Croatian writer Dubravka Ugrešić gave to *Novi list* in September 2000 is cited as one such example of broadbrush criticism of Croatian librarians which fails to distinguish between individual librarians accused of book cleansing and the library profession as a whole. The usage of certain formulations and specific examples leaves the reader with the impression that the profession is erecting a defensive bunker around itself by individualizing responsibility and an impermeable fortress by not reacting publicly, by not even trying to reach out to the public in order to improve the image of the profession. This is further reinforced by citing the case of the dean treating a collection improperly: more or less it is like saying that non-professionals have no idea what they are doing, while librarians do know but cannot be bothered to communicate it.[108] If the media were reporting about "book purges" at the hands of librarians and these reports damaged the reputation of the profession, why did the Association not react in public by condemning these acts and by instructing the public, through workshops or panels or presentations about the practice of weeding, instead of reacting with an internal measure? There is clearly a discrepancy between the diagnosis and the cure. If it is a matter of a couple of cases, was it necessary to form a committee?

The two IFLA/FAIFE reports are important because they provide an assessment from the librarians' point of view of the period that is scrutinized in this research (1990–2000). I will now analyze the most important newspaper articles in which librarians are presented, in the language of the report, as "persons responsible for extensive book purges in the war and post-war years". Since the report does not mention any specific article (except for the interview with Dubravka Ugrešić) and only one "case", that is, Korčula, I will focus on those writings from my own and Ante Lešaja's archive (digitized on the CD attached to the book, but paper copies of the articles could also be consulted during the exhibition "Discarded" in Zagreb in 2015) that I consider relevant.

2.3. Newspaper Accounts about the Discarding of Books from Croatian Libraries

Ante Lešaja counted for the period 1990–2009 a total of 140 articles written on the topic of book destruction (interpreted in the broadest possible sense). Book destruction is mentioned in three magazine issues, nine books, and fifteen manuscripts. Seventy-two writings were dedicated to the the "Korčula case" in the same period (Lešaja 2012, 74). As mentioned in the introduction, Lešaja's focus is on all manners of handling books conducive to their physical destruction. I am, however, interested in the discarding of books from public libraries as a result of the social, economic and political changes

---

108 The report "IFLA/FAIFE World Report: Libraries and Intellectual Freedom. Croatia" can be read online: https://www.ifla.org/files/assets/faife/publications/ifla-world-report/croatia.pdf. Last accessed on March 18, 2019.

stemming from the dissolution of Yugoslavia and the collapse of communism, which was interpreted as a standard weeding process by some and as "libricide" by others. This is how Davorka Vukov Colić frames the issue in her article "The Judiciary and Culture. Through Silence into a Painless Society" *(Sudstvo i kultura. Šutnjom u bezbolno društvo)*, published in the biweekly *Zarez* on October 15, 1999:

> "The removal of unsuitable books is only a part of a much wider process of adjusting culture to new times and a new ideological environment, connected with other similar occurrences in the public sphere, such as the rewriting of history or the toppling of monuments, or the renaming of squares and streets. A process that is more or less completed today". (Davorka Vukov Colić, article "The Judiciary and Culture. Through Silence into a Painless Society" *(Sudstvo i kultura. Šutnjom u bezbolno društvo)*, published in the biweekly *Zarez* on October 15, 1999).

This process was not limited to public institutions and the public sphere; individuals as well were tidying up their homes and libraries. As my interviewee IR remembers:

> "Everyone was getting rid of all that. They were getting rid of their private libraries, too. Even my grandmother threw away 'The Capital', I think immediately in 1991 or 1992. So that the Ustasha don't come and find it" (IR, theatre critic, personal interview, Zagreb, September 24, 2015).

The painter Edo Murtić remembers the 1990s in an interview for the magazine *Blic*:

> "Apart from those who did it out of primitivism, or those who 'cleansed' public and school libraries following the directives of the state, or in the Lexicographic Institute were recycling "The Encyclopedia of Yugoslavia", there were older people who were doing it because deep in their conscience they had the fear of Nazism and Ustashism. They were afraid that someone in their house would see these books. It is about the fear of something you think might happen to you".[109]

Unfortunately, it is not possible to establish the exact number and titles of volumes that were discarded from public libraries as a result of what Davorka Vukov-Colić called "adjustment". There are

---

[109] The interview was published on February 9, 2003, in Blic and was then reprinted in the monthly Identitet61, February 2003, 8-11. I am quoting from Lešaja (2012), 167.

The Discarding of Books in the 1990s   99

several reasons for that: first of all, the National and University Library in Zagreb started systematically generating the data (though not even explicitly on discarding) about public libraries' collections only in the year 2000 (Nebesny and Švob nd, np). Even if such statistics were available, it would consist of numbers and percentages, but would remain silent on the titles of the discarded books and the reasons for their being discarded. This information is usually contained in the discarding protocol that libraries have to fill out in the process. However, neither the protocol nor the lists of books suggested for discarding that libraries are supposed to send to the National and University Library are usually kept for longer than 10 years. Library catalogues do record changes in the collection such as discarding, but do not track the reasons for it. Ante Lešaja's estimate of 2.8 million fewer books stocked by Croatian public, school and general scientific libraries in the first half of the 1990s is probably the closest a researcher can get to the number of removed books. When it comes to their titles and content, the only option would be to select a couple of representative titles, to search for them in each of the 269 libraries, and to check in the card catalogue or inventory list whether they were discarded and when, provided that all the changes were tracked in real time and not inserted retroactively. Again, this would not provide any details on the reasons for discarding, which, even if they were listed, would fall under the category of lost, damaged beyond repair and outdated.[110] As Vukov Colić writes in the abovementioned article, neither the Ministry of Culture nor the National and University Library has ever stated the number of books discarded since 1991. However, information about the Zagreb City Library was published in the article "Zagreb City Libraries. Mice in the Covers" *(Knjižnice grada Zagreba. Miševi u koricama)*, by the same author:

---

110 These are listed in the "Regulations on the weeding and discarding of library materials" *(Pravilnik o reviziji i otpisu knjižnične građe)*, NN 21/2002, which replaced the "Instructions on the weeding and discarding of library materials" *(Naputak za provođenje revizije i otpisa građe u knjižnicama Republike Hrvatske)* published in *Vjesnik bibliotekara Hrvatske* 3-4/92.

Public libraries in Zagreb in the period 1988-1998

Year	Acquisition of books	Discarding of books	Collection total
1988	150.849	65.942	1.429.525
1989	141.490	69.749	1.511.518
1990	116.660	40.064	1.595.466
1991	93.140	42.690	1.643.278
1992	72.962	37.339	1.681.052
1993	36.364	39.464	1.678.248
1994	48.704	68.487	1.656.669
1995	70.252	27.242	1.702.073
1996	78.027	60.776	1.721.870
1997	80.684	26.967	1.764.870
1998	61.413	42.019	1.764.870

Table 1. Collection development in public libraries in Zagreb between 1988 and 1998

Source: Davorka Vukov-Colić. "Miševi u koricama". Zarez, 1/V, April 16, 1999.

I am reporting the full table because it gives the reader an idea of how the statistical data for the whole country would look like if it were available. From the table it is apparent that the total number of books decreased between 1992 and 1994 and that in 1993 and 1994 the number of discarded books was higher than that of acquired volumes. A caption under the table explains that acquisition during the war decreased, while discarding in the year 1993 and 1994 increased due to the discarding of "books in Cyrillic, as well as Marxist and other literature from the previous system". It is interesting to note the speed with which the discarding was carried out, considering that it took place during the war, when limited funds were available for the purchase of new books. Vukov Colić summarizes it as follows:

> "With the collapse of socialism, in other transition countries monuments celebrating this ideology were also disappearing, as well as metres of books by authors that glorified it. [...] Here, too, no one was expecting that Stipe Šuvar's sociological disquisitions would be still standing out on the

The Discarding of Books in the 1990s 101

shelves of public libraries, which at some point was a tacit obligation in high school libraries, a couple of copies of Plechanov, 30 copies of *Pirgo* by Anđelka Martić[111], as when it was on the reading list, or 10 copies of Lazarević[112] that no one borrows and is not on the list of readings. Libraries in fact needed to be cleaned up. Apart from that, books are consumables and the dilapidated ones need to be replaced by new copies. [...] All in all, the cleaning up of libraries in Croatia was rushed and in 1992 in Zagreb alone 54,956 books were discarded, while the City Library discarded 23,000 volumes in 1994 or 10% (international standards allow 5% in exceptional cases, like an earthquake or a flood)".[113]

Based on the data in the table above, discarding in public libraries in Zagreb reached its peak in 1994. In the same year Anton Lukežić from Rijeka sent a letter published in *Novi list* on July 12, 1994. This citizen's writing was triggered by what he characterizes as a "crusade" (*križarski rat*) against "unsuitable books" (*nepodobne knjige*) happening in the Croatian Parliament since 1990, where discussions about the withdrawal of textbooks and language manuals had been taking place. He then mentions two examples of anti-Serbian and anti-Cyrillic hysteria: a librarian from Zagreb who stated on TV that "the process of removal of 'unsuitable books' from her library is approaching to an end" and the scandal that broke out in the media when a teacher in Bribir used a booklet published in ekavian[114] in Belgrade during her class. Lukežić reminds the readers of some historic examples of book burning and censorship and concludes that "despite Serbia being an aggressor, I am not in favor of 'burning' books that are not printed in a 'pure' Croatian language".[115]

---

111 Set during the Partisan struggle in World War II, Pirgo is the story of the friendship between a boy named Željko and a fawn. From 1989 onwards, it was no longer on the reading list. It was reprinted again in 2003 by "Golden marketing" on the occasion of the 50th anniversary of the publication of the first edition.
112 Laza Lazarević (1851–1891) Serbian writer and physician. His stories *Na bunaru* (At the Well), *Sve će to narod pozlatiti* (People will reward all this), *U dobar čas hajduci* (Bandits) and a selection of short stories were suggested as readings in the 1950s and 1960s (see Narančić Kovač and Milković 2018).
113 Davorka Vukov Colić. "Sudstvo i kultura. Šutnjom u bezbolno društvo". *Zarez*, I/16, October 15, 1999.
114 Pronunciation of the proto-Slavic jat as "e" common among Serbian speakers. Croatian speakers mostly resort to ijekavian pronunciation. E.g., *vreme/vrijeme* (time or weather), *mleko/mlijeko* (milk), *lepo/lijepo* (beautiful).
115 Anton Lukežić. „Tko pali knjige, palit će i ljude" (Who burns books, will burn people, too). *Novi list*, July 12, 1994.

Another reaction to the atmosphere in Zagreb (and in Croatia) was published in the Slovenian daily *Delo* in January 1993. Nikica Mihaljević, the author of the three-part article "Miroslav Krleža knew: Woe to us, who are your poets: literary life in 'old' and 'new' Croatia" *(Miroslav Krleža je vedel: Gorje nam, ki smo vaši pesniki: književno življenje v 'stari' in 'novi' Hrvaški),* compares the situation on the streets of Ljubljana and Zagreb:

> "Recently in Ljubljana, on Plečnik Square I came across a street bookseller [...] It did not cross anyone's mind to admonish the man for selling 'Serbian books'. For me this was a welcome surprise because in Zagreb something like that cannot even be imagined. It was equally impossible to imagine, only a couple of years ago, that in the centre of 'cultured' and 'civilized' Zagreb books would be cut into noodles and libraries 'cleansed' from everything Serbian and Cyrillic and from everything 'non-Croatian'. The future of Slovenian books is also not bright at all".[116]

This article is a noteworthy source not only because it describes the prevalent atmosphere in Croatia in the early 1990s, but also because the reactions it provoked in the Croatian press show how someone's patriotism was measured. As such, it forms an invaluable contribution to the study of the media in the "leaden 1990s". Before examining these reactions in the form of four newspaper articles, I would like to quickly summarize the findings of Nina Ožegović's research on the ways in which the media presented cultural content in the transition period because I think her classifications could be tested against the four reactions to Mihaljević's article(s). She divides media production during transition into three phases: war and postwar (1991–1995), explicit political and ideological polarization (1995–2000), and spectacularization and trivialization (2000–2005). The first phase is characterized by

> "the political manipulation of cultural content (language as an instrument of political fighting, libricide and the destruction of partisan monuments), warmongering rhetoric and hate speech and the model of the satanization of the individual" (Ožegović 2018, 2102).

In the second phase (1995–2000), the conflict between state-building *(državotvorni)* and independent media, or between intellectuals

---

116 I am quoting the article as it is reported in Lešaja (2012), 162–163.

supporting and opposing the dominant political option, reached its peak, "spiced" with the strategy of scandal. The concept of *državotvorni* (literally, state-forming) media is rather curious: nation and state-building assumed such crucial importance in the discourse of the dominant party that a new word was introduced to describe it. Initially used to describe those Croats who put the national interest above everything else (including human rights or the freedom of speech), the word soon became an inclusion/exclusion device. State-building media were labelled responsible because they supported the government and refrained from reporting about the "dark side" of things, while independent media were considered irresponsible in their criticism directed at the elites (Ramet and Matić 2007, 233). Finally, the third period (2000–2005) was marked by the trivialization and reduction of contents to "what sells", leading to a loss of critical sharpness and credibility (Ožegović 2018, 2109–2112). Ožegović's characterization of the "first phase" as imbued with "hate speech" and the "satanization of the individual" is confirmed, albeit on the basis of a small sample, in the reactions to Nikica Mihaljević's article in *Delo*.

The first was an article by Denis Derk, *Hrvatska pisana mržnjom* (Croatia written by hatred), published on January 26, 1993, in *Večernji list*, where another commentary by Branimir Donat followed on February 7, *Informatorova lažna dostava* (The informer's false delivery). On January 30 a piece by Darko Brdarić, *Tatarski biftek od sirove mržnje* (Steak tartare of pure hatred) appeared in *Vjesnik*, and finally, on March 6 Tomislav Sabljak published *Moj prijatelj terorist* (My friend, the terrorist) in the same daily. Donat calls Mihaljević an "ideological psychopath" who "truly hates Croatia" and "cries Yugo tears", a literary nobody ("nitkica", a wordplay on the author's name since *nitko* means nobody). He does not even try to present counterarguments to Mihaljević's claims, but simply *ad hominem* attacks. With one sentence he dismisses the claim that Serbian books are being destroyed in Croatia: "In his original hatred towards Croatia Mihaljević continuously confabulates, so he is also saying that all books in Cyrillic Croatia ended up in the paper factory". Derk follows a similar pattern and additionally negates the "cleansing" of Croatian libraries ("we cannot forget his factually false claims that libraries were cleansed from everything Serbian and Cyrillic [...] because it is simply not true"). Darko Brdarić writes that Mihaljević is trying to present the

> "never confirmed statements about the cleansing of libraries as an existing practice and chauvinism in action [...] This amount of hatred towards the Croats and Croatia we did not have the chance to read since 'Politika ekspres'[117] stopped coming to Zagreb".

Finally, Sabljak asks himself why *Delo* is using the services of a man "whose only friend is a terrorist with a pointed gun" (Mihaljević mentioned a friend who is a Serbian poet); he is curious as to

> "why [...] a newspaper like "Delo" from Ljubljana even accept[ed] such a notoriously unchecked delivery of a former snitch [...] Perhaps some political forces in Slovenia need to occasionally point a finger at somebody less democratic than themselves, jealously safeguarding that one half-step before Croatia".

Sabljak also states that

> "in Croatia no one destroyed a single copy of a Serbian book, but a lot of worthless Serbian books ended up in storerooms. It is common knowledge that acquisition in public libraries in most cases was led by self-declared Yugoslavs, or the children of military personnel or Serbs. And in the departments for adults and children year after year there were ever more hundreds of worthless Serbian titles, even books with anti-Croatian content".

He also mentions the discarding at the Ljubljana City Library and the fact that on that occasion no one even tried to accuse the Library of cultural genocide. This discarding will be mentioned in subchapter 2.5.

All in all, the four articles do not contradict Mihaljević's statements, but rather resort to a series of logical fallacies such as *ad hominems*, generalizations, *ignoratio elenchi* and *tu quoque* to discredit the author of the text. A couple of years later, in 1998, another article appeared on the prevailing atmosphere in Croatia, where "individuals are taking up the role of nationally 'conscious' censors, so libraries need to put disputed books in less visible places". This article, published in *Delo* by Ratko Čangalović, was titled *Hrvatske*

---

117 Politika ekspres was a Serbian daily published in Belgrade until 2005.

The Discarding of Books in the 1990s 105

Knjižnice otpisuju nepodobnu literaturu. Kad gore knjige, pucaju kosti (Croatian libraries are discarding unwanted literature. Where books burn, bones break) and was reprinted in *Novi list* on April 29, 1998.[118] This time no reaction followed, be it from journalists or professional librarians. In fact, professionals reacted only sporadically: on May 23, 1998, in *Večernji list* the statements of Anka Katić-Crnković, the director of the Zagreb City Libraries (which comprise the City Library, 27 other libraries and two bookmobiles) and the acting director of the National and University Library, Josip Stipanov, were reported under the title *Kome služe izmišljotine o vandalizmu hrvatskih knjižničara. Knjige srpskih pisaca nitko ne baca s polica* (Who needs the fabrications about the vandalism of Croatian librarians. No one throws books by Serbian authors from the shelves). Katić-Crnković was quoted as saying:

> "it is a matter of politicization, of abuse of the library profession for political aims. A regular activity (and what is more, an obligation regulated by law) of libraries to periodically weed their collections and discard damaged and stolen, that is, non-returned books in the case of Serbian and Cyrillic volumes is being presented as a cleansing of unsuitable books. [...] The weeding and discarding of Serbian books are being carried out according to the same professional and legal regulations as all other books, Croatian or foreign; no special treatment of Serbian books was ever prescribed nor implemented".

"Paradigmatic" is how the author of the article, Mirjana Jurišić, formulates the question:

> "What is the purpose of fabrications about the alleged Croatian bonfires of Serbian books, while these same media never voiced any concern over real fires caused by Serbian grenades thrown on the libraries in Vukovar, Vinkovci, Slavonski Brod, Karlovac, Zadar, Dubrovnik and many other Croatian libraries, where tens of thousands of Croatian books, original manuscripts, documents and other materials valuable for the history and culture of this people disappeared forever"?[119]

---

118 As Lešaja notes on p. 304, the said article was probably inspired by Nina Domazet's "Nacionalni čistunci haraju policama" (National cleaners are pillaging shelves). *Novi list*, April 11, 1998. Ratko Čangalović published another article in *Delo* on the occasion of the discarding carried out in the elementary school in Vrsar: "Zagrepška šepetanja. Nazor in Krleža na smečišču" (Zagreb whispers. Nazor and Krleža in the dump), March 12, 2004.

119 Mirjana Jurišić. "Kome služe izmišljotine o vandalizmu hrvatskih knjižničara. Knjige srpskih pisaca nitko ne baca s polica". *Večernji list*, May 23, 1998.

The same analogy was put forward by librarian Đurđica Jureša in a reaction to Kangrga's article, published under the title "Croatian Libricide. Barbarism and Renaissance" (a comment on the "Korčula case") in *Vjesnik* on April 21, 1998: "Mr. Kangrga raises his voice to defend the discarded Cyrillic books, but he did not say a word when the books of the fatherland in which he is living were burning."[120] The Korčula case, which happened in the late summer of 1997 and periodically resurfaced in the press until 2003 due to the judicial proceedings connected to it, will be mentioned in more detail in the following review of Lešaja's research.

First, the case that practically inaugurated press coverage of the topic of library cleansing should be mentioned. In April 1993 an article by Denis Derk in *Večernji list*, titled *I Balzac na smetlištu* (Balzac in the Dump, too), reported on an employee of the Centre for Culture in Slatina, Tomislav Matošević, who ordered the dumping of around 2000 books (the article mentions two estimations, i.e., 1650 or 3153 books). The books allegedly included Belgrade editions of classics such as Balzac, which Matošević classified as "ideological literature". He was apparently unqualified for the job, but he was employed on the recommendation of the Government commissioner Ante Šimara and given the task of weeding the library collection. He was later dismissed from his job because of protracted unjustified absences.

These articles demonstrate how the media debate about the "cleansing" of libraries was led in the early 1990s, but also later (Jurišić's article and Jureša's reaction are both from 1998, in the wake of the Korčula scandal). First a journalist (Mihaljević) is demonized in the media for having written about the nationalist tendencies in Croatia. A year later a librarian (the unknown librarian from Lukežić's letter) publicly states "unsuitable" books are being removed, which is then negated by another librarian four years later (but the two are presumably speaking about different libraries). Finally, a librarian (Jureša) and a journalist (Jurišić) compare the

---

120 Đurđica Jureša. "Akademik Kangrga brani knjige na srpskom, ali nije izustio ni slova dok su gorjele hrvatske knjige" (Academician Kangrga defends books in Serbian, but he did not say a word when Croatian books were burning). *Vjesnik*, April 21, 1998.

The Discarding of Books in the 1990s 107

removal of Serbian books with the damage perpetrated by the Serbian and Montenegrin Army during the war. What this analogy seems to suggest is that it is ok to throw away Serbian books, considering what has happened a couple of years prior.

Apart from these articles, which I think summarize the media coverage of discarding prior to the "Korčula case" pretty well, three lengthier accounts on "libricide" appeared in 2000, 2003 (2005) and 2012 respectively. I will now examine them chronologically.

2.4. Ante Lešaja's *Libricide* and Other Sources

The first contribution is also the shortest, a book chapter titled "Culture of Death" *(Kultura smrti)* in Viktor Ivančić's book *Točka na U. Slučaj Šakić: Anatomija jednog skandala* (Dot on the U. The Šakić Case: Anatomy of a Scandal, 2000). In it, the author alternates paragraphs on the removal of books in the Serbian language and Cyrillic script from Croatian school, public and special libraries, such as the library of the elementary school "Nikola Hribar" in Velika Gorica (where 400 books were apparently burned), "Ivan Vidali" in Korčula, or the library of the Centre for Culture in Slatina with paragraphs about the Nazi "action against the un-German spirit". Ivančić writes that "during the first decade of Croatian revolutionary state-building *(državotvorstvo)*, the concept of "re-establishment" of the national culture was exclusively based on reductionism" (Ivančić 2000, 175). The latter manifested itself not only in the "destruction *(uništavanje)* of books and the cleansing *(čišćenje)* of libraries", but also in the "redefinition of the standard language, mostly reduced to the elimination *(odstranjivanje)* of 'foreign' words'", "the nationalization *(nacionaliziranje)* of school readings", the "prevention *(sprječavanje)* of the translation of foreign literature", the "non-distribution *(bunkeriranje)* of films and tv series", "informal bans *(zabrane)* on theatre plays", the "silencing" *(prešućivanje)* of artists whose work was not in line with the "'new Croatian spirit'", the "blocking *(onemogućavanje)* of individual artistic actions" and the "removal *(uklanjanje)* of 'former' and 'foreign' cadres from central cultural institutions" (175). Ivančić concludes that the establishment of the Croatian national culture equalled an "elimination program"; a couple of sentences further on he is even more categorical in saying that a culture "that understands *elimination* as a 'creational act' necessary to establish itself as a national culture is a *culture of death*" (176; emphasis in the original).

Three years later the *Prosvjeta* magazine of the homonymous Serbian Cultural Society *(Srpsko kulturno društvo)* — the Society is also called Prosvjeta — published a special issue on "Bibliocide — Culturecide: Where one burns books, one will soon burn people" (the Croatian version saw the light of day in 2003, while the English translation followed in 2005). Rade Dragojević, the editor of the English language edition, introduces it by writing that the English translation

> "was not due to malice, nor to damage the reputation of the country in which we live by airing its 'dirty laundry' before foreigners. The reason [...] lies in our desire to stress the inacceptable nature of bibliocide by internationalizing the problem, and the fact that we are publishing in English only shows that our society is maturing and we are not afraid of outside assessments of shameful episodes from our recent past" *(Prosvjeta* vol. 12 (37) n. 71 (681), 2005, 4-5).

Apart from the introductory remarks by Dragojević, the issue includes a couple of articles written especially for the occasion by authors who have most intently followed libricide in the 1990s such as Dragojević, Lasić and Lešaja, as well as reprints of articles published in *Feral Tribune*, *Novi List* and *Tjednik*. Finally, it includes a bibliography on "bibliocide as social pathology" prepared by Ante Lešaja (60–66).

"Bibliocide — Culturecide: Where one burns books, one will soon burn people" is rather journalistic in its style, and it does not always offer references for the stated facts. An example is the Nazi-inspired exhibition of "degenerate art", or "objectionable literature" *(entartete Kunst)*, allegedly organized somewhere in Croatia *(Prosvjeta* vol. 12 (37) n. 71 (681), 2005, p. 5), which most likely never took place.[121] This and, for instance, the variation in media reports

---

121 Since I was not able to find any information about the alleged exhibition, I turned to the author of the article in *Prosvjeta* where it was first mentioned. He was not able to substantiate this claim with proofs.

on the number of books dumped on the island of Korčula that ranged from a low of 100–150 to a high of 400–500, suggest the wisdom of caution in the use of some data, but also point to the important role the media have in not only *mediating*, but also co-creating a particular story. Similarly, bibliocide was sometimes referred to as "book burning" in the media, probably metaphorically, but this might create confusion among (un)informed readers, as well as fuel hearsay.[122]

Ante Lešaja's encyclopedic study *Knjigocid: Uništavanje knjiga u Hrvatskoj 1990-ih* (Libricide: The Destruction of Books in Croatia in the 1990s) is the result of two decades of research. The study contains references to a number of newspaper articles, public speeches, politicians' statements, instructions and other proceedings that have appeared in the 1990s in connection with what the author calls "libricide" *(knjigocid)*, or the systematic destruction of books. Although it focuses (solely) on Croatia, due to its meticulousness and completeness, Lešaja's work constitutes a valuable starting point for anyone interested in cultural heritage destruction in Croatia, the former Yugoslav area and beyond. As the author writes in the introduction to the volume, his intention was to present to the public the documents and newspaper articles he has collected over a period of twenty years, without wishing to engage in a theoretical discussion (16), albeit he does provide theoretical insights on the nature of the social turn in the 1990s. By arranging these previously scattered documents, the author "lets them speak" and limits his interventions to a minimum. Lešaja often reprints entire letters, newspaper articles and documents, like, for instance, the "Binding Instruction on the Usage of School Library Book Inventories". Due to the number of newspaper articles reprinted in the book and available as scanned copies on the CD attached to the volume, it could be said that *Libricide* offers an insight into the media presentation of cultural content in the period 1991–2010.

The term *knjigocid*, translatable as libricide, bibliocide or even bookicide, was first used in the Croatian press by the weekly *Feral*

---

[122] Lešaja for instance writes he was informed about the burning of books in front of a school in Slavonska Požega, but the informer asked for discretion (159).

Tribune in 1998 to describe the hasty removal of a number[123] of books from the library in Korčula on the homonymous island and their inappropriate disposal in a waste container (Lešaja 2012, 24). Most of these books were discarded as "outdated" and included classics like Lev Tolstoy, Nikolai Gogol, Émile Zola and Luigi Pirandello; Serbian authors such as Branko Ćopić, Branislav Nušić and Jovan Jovanović Zmaj; and Croatian authors Ivana Brlić-Mažuranić, August Cesarec and Anđelka Martić (344). It is this event, to which he had a personal connection — as a retired university professor Lešaja took part in the revitalization and development of the library in his native Korčula — that mobilized the author and motivated him to conduct more extensive research on the topic. He acted (and still does) as an archivist of all the data he could gather about the destruction of books, but he was also actively involved in requesting sanctions for the responsible librarian and people who destroyed cultural monuments in general and obtaining an official condemnation of the act by state authorities, both of which did not happen. In one of the texts available on the CD, in which the author summarizes the developments in the "Korčula case", he writes that the main reason behind his persistence in requiring a reaction from the Ministry of Culture and sanctions for the irresponsible librarian is for the whole phenomenon not to be forgotten, primarily by those whose task it is to act against the destruction of books. The final aim of the book is, in fact, "to contribute to collective memory".[124]

---

123 See footnote 26. The number cited by the journalist Igor Lasić is 150, but in the press the number sometimes rose to 400-500 (see for instance "Milan Kangrga proglašen krivim" (Milan Kangrga declared guilty). *Novi list*, March 30, 1999 (the cited number is 400 books); "I knjige se mogu ubiti" (Books can be killed, too). *Novi list*, May 10, 1999 (once more the reported number is 400 books); "Poništena presuda Kangrgi" (Annulled verdict to Kangrga). *Novi list*, September 10, 1999 (500 books). Within six months in the same daily newspaper the number of books allegedly thrown into the garbage rose from 400 to 500, not to mention that there is a considerable difference between 100-150 and 400. The confusion is partially due to the fact that the responsible librarian retroactively produced a couple of lists, each with a different number of volumes. Kruno Lozica, an inhabitant of Korčula, took 42 books out of the trash, while another person took 9, and Lozica's estimate was that there were around 100-150 books in total.

124 The title of the text is "Razrješavanje 'slučaja Korčula'" (Resolution of the "Korčula case"), p. 11.

The Discarding of Books in the 1990s 111

Lešaja's book is divided into four parts: the first two are devoted to the phenomenon of the destruction of books in Croatia, including a section on destroyed monuments; the third part focuses on the judiciary and the way it handled "libricide"; while the fourth and last section is on "exclusionism" *(isključivost)* in the 1990s. As Lešaja emphasizes, the removal of "unsuitable" *(nepodobne)* books was a systematic process justified with standard library procedures such as weeding and discarding, and is thus comparable to the deliberate dynamiting of anti-fascist monuments and later blaming the Serbs or strong wind for the action.[125] The destruction of socialist monuments and the (ab)use of history textbooks have in fact already attracted some (scholarly) attention.[126] All these phenomena are, according to Lešaja, a direct consequence of the "exclusionism" *(isključivost)* of the 1990s, which had specific targets: Tito's Yugoslavia as a state community, socialism as ideology and practice, the National Liberation Struggle and anti-fascism (1941–1945), the Serbs as people (including the Croatian Serbs), the working people, that is, the working class, and any type of disagreement with governmental policies (502). Lešaja argues that the "exclusionism" promoted during the "social overturn" *(društveni prevrat)* of the 1990s was nothing but an expression of the fundamental social conflict, a change in the economic system that allowed a very limited number of people to grow rich at the expense of a much wider population. The author estimates[127] that in the given period approximately 2.8

---

125 Here I am referring to the Monument to the Victory of the People of Slavonia *(Spomenik pobjedi naroda Slavonije)* by Vojin Bakić, unveiled in 1968 in Kamenska and dynamited by the Croatian army in 1992. The responsibility for the act was attributed first to the Serbs and then to a strong wind. For more information, see Lešaja (2012), 48 and the documentary by Bogdan Žižić, *Damnatio memoriae ili Udar na sjećanje* (2001), HRT, 60'.
126 See, for instance, Najbar-Agičić and Agičić (2007), as well as the vast research conducted by the Georg Eckert Institute for International Textbook Research, or the Joint History Project Sponsored by the Center for Democracy and Reconciliation in Southeast Europe (CDRSEE). The destruction of anti-fascist memorials has been analyzed in the previously mentioned documentary film by Bogdan Žižić in *Udar na sjećanje/Damnatio memoriae* (2001), Hrženjak ed. (2002), Kirn and Burghardt (2012), etc.
127 Despite his insistence, Lešaja never got the data on discarding from the National and University Library, perhaps because it does not exist. Consequently, his

million books (280) were removed from Croatian libraries: books printed in Cyrillic, published in Serbia or by a Serbian author, as well as those dealing with a "leftist" topic. Approximately 55 percent of the discarded books originated from school libraries (280). The concrete examples he examines include the discarding of 23,069 books from the Zagreb City Library in 1994 (295–312); the founding of the library of the Serbian Cultural Centre Prosvjeta, which he calls an "extorted consequence and the result of book 'cleansing'" (312–328); and the "cleansing" of school libraries like the Gymnasium in Pula (1996), S. Ivan Žabno (2000), Vrsar (2004), Gornjogradska Gymnasium in Zagreb (2004), the First Croatian Gymnasium in Rijeka (2006) (355–370) and the "Korčula case".

As stated before, the point of departure for Lešaja's research was the previously mentioned "Korčula case", which is the only one that ended in the courtroom and received extended media attention. The librarian responsible for the act in Korčula pressed charges for defamation against *Feral Tribune*, the philosopher Milan Kangrga (for the article *Hrvatski knjigocid. Barbarizam i renesansa* — Croatian libricide. Barbarism and Renaissance, published on March 30, 1998) and the journalist Igor Lasić, author of the article *Djevojčica sa žigicama* (The Little Match Girl), dated March 1, 1999. Two lawsuits out of four were later withdrawn (the first one against *Feral Tribune* and Igor Lasić),[128] but the episode constitutes a paradigmatic example of prosecution against the critique of libricide (404). Lešaja in fact devotes an entire chapter to the legal proceedings, showing that the judiciary in 1990s Croatia was hardly independent (383–413). As he argues, it was instrumentalized and used to serve the dominant nationalist platform; the frequent (mis)use of the category "emotional distress" *(duševna bol)* in lawsuits is a case in point (391). Lešaja divides the public reactions to "bibliocide" into two groups: the mostly condemnatory stance taken by concerned

---

estimations are based on the total number of volumes in Croatian libraries and their oscillation over the years.
128 Kangrga was first found guilty, but the lawsuit against him was finally dismissed in 2002. For a detailed chronology of the case, see also *Kulturocid. Sudski process protiv Milana Kangrge*, (Culturecide. The Court Case against Milan Kangrga), a text by Lešaja published in *Republika*, n. 490–491, 2010.

The Discarding of Books in the 1990s   113

citizens and journalists, and the relative ("provided that it happened") or formal (principal) condemnation of such acts by public institutions and professional associations (147). As he stresses, the Ministry of Culture reacted twice when the Minister was Božo Biškupić (HDZ) and twice during the mandate of Antun Vujić (SDP) with statements on the "Korčula case" (147–148). Nevertheless, the various open letters asking for the condemnation and sanctioning of the destruction of monuments and books, including one signed in 2004 by 42 citizens and addressed to the upper echelons of power, remained largely unanswered. What characterizes the attitude both of the Ministry of Culture and professional associations such as the Croatian Library Association *(Hrvatsko knjižničarsko društvo)*[129] and the Croatian Council for Libraries *(Hrvatsko knjižnično vijeće)*[130] is the minimization of acts of "libricide" as sporadic, singular episodes; their relativization by comparing them with the action of the "aggressor"; and partial justification by questioning the actual value of the discarded books. To summarize, Lešaja stresses the persistence of such stances and a complete lack of assumption of responsibility (150). What is more, when a case of murky discarding was reported to have happened in Bugojno (Bosnia and Herzegovina) in 2005, the Ministry of Culture immediately condemned the "bibliocide" directed against Croatian books (152–154). In August 2005 Serbian and Croatian books were allegedly thrown into the garbage. The Croatian Minister of Culture, Božo Biškupić reacted by sending a letter to the Bosnian Minister of Culture, Gavrilo Grahovac, severely condemning such an "act of vandalism". It was later found out that the news was not entirely trustworthy. Nevertheless, what is important to note here is the readiness of the Minister to react to an action happening in a neighboring country in order to protect Croatian books, but while the same was happening to Serbian (and other) books in Croatia the Ministry remained silent.

---

129   The Croatian Library Association is a professional association dedicated to the development of librarianship.
130   The Council for Libraries is a professional and advisory body composed of seven members operating within the Ministry of Culture.

Interestingly and not surprisingly, the appearance of Lešaja's book in 2012 aroused some interest in the Serbian media. As much as former Yugoslav countries would like to distance themselves as much as possible from one another, gloating over the "misdeeds" of a neighbor is often done in an all-Yugoslav frame of reference, with the purpose of cleaning up one's reputation and possibly relativizing one's own faults. In an unpublished compilation and analysis of the reception of his book, Lešaja concludes it was favorably received in Croatia, but also in Bosnia and Herzegovina and Serbia where it was presented (he refers to three negative reactions to the book). Interestingly, no comments on the volume were issued by the librarians' associations and by the respective Ministries (172-177).[131]

Lešaja's 600-page study abounds with sources, mostly newspaper articles on the topic of book destruction, which allows it to successfully capture the cultural climate of the 1990s. The 1990s that the author refers to, however, are slightly protracted: namely, the whole period between 1990 and 2010 (potentially even until today) is subsumed under the term 1990s because "the inertia of destruction or discrimination of 'unwanted' books is still 'at work'" (Lešaja 2012, 69). While it is undeniable that some of the structural problems that lead to the "destruction" of books are still in place — lack of correspondence and coordination between libraries, non-professionals employed as librarians (particularly in smaller communities), inadequate communication with the patrons — overstretching the terms "destruction" and potentially even "the 1990" might have negative consequences on the interpretation of the phenomenon. It is equally true that many of the cultural patterns developed as a consequence of the extreme nationalism professed in the actual 1990s is still present in Croatian society, but empirical evidence

---

[131] Pp. 172-177 of Lešaja's unpublished text "Odjeci (Recepcija) knjige i fenomena uništavanja knjiga (i spomenika NOBe/socijalističke revolucije) (od objavljivanja knjige polovicom 2012. do 2018)" (Reception of the book *Knjigocid. Uništavanje knjiga u Hrvatskoj 1990.-ih* and of the phenomenon of the destruction of monuments to the People's Liberation Struggle/the socialist revolution from its publishing in mid-2012 to 2018). I would like to thank Ante Lešaja for sending me this document.

seems to be suggesting that the nation building process is over.[132] In other words, if we wish to separate the discarding of Serbian books as some sort of a "subsidiary nation building strategy" or a form of auto-censorship from sloppy and unprofessional discarding, terminological clarity is a precondition. In general, this would avoid rhetorical tricks and unnecessary confusion that is now present across professions, languages, areas, and periods. As a side note, the librarian who without any doubt threw books into the bin sued the weekly *Feral Tribune* because in one article they wrote that she had burned the books. A similar confusion is also visible on the two Wikipedia websites that have already been mentioned.

In any case, both Lešaja's book and the special issue of *Prosvjeta* undoubtedly contributed to the examination of a largely unresearched phenomenon, but also to the analysis of contradictions and unlawful practices of some institutions in a country that sought to establish its international image as a Western democracy defending Christian values against "Byzantine despotism".

Now that all the most important newspaper articles and other writings about "libricide" in Croatia have been outlined, let us turn our attention to Slovenia.

2.5. Discarding in Public Libraries in Slovenia: Data and Perceptions in Comparison

Discarding in Slovenian libraries is regulated by the Librarianship Act (*Zakon o knjižničarstvu*, Official Gazette 87/2001)[133] and the Instructions issued in 2012[134] by the National and University Library *(Navodilo za izločanje in odpis knjižničnega gradiva)*. Most libraries in Slovenia are using the COBISS catalogue system COBISS (Cooperative Bibliographic Systems and Services), through which acquisition and discarding is also coordinated. In other words, what a library might discard as obsolete might be of interest to another library (Poličnik-Čermelj and Žagar 2007, 54). A book can become

---

132 See footnote 74.
133 The 2001 Act replaced the Librarianship Act from 1982 (Official Gazette of the Socialist Republic of Slovenia n. 27/82).
134 These instructions went to replace the ones from 2003.

obsolete due to its superseded content, sociopolitical changes (and how these affect the curriculum), technological development, changes in language (grammar, script) and the replacement of old with new editions (55). The National and University Library stores and collects all materials that are considered a "cultural monument", which includes volumes written before 1800, but also legal copies and books that complement *Slovenica* (and *Jugoslavica* until 1991).[135] This is the reason why, when a library discards certain volumes, it is obliged to send a list to the National and University Library, which has fourteen days to check and notify the library whether it requires any of these books. Following the selection at NUK, public libraries should offer their discarded materials to regional libraries, faculty libraries to university libraries, school libraries to other school or public libraries and special libraries to other special and university libraries (60).

Unlike Croatia, in Slovenia there were no public reports on discarding that is not carried out according to professional guidelines. Nevertheless, on November 21, 1989, an article in "Dnevnik" announced that due to a lack of space in the Ljubljana City Library "10 tons of books found themselves in the dump".[136] On the same day *Delo* wrote that a considerable part of the books that were waiting to be recycled would be taken over by the Society of Bibliophiles of Slovenia, which also accused the library of not being cooperative.[137] A short scrutiny of this case is needed in order to better frame the Croatian case and the public perception of discarding operated by libraries in general. This is in fact the event that Tomislav Sabljak mentioned in his rebuttal to Nikica Mihaljević (which I addressed in subchapter 2.3), in which he said that "no one even thought of labelling it as cultural genocide". As mentioned in subchapter 2.2, the disposal of discarded materials is a sensitive issue

---

135 Slovenica is a collection of volumes in Slovenian or other languages written on Slovenia and the Slovenians, but also books by Slovenian authors and publishers.
136 Danilo Hinič. "Zaradi prostorske stiske Mestne knjižnice deset ton knjig na odpadu" (Due to a lack of space in the City library, ten tons of books end up in the dump). *Dnevnik*, November 21, 1989.
137 Mojca Kaučič. "Na stotine knjig komaj rešili pred uničenjem" (Hundreds of books barely escaped destruction). *Delo*, November 21, 1989.

The Discarding of Books in the 1990s 117

for every library. Libraries are encouraged to sell, donate and exchange them rather than recycling or destroying them because large quantities of books in the trash can provoke a "weeding controversy" and reactions such as "libraries are throwing valuable books away". If this is inevitable, it is important that libraries communicate to the public the reasons behind their decisions and when possible, include the patrons in the process. An example of such a project that can detaboo the standard library practice of weeding and discarding will be presented in section 3.2.1.

The Ljubljana City Library reacted a day after the abovementioned articles were published with a letter signed by the Director of the "Oton Župančič" Library, Damijana Hinz, and the Head of the Unit of the City Library, in which they gave a summary of the considerations that led to the recycling of a vast number of books and dismissed the claims of the Society of Bibliophiles.[138] Namely, during the renovation of the Oton Župančič library, the staff undertook "a thorough cleansing of the library stock", the first since 1911. In the storage in Topniška Street 60, the library had 45,000 volumes that had been weeded, and when the library lost half of this space (it is not stated why) it was decided to discard 35,000 volumes by respecting all the professional standards and regulations. The letter also accentuates that public libraries are not archives; that they have to periodically (at least once a year) weed their collections; that the books have been offered to several other libraries and to the Trubarjev antique store (which selected 2500 volumes); and, most importantly, that all the documentation about it is available in the "Oton Župančič" library. The letter ends with the sentence: "we are of the opinion that the journalists and the public should trust the professional judgments of library employees, also because for the abuse of this trust sanctions are foreseen". A couple of other newspaper articles on the issue followed, including an answer from the Bibliophile Society accusing the library of "bibliocide".[139] This case

---

138 Damijana Hainz and Brane Čop. "Knjige na odpadu" (Books in the dump). *Delo*, November 22, 1989.
139 Further articles on the topic include: Miran Čubic. "Poblazneli svet" (Crazy world). *Dnevnik*, November 22, 1989; "Zagovora knjižničarjev ne sprejmemo": Odgovor Slovenskega bibliografskega (pravilno bibliofilskega!) društva na

did not, however, remain a media debate, but it was taken up by the (now retired) librarian Irena Kernel in her scientific article *Kam z izločenim knjižničnim gradivom?* (What to do with weeded library materials?). It is an article directed at professionals in which she compares the annual weeding statistics in the "Oton Župančič Library" with the prescribed standards and dwells upon the number of volumes that should be donated to other libraries. In the article she draws the readers' attention to bombastic titles such as the "Hundreds of books barely escape destruction" and "10 tons of books end up in the dump", as well as inaccuracies due to a sensationalist style of writing: libraries do not consider books in kilograms, but number of copies. She also warned against some inconsistencies in the newspaper article: if it is assumed that 1 ton comprises approximately 2000 copies (where one book weighs 400 or 500 g) and that out of the 100,000 tons of paper annually collected in Slovenia 5 percent are books (5000), how does the author get to the conclusion that 1 ton of books is destroyed per day? If the library were to give up discarding, it would need 600m² of additional space every year (Kernel 1999, 30).

Based on annual reports on public libraries issued by the National and University Library (NUK) in Ljubljana (*Slovenske splošnoizobraževalne knjižnice: poročilo za leto ...*, where the ellipses represent the year of the report), in the past two decades the annual discarding percentages did not exceed the standard 3-5 percent. Apart from distinguishing between books, periodicals and other materials, these reports do not include any other (for example, thematic or disciplinary) specification of the books in question. The reports for 1991, 1992, 1995 and 1996 were edited as monographs, while from 1997 onwards they were issued as part of the series

---

poziv delavcev Knjižnice Oton Zupančič, naj novinarji in javnost zaupajo njihovi "strokovni presoji" ("We do not accept the librarians' defense": Response of the Slovenian Bibliographic Society (properly bibliophile) to the call of the workers of the Oton Župančič Library, directed to journalist and the public, to accept their "professional judgment"). *Delo*, November 28, 1989; Mojca Kaučič. "Knjige z odpada bodo dobile nove lastnike v Bukvarni" (Books from the waste will get new owners in Bukvarna). *Delo*, December 6, 1989. For a list of newspaper articles (25) published between 1989-1998 in *Delo* and *Dnevnik* about the weeding of books from libraries see Kernel (1999).

The Discarding of Books in the 1990s 119

Slovenske knjižnice v številkah. Data from 2000-present for all types of libraries can be found online.[140] The figure below shows how this data, based on the compiled questionnaires that libraries send to the National and University Library is usually presented:

Discarding in public libraries in Slovenia in 1990

Municipality	Books	Magazines	Other
1. Ajdovščina	285	0	0
2. Brežice	51	0	7
3. Celje	21049	35	21084
4. Cerknica	134	0	134
5. Črnomelj	9	30	0
6. Domžale	570	46	67
7. Dravograd	136	26	1
8. Gornja Radgona	122	36	0
9. Grosuplje	453	109	23
10. Hrastnik	120	40	0
11. Idrija	356	47	0
12. Il. Bistrica	85	41	0
13. Izola	207	19	0
14. Jesenice	5546	105	0
15. Kamnik	223	0	0
16. Kočevje	814	91	17
17. Koper	3179	0	0
18. Kranj	1629	959	29
19. Krško	96	5	0
20. Laško	53	0	0
21. Lenart	68	2	0
22. Lendava	892	0	0
23. Litija	0	0	0
24. Lj. Bežigrad	1152	0	0
25. Lj. Center	67858	0	0
26. Lj. Moste	1747	550	272
27. Lj. Šiška	3237	16	209
28. Lj. Vič	0	0	0
- Lj. bibliobus	2572	0	0
29. Ljutomer	1045	40	4
30. Logatec	218	15	0

140 *Statistični podatki o knjižnicah* 2000-2017: http://bibsist.nuk.uni-lj.si/statistika/. Last accessed on February 28, 2019.

31.	Maribor	4725	644	0
32.	Metlika	0	36	0
33.	Mozirje	0	0	0
34.	Murska Sobota	3696	0	0
35.	Nova Gorica	1267	172	0
36.	Novo mesto	15774	0	0
37.	Ormož	54	0	0
38.	Piran	116	-	0
39.	Postojna	21	0	0
40.	Ptuj	1774	-	-
41.	Radlje	51	2	1
42.	Radovljica	2358	-	0
43.	Ravne	500	0	0
44.	Ribnica	0	0	0
45.	Sevnica	0	13	0
46.	Sežana	60	0	0
47.	Slov. Bistrica	342	29	0
48.	Slov. Gradec	310	35	0
49.	Slov. Konjice	312	0	0
50.	Šentjur	0	0	0
51.	Škofja loka	484	-	0
52.	Šmarje	0	0	0
53.	Tolmin	0	0	0
54.	Trbovlje	0	0	0
55.	Trebnje	0	0	0
56.	Tržič	83	29	0
57.	Velenje	303	4	12
58.	Vrhnika	399	0	0
59.	Zagorje	570	0	0
60.	Žalec	15	25	0
TOTAL:		147120	3201	21860

Table 2.   Discarded material from public libraries in Slovenia in the year 1990.

Source: Splošnoizobraževalne knjižnice v letu 1990 (Posnetek po vprašalniku). Edited by Silva Novljan, national and University Library, Ljubljana, September 12, 1991.

Even if later reports also included an additional column showing the percentage of the overall collection discarded each year, it is silent on the type of discarded materials, as well as the reasons leading to it.

The Discarding of Books in the 1990s   121

	County	Books	Serial Publications	Non-book Materials	Total	% of Total Collection
1.	Celje	15.598	1.480	-	17.078	5,03
2.	Koper	1.336	221	17	1.574	0,00
3.	Kranj	2.481	214	46	2.741	0,81
4.	Lj. Bežigrad	683	25	126	834	0,70
5.	Lj. Center	8.861	0	280	9.141	3,37
6.	Lj. Moste	278	481	1.179	1.938	1,37
7.	Lj. Šiška	261	465	256	982	0,73
8.	Lj. Vič	290	388	382	1.060	0,67
-	Lj. Bibliobus	9.357	0	435	9.792	20,31
9.	Maribor	7.813	975	25	8.809	2,49
10.	Murska Sobota	0	0	0	0	0,00
11.	Nova Gorica	1.397	381	18	1.796	0,71
12.	Novo mesto	3.585	78	1.113	4.776	1,12
13.	Ptuj	725	1.009	0	1.734	0,91
14.	Ravne	543	221	0	764	0,35
1.	Ajdovščina	123	68	0	123	0,18
2.	Brežice	159	50	11	220	0,40
3.	Domžale	835	65	380	1.280	1,25
4.	Gornja Radgona	18	0	7	25	0,10
5.	Grosuplje	150	74	50	274	0,50
6.	Jesenice	0	0	0	0	0,00
7.	Kamnik	1.888	5	0	1.893	2,36
8.	Krško	18	13	16	47	0,08
9.	Lendava	254	0	0	254	0,33
10	Radovljica	358	154	29	541	0,57
11.	Sežana	293	-	-	293	0,44
12	Slov. Bistrica	646	25	46	717	1,05
13.	Slov. Gradec	483	6	26	515	1,32
14.	Slov. Konjice	296	30	0	326	0,92
15.	Škofja loka	104	63	0	167	0,16
16.	Šmarje	0	0	0	0	0,00
17.	Tolmin	0	27	0	27	0,04
18.	Velenje	938	126	888	1.952	2,04

19.	Žalec	97	140	12	249	0,45
1.	Cerknica	197	45	32	274	0,68
2.	Črnomelj	2.865	42	3	2.910	9,03
3.	Hrastnik	850	59	10	919	2,99
4.	Idrija	233	76	0	309	0,42
5.	Il. Bistrica	85	39	-	124	0,34
6.	Izola	278	0	0	278	0,71
7.	Kočevje	3.878	289	61	4.228	8,77
8.	Laško	23	52	2	77	0,19
9.	Lenart	109	46	0	155	0,42
10.	Litija	16	133	18	167	0,32
11.	Ljutomer	23	66	0	89	0,21
12.	Mozirje	0	2	0	2	0,00
13.	Ormož	-	42	-	42	0,11
14.	Piran	1.590	122	0	1.712	3,58
15.	Postojna	1.608	91	9	1.708	2,24
16.	Radlje	154	20	1	175	0,52
17.	Ribnica	34	16	32	82	0,29
18.	Sevnica	22	36	3	61	0,36
19.	Šentjur	0	3	0	3	0,01
20.	Trbovlje	0	32	0	32	0,08
21.	Trebnje	112	5	2	119	0,31
22.	Tržič	50	25	5	80	0,19
23.	Vrhnika	2.389	320	34	2.752	4,11
24.	Zagorje	318	34	0	352	0,92
1.	Dravograd	199	35	0	234	1,92
2.	Logatec	412	100	12	524	1,66
3.	Metlika	0	52	0	52	0,30
	TOTAL:	75.313	8.566	5.566	89.382	1,52

Table 3.   Discarding from public libraries in Slovenia in 1993.

Source: Novljan, S. (1994), "Pogoji dela zaostajaju za rastjo potreb" (Splošnoizo braževalne knjižnice v letu 1993) (Working Conditions Lag Behind the Growth of Needs, Public Libraries in Year 1993), National and University Library Ljubljana.

In the given example, 20.31 percent of the collection of the Ljubljana bookmobile and 9.03 percent of the collection in the Municipality of Črnomelj were discarded in 1993. Whether these percentages represent a long-overdue weeding or "murky" discarding, it is hard to say. In order to know what exactly was discarded in that particular year, one would need to have access to the inventory of discarded materials of each library and check each entry one by one, provided that such data is available, considering that in most cases this information is not stored that long. In Slovenia alone there are more than 250 public libraries and more than 900 libraries in all, which makes it a virtually impossible task with highly uncertain outcomes and low prospects for success. Most of the annual reports in the period 1990–2000 were prepared by the now retired librarian Silva Novljan. In a conversation with me, Mrs. Novljan confirmed that during her monitoring of public libraries in the years 1990–2007 these statistical reports were issued every year. From 1997 onwards the data about discarding was not included in the summary reports, even if the questionnaires directed at libraries contained it. Nevertheless, libraries would often leave this field blank. According to Novljan, this is potentially due to several factors: since libraries sometimes did not dispose of enough books per patron they did not discard regularly, or they would weed without discarding because of a lack of staff members. As it turned out later, the discarded books were often labelled as donations to other, newly opened libraries or libraries affected by calamities, including libraries in former Yugoslav states, refugee centers or libraries aimed at Slovenians living abroad. Based on the data available at the National and University Library, Slovenian libraries do not discard enough. Special, university and school libraries discard even less than public ones because of a lack of staff and lack of training (Poličnik-Čermelj and Žagar 2007, 57–58).

My research partly consisted in semi-structured interviews with librarians from the National and University Library, the Ljubljana City Library and some specialized libraries, antique dealers, a former employee of a paper recycling center and the members of one Serbian cultural society operating in Ljubljana. Most interviewees were over fifty, some were retired or in other jobs, while others are still in service. When asked if there were books that became ideologically or linguistically "unsuitable" after Slovenia declared independence, librarians mostly claimed they would have known if unlawful discarding had happened. They all agreed there were neither instructions nor recommendations issued to the libraries by the Ministry of Culture or Education, and in most cases library policies depended on the director and the course he or she decided to take. Some non-librarians among the interviewees hinted at potential irregularities, without presenting clear proofs. Moreover, the lack of evidence (if any) was sometimes ascribed to the "typically Slovene" covert way of doing things, or doubts were expressed on whether all discarding was done by the book with the comment "if they were erasing people, it is hard to believe that books were left untouched". The "Erased" is the name used in the media for a group of people who were citizens of former Yugoslavia, but remained without a legal status after Slovenia declared independence, either because they did not apply on time or were refused Slovenian citizenship or permanent resident status. On February 26, 1992, 25,671 people were erased from the permanent residents-registry. The case was even brought to the European Court of Human Rights, which ruled in favor of the applicants.

On the other hand, the interviewed librarians stated that weeding (and discarding) were carried out according to the existing rules: books in Serbo-Croatian and/or Cyrillic script or dealing with "socialist" themes were discarded if they were duplicate copies or they had not been borrowed for a number of consecutive years. Statements like "weeding in Slovenia was not political" or "we did not have war and hatred like you [in Croatia]" were quite common.[141] A similar "othering" process to the one observed in the IFLA/FAIFE report on Croatia (addressed in subchapter 2.2) could also be observed in sentences such as:

> "if something like that happened, it was probably in schools where no professional librarians are employed, but bad teachers take over the role. Probably it did come to the discarding of Cyrillic volumes, but not because of ideological reasons, but because the users were no longer able to read them. The Cyrillic script was a problem even for my generation, which attended elementary school in the late 1960s. In fact, we only learned Serbo-Croatian for a year and a half. What happened with other inhabitants of Slovenia that came from other Yugoslav republics as library

---

141 This and other statements are all taken from interviews and personal conversations with the author, unless otherwise indicated.

users, I do not know. I do not remember any analysis of library users in the 1990s" (EKD, librarian, e-mail correspondence, March 26, 2015).

When it comes to school libraries, which were not the focus of my research, Dimitar Anakiev[142] mentions in his 2011 article "Omarska, pakao za ljude" (Omarska, hell for people) that in 1996 he witnessed the burning of Serbo-Croatian books in a small town in Slovenia. He writes that he saw books numbering in the "hundreds, thousands, who could tell, in the so-called Serbo-Croatian language" that were burning, and he later found out from the school director's wife that "the ethnic libricide was ordered from Ljubljana for the whole of Slovenia".[143]

One case of missing books nevertheless found its way to the Slovenian press, namely, the books from the library of the Yugoslav People's Army (YPA). It is uncertain what happened to approximately 300,000 books that the withdrawing YPA left in Slovenia. The issue was first raised in 1998 by one of my interviewees, the publisher and used book dealer Dušan Cunjak. The man "who sold the Slovenes more than 2 million old, used and cheap books" contacted the Slovenian Ministry of Defence inquiring about the fate of these volumes. The Ministry first responded by saying that they took over the books and placed them in the Central library of the Ministry: "regarding the fate of the books from the former libraries of the Yugoslav People's Army, we inform you that most of the volumes are kept in the Central library of the Ministry of Defence of the Republic of Slovenia in Ljubljana". Three years later "Mladina" reporters were told the handover never took place:

> "The library of the Ministry of Defence of the Republic of Slovenia, established in 1993, did not take over the books in possession of the YPA. When the library was established no formal handover from those responsible for the books at the Ministry of Defence to the Central library took place".[144]

---

142 Dimitar Anakiev became famous for his socially engaged films, particularly on the "Erased" in Slovenia, to which he also belonged.
143 Dimitar Anakiev. "Omarska, pakao za ljude". *E-novosti*, January 15, 2011. Retrieved on April 20, 2019, from: http://www.e-novine.com/stav/43912-Omarska-pakao-ljude.html.
144 Dušan Cunjak. "Kje so knjige?". *Mladina*, May 7, 2011. Retrieved on March 20, 2015, from: http://www.mladina.si/87893/m-knjige/?utm_source=tednik%2

It is hard to establish what exactly happened (some people even claim the Army took the books and brought them to Belgrade), but a couple of years ago the Serbian Cultural Society "Mihajlo Pupin" was given 15,000 volumes, mostly in Cyrillic, that were allegedly stored in some boxes in a military facility for more than fifteen years. *Mladina* reporters unofficially found out that some of the books were inherited by the Central library of the Ministry of Defence; a part went to the barracks and other ministries and some were sold to the NUK.[145] My interviewee, however, says:

> "Librarians in the military barracks warned me that they were burning books. It was not the librarians who burned them, for them books are like their children, it was the soldiers, the commanders." (DC, antiquarian, personal interview, Ljubljana, March 30, 2015)

The problems in establishing the exact number and content of the books that were taken, burned, trashed or saved during the withdrawal of the Yugoslav People's Army from Croatia were also recognized by Lešaja (Lešaja 2012, 82). The various barracks and other facilities operating within the YPA were equipped with not only military literature, but also encyclopaedias, maps and sometimes rare and valuable volumes. Apparently one of the few collections that remained intact is that of the garrison library in the Gripe fortress in Split, since 1991 the library of the Croatian Navy.[146] In Zadar, there were four military libraries with approximately half a million volumes (139). Books and maps were burned by the withdrawing YPA in the barracks "Đuro Đaković" and "Marko Orešković". The reports on the event by the academician Tihomil

---

F200118%2Fclanek%2Fm-knjige%2F&utm_medium=web&utm_campaign=oldLink.

145 I unsuccessfully tried contacting the now retired librarian who became the Head of the library of the Education Center at the Ministry of Defense in 1993. She set up the first special military library in independent Slovenia and contributed to its digitalization.

146 Sanja Stapić. "Jedina knjižnica bivše 'JNA' koja je preživjela rat. Knjige za HRM" (The only library of the former 'YPA' that survived the war. Books for the Croatian Navy). *Slobodna Dalmacija*, May 5, 1992.

The Discarding of Books in the 1990s 127

Maštrović[147] and the Director of the Zadar City Library Ivan Pehar slightly differ:

> "Led by hatred towards all that is Croatian, Serbian criminals took out tens of thousands of books in Latin script from the libraries of the military academies in Zadar, piled them up, poured gasoline over and burned them. [...] Out of the once rich library with nearly 80,000 volumes only a heap of ashes remained to be found by the liberators". (Maštrović)

> "From around half a million volumes, the employees of the Zadar City Library and other cultural workers from Zadar managed to save around 70,000 books, a great number of magazines, manuals, ballistic charts and around 100,000 specific topographic maps. Around 10,000 volumes were left undamaged in the former Army Hall Zadar. The entire collection was elaborated and given to the Croatian Army. In the 'Đuro Đaković' barracks books were burning for 23 days—encyclopaedias and fiction that were systematically chosen as the most valuable. In the 'Marko Orešković' barracks we found burned maps and schemes, 150,000 of the most valuable books were selected and taken, as well as the entire collection of the Air force academy". (Pehar)[148]

One of the two antiquarians I interviewed remembers that sometimes officers were looking for military literature that had been thrown away:

> "Officers were coming to our shop to buy manuals that were thrown away earlier. A classical Croatian story. The professional literature of the Yugoslav People's Army was top-notch, but it still ended up in the trash, despite possessing a "top secret" seal" (TV, antiquarian, personal interview, Rijeka, March 14, 2015).

When asked whether they knew about some cases of unlawful discarding practices in Croatia, almost none of the interviewed librarians in Slovenia professed familiarity with the situation in the neighboring country.

Based on research conducted in 1998 by the Department of Library and Information Studies and Book Studies at Ljubljana University, the interest in other South Slavic literatures diminished

---

147 Tihomil Maštrović was the Director of the Croatian National and University Library between 2007–2011.
148 Tihomil Maštrović, "Zločin ćiriličnog uma" (The Crime of a Cyrillic Mind). *Večernji list*, October 1, 1995; Pehar, I. (1994), "Nestali, uništeni, oštećeni fondovi 1991–1994" (Disappeared, damaged and destroyed collections 1991–1994). *Vjesnik bibliotekara Hrvatske*, n. 3/4, pp. 119–121.

considerably after the breakup of Yugoslavia[149] (Žnideršič et al. 1999, 38–45). The level of knowledge of the Cyrillic alphabet deteriorated, so books in this script were gradually discarded and donated to the various Serbian societies operating in Slovenia, to refugee centers and/or sent to Serbia. Some of the discarded books were also donated to Croatian and Bosnian libraries that have been destroyed or burned down during the war. These events coincided with an increase in the number of publishing houses and, consequently, published books. In the 1980s there were around 20 publishing houses in Slovenia, together with the publishing departments of some cultural institutions and associations. In the first half of the 1990s the number grew to approximately 200, to be stabilized and regulated by the market to roughly 50 towards the turn of the Millennium. The number of published works increased from fewer than 2000 annually in Slovenia before 1990 to almost double that total in the next decade (Gabrič 2006, 164–165). The diffusion of computers also led to the informatization of library catalogues. Library collections grew, which is why they sometimes had to move to larger premises, often a good opportunity to weed. Similarly, a lot of materials were weeded prior to the growth of the informatization process in order to avoid double work. The collections in public libraries in Slovenia kept growing between 1990 and 2015, while the number of members registered minor oscillations, with the number first growing for four or more consecutive years and then dropping only to rise again etc. (Kodrič-Dačić 2016, 11).

The table below, compiled from data that the National and University Library in Ljubljana acquired from public libraries over the years, shows that the collection kept growing and the percentage of discarded material stayed below 4 percent. That is, the number of newly acquired volumes was higher than the quantity of discarded materials and books. From 1997 onwards the data about discarding was not included in the yearly report, presumably because libraries were not discarding enough and would leave that field

---

149 Most Slovenian public libraries started using the COBISS system in 1993, which means that the data about the most and least borrowed books is theoretically available in digital form from that year onwards. Prior to 1993 date cards were used.

The Discarding of Books in the 1990s   129

blank in the questionnaires sent to the NUK. The data in the annual reports was not always presented equally in the summary reports: in some cases, the given numbers concern all materials in the collection (such as periodicals, newspapers, maps, films, CDs etc.), not only books, which is why the number referring solely to books was put between brackets when available. Furthermore, for the year 1998 the category "books" also included periodical publications. These considerations are relevant, but not crucial for the purposes of this research. What the table demonstrates is a steady growth of the stock and discarding is even below the norm (3–5 percent of the basic stock).

Public libraries in Slovenia

Year	Acquisition	Discarding	Total Collection
1990	307.085 (282.416)	172.181 (147.120) 3,3% (3%)	5.248.421 or 5.048.176
1991	290.856 (251.630)	75.421 (62.205) 1,25%	5.427.770 or 5.428.456 (5.121.149)
1992	265.669 (221.000)	103.947 1,85%	5.612.685 (5.131.427)
1993	260.367 (221.774)	89.382 1.55%	5.780.399 (5.284.919)
1994	288.118 (247.434)	77.172 1,29%	5.992.856 (5.472.899)
1995	333.231 (290.343)	71.211 1,13%	6.323.488 (5.710.287)
1996	359.364 (317.517)	126.168 1,94%	6.503.684
1997	372.506 (330.895)	No data	6.753.274 (6.159.079)

1998	399.446 (366.814*)	No data	6.761.030 (6.496.548)*
1999	440.077 (382.537)	No data	7.150.926 (6.604.778)
2000	431.448 (366.435)	No data	7.383.654 (6.775.406)

Table 4. The development of the collection in Slovenian public libraries in the period 1990–2000

Source: I compiled the table based on the data in the various annual issues of *Splošnoizobraževalne knjižnice v letu...*, National and University Library, Ljubljana.

2.6. The Discarding of Books in Public Libraries in Croatia and Slovenia during Transition: Possible Lines of Interpretation

In her 1990 article "Epoch on the junkyard" *(Epoha na smetlištu)*, which I have already cited in the introduction, the journalist Jasmina Kuzmanović describes the removal of monuments, the "most obvious political iconography of an epoch", and books intended as "ideological paraphernalia" in Eastern Europe after the collapse of communism. No negative emotions are involved in the process of removal, she writes, because "what is leaving are not books in the true sense of the word, but the ideological paraphernalia of previous systems".[150] In Croatia, events are unfolding pretty much as elsewhere:

> "first the initiative to bring back the monument to ban Jelačić, followed by the intervention into the ideologically-colored names of squares and streets. Last in the row is the great tidying up of governmental offices, and then I guess of municipalities, libraries and community centres".

Until that point, the "cleansing" of libraries is not an exclusively Croatian phenomenon: an article by Micha Haarkötter, published in the German daily *Die Tageszeitung* (commonly known as taz) on

---

150 Jasmina Kuzmanović, "Epoha na smetlištu" (Epoch on the junkyard). *Danas*, December 4, 1990.

The Discarding of Books in the 1990s 131

August 10, 1994, also reports about the "cleansing" of public libraries in the former German Democratic Republic, the "modernization of school books" and the "destruction" of books, most of which originated from the so-called "worker's libraries". He writes that "reunification began in the cultural field with the biggest book destruction of the postwar period".[151] Four years after Kuzmanović's article was written, Croatia is an independent state and unlike East-Central European postsocialist countries, it is at war and does not have control over parts of its territory. In July 1994, the reader Anton Lukežić wrote a letter to "Novi list" in which he expresses his disagreement and concern about "the crusade against unsuitable books that has been going on for four years in the Croatian Parliament". As examples of unsuitable books, the sale and distribution of which is being discussed in the Parliament he cites the *Orthography manual of the Croatian or Serbian language* by Vladimir Anić and Josip Silić and the book *Anglicisms in the Croatian or Serbian language: Origin, development, meaning*. Lukežić then mentions that a librarian announced on TV that her library was about to complete the removal of "unsuitable" books. Although it is not clearly stated, it is implied that unsuitable books are those that make references to or are written in the so-called Serbo-Croatian language. This example illustrates that the "tidying up" that Kuzmanović announced in 1990 in Croatia involved not only "ideological paraphernalia" but also, for one reason or another, "unsuitable" books. At the end of 1999 the journalist Davorka Vukov Colić was able to ascertain that "the removal of unsuitable books is only a part of a much wider process of adjusting culture to new times and a new ideological "environment" that is "more or less completed today"[152]. These three articles provide the framework for the analysis of the developments in the removal "à la Croate". Like in other postsocialist

---

151 Micha Haarkötter. "In aller Stille abgewickelt. Vom verschwinden der DDR-Betriebs-Bibiotheken" (Liquidated in silence. About the disappearance of GDR company libraries). *Die Tageszeitung*, August 10, 1994. All translations from German are my own, unless otherwise indicated.
152 Davorka Vukov Colić. "Sudstvo i kultura. Šutnjom u bezbolno društvo" (The Judiciary and Culture. Through Silence into a Painless Society). *Zarez*, October 15, 1999.

states, libraries and other institutions needed to be adapted to the new system, but due to the prevalence of language policies promoting a clear differentiation between the Croatian and Serbian languages (which, as mentioned in subchapter 1.5, was not first formulated in 1990) the removal process involved a larger corpus of books. Yet, this is not the only specificity of the Croatian case: it is the frame within which the debate was conducted. An anti-communist mood characterized pretty much all postsocialist states in the 1990s (and to a large extent it still does), but in Croatia the public discourse was further polarized by the state of war and a certain "anti-Serbian and anti-Yugoslav hysteria". By the time the topic of the "cleansing" of libraries resurfaced again with the mediatic exposure of the "Korčula case" the frame had partially changed, but the anti-Serbian mood did not: the throwing of books, many of which were published in other parts of former Yugoslavia, into the garbage coincided with the statement by the Ministry of Finance about "cleaning libraries from books in Serbian and similar languages". However, the country was no longer at war, and Tuđman's authoritarian style of government could no longer be justified with an "external threat". Going back to Ožegović's classification of the ways in which the media presented contents, Korčula would fall under the second phase (1995–2000), a period in which the strategy of scandal was often used as an instrument in the conflict between state-building *(državotvorni)* and independent media, namely, intellectuals supporting and opposing the dominant political option. In other words, the conflict with an external enemy (the so-called rump Yugoslavia) was replaced by an internal, Croatian confrontation between critically minded intellectuals and the supporters of the regime. In such a highly polarized environment, writing about Korčula became a metonym for fighting against a regime where corruption and political crime was the order of the day. It embodied the criticism against cultural policies, the impunity of crimes and historical revisionism. I believe this is reflected in the answer the journalist IL gave me to the question whether the case might have been "overblown" in the media:

The Discarding of Books in the 1990s 133

> "I think it was exposed too little. I personally never had in mind a media scandal that could in any way be lucrative, but simply writing about something that the mainstream does not want to ask and question. Besides *Feral* [*Tribune*] no one even wanted to take it into account as relevant. The perpetrators did not have to face any particular consequences, apart from some kind of scandal, and that also says something about the final balance sheet of the media writings about that" (IL, journalist, personal interview, Zagreb, October 7, 2015).

Feral Tribune (also known as *Feral*) asserted itself as an uncompromisingly critical media outlet that was among the first to report about Croatian crimes during the war in Bosnia, so it was often the target of governmental attempts at silencing it. First, in 1994 a special tax for pornographic material was imposed on the weekly (overruled by the Constitutional Court in 1995). This was followed by a law prohibiting the public criticism of high-ranking politicians in 1996. Due to accumulated financial problems *Feral Tribune* was discontinued in 2008.[153] Journalists writing for *Feral Tribune* often had to deal with lawsuits, and the "Korčula case" was no exception in this respect.

Professional librarians were more like extras, background actors in the whole issue. While, on the one hand, this could be explained by the fact that the debate did not unfold among professionals, on the other it is hard to understand that a profession (judging by the IFLA/FAIFE report) that felt attacked and negatively affected by the scandal did not feel the need to intervene. A resolute, quick and data-supported reaction such as the one displayed by the librarians from the "Oton Župančič" Library could have avoided the politicization of the issue. On the contrary, up until today there is no official data about discarding in the 1990s which only further mystifies the issue. As far as I am aware there was also no attempt from the side of librarians to deal with the controversial discarding in the 1990s through scientific publications. Based on my correspondence with Ante Lešaja, who carefully followed the reactions

---

153 On the 25 years of history of the political-satirical weekly see Pavelić (2014).

to the publication of his book from 2012 until today, no response whatsoever from the library profession was to be registered.[154] Librarians are obviously not a homogeneous body, but a declaration from an official body representing them has a certain symbolic weight. What is concerning is that, based on what Lešaja writes in *Bookicide*, in the 1990s many were afraid to speak out on "murky" discarding for fear of losing their jobs. So, were the known cases individual excesses or was it a widespread occurrence? IL continues:

> "In parallel, there was some resistance because librarians are far from a homogeneous body that functions automatically on demand. They are to be given a great deal of credit for saving a lot of books, but also for the fact that some cases even made it to public view. The dimensions of this [phenomenon] are really so big that we could say that it is something special. There was even war here and in such circumstances, it is easier to carry out such abominations, which are easier to realize as systemic actions, as initiatives of the regime. In other postsocialist countries comparable things also happened, but with less intensity, I suppose. It is wrong to divide things, there is no either/or, things happen in parallel and are mutually conditioned. I am afraid it is a kind of an alibi if we are justifying it with the war" (IL, journalist, personal interview, Zagreb, October 7, 2015).

While it is TV's opinion that

> "I judge these as excesses. It is my belief because I know people, librarians. From everywhere, right? Today they are ordering books from us, Serbian editions of all books. Except for those that are on the compulsory reading list. But if it is professional literature, for all professions, all fields, there are no problems" (TV, antiquarian, personal interview, Rijeka, March 14, 2015).

Indeed, as IL argues, the Croatian "libricide" can hardly be disentangled from the context of the war, but also the general atmosphere in those years that is poignantly described in the previously cited excerpts from texts by Anton Lukežić, Nikica Mihaljević and Dubravka Ugrešić. The librarians in Slovenia I spoke with also expressed their doubt as to how hard it probably is to stay impartial

---

154 In a conversation over the phone, an employee of the National and University Library in Zagreb told me, when I mentioned Lešaja's book, something like "let it be".

The Discarding of Books in the 1990s 135

during an armed conflict and with pressure coming from "above" and "below". I have already given some examples of the occurrence in subchapter 1.6, which is why I would now like to complement these insights with some anecdotes from antique stores, where it is also possible to "take the pulse" of the clients and the reactions from "below" that antiquarians (and librarians) are sometimes exposed to:

> "What we had in the antique shop is reactions to books [...] People were coming from emigration [...] And then came this guy and then he saw something and then he said, like, I see you have a lot of communist literature, I don't know if this is by chance or if here everyone is affected by communism. All of this should be disinfected very well. [...] That was an excess" (TV, antiquarian, personal interview, Rijeka, March 14, 2015).

In Ljubljana a customer had a problem with "communism" being sold at Christmas time:

> "Because here in my shop there is no politics. Everything is on sale, I take everything as long as it is of a good quality. There was a volume from the Nazi period and a man came in saying that this should not be sold. Also, before New Year I had a calendar of the 11th Congress of the League of Communists of Yugoslavia, leather-bound and with original photos and a man comes in just before New Year's and asks me if I know that it is Advent time. I say yes, and? Well, how can you sell this Communism?" (RG, antiquarian, personal interview, Ljubljana, March 11, 2015).

The antiquarian I interviewed in Rijeka, on the other hand, had to learn that too much Cyrillic in one book will not help sell it:

> "They come and they ask: *Do you have Russian?* And I say yes. *Man, but this is in Cyrillic. If at least the translation was in Latin.* And I say well ... If you read the Russian Cyrillic script ... You tell me why it is a problem to read the Serbian one" (TV, antiquarian, personal interview, Rijeka, March 14, 2015).

In this chapter I outlined the distinctive features of the debate on "libricide" in Croatia and the lack thereof in Slovenia. Despite the limits the researcher encounters in terms of the available official data when examining discarding more than a decade later, witness accounts on the matter in written and oral form provide more than enough material to examine. Rather than establishing the actual number or titles of discarded books, what my research tackled is how and why certain debates and perceptions came into being and on what grounds they were instrumentalized for other goals. In the following section, the focus will be on the aftermath of these discussions through the medium of (discarded) books. As has been argued before, when discarded, books are not necessarily physically destroyed and they continue circulating. Furthermore, books are reproducible (unless they are rare volumes and manuscripts, but these are generally not the kind of books a public library deals with), which means that discarding certain volumes *en bloc* will unlikely lead to their physical elimination, but rather to the constitution of a category of the "other", the discarded.

3. The Afterlife of Discarded Books between Dumps, Library Shelves and Art

When discarded from a library, regardless of whether professional standards were respected in the process or not, many books continue circulating: some enrich private or public libraries, others end up in used book stores or flea markets, some are read, while others are turned into artistic objects or furniture. Chairs or coffee tables made with books can be seen in libraries, sometimes in archives, and in an increasing number of cafés. Even if they do end up in the rubbish dump, this does not have to be their final destination. As with other objects, books can navigate between the library, the dump, the flea market, and the museum, and this is not a one-way road. Archives and trash dumps, argues Aleida Assmann, can be considered "emblems and symptoms for cultural remembrance and oblivion," and as such they have attracted the attention of scholars and artists (A. Assmann 2002, 71). There is a "reverse affinity" between archives and rubbish dumps: while the former are repositories of things past worth preserving, the latter are repositories of things past left to decay. They are also connected by a common boundary which can be crossed by objects in both ways; what does not "qualify" to be stored in an archive usually ends up on a rubbish dump, but what is also discarded from an archive can equally end up there. What is more, sometimes objects can be relocated from a dump to an archive. "In the totalitarian context the dump becomes an emblem of a subversive counter-memory that cannot be controlled by the institutions of political power, figuring as a perpetual source of creative energy" (A. Assmann 2002, 81). Waste archives can thus be seen as refuges for the forgotten and rejected which are *ipso facto* remembered. The objects themselves "may remind us, may trigger our memory, because they carry memories which we have invested into them" (J. Assmann 2008, 111).

To see books in overflowing waste bins between banana peels and used diapers is not a pleasant sight—it provokes disgust and public outrage, a bit less so if they are spotted in paper bins. It is a matter of fact that most people do not like to throw away books.

This is no less true of librarians, who are expected to do it as part of their job. Can books even be classified as waste? In his "Rubbish Theory" (1979) Michael Thompson argues that rubbish is a consequence of a change of values in a given society. According to Thompson, objects go through three stages: transient value, zero value and permanent value. Transient is the use-value of artefacts which gradually drops to zero, turning them into rubbish. If they acquire an aesthetic, museological or historical value, objects enter the permanent value category (Moser 2002, 93). As was discussed in Chapter Two, it is books in the trash that create an emotional reaction. And that is because value is not a purely economic category. Even if their material value drops to zero, their symbolic value as important cultural artefacts is still high. In fact, rubbish can be seen through different lenses: economic (if an object no longer has a functional value, it becomes obsolete and is replaced), art (grounded on values such as truth, beauty and meaning) and personal and cultural memory (grounded on an identity value that provides the criteria of relevance).

Waste, argues Walter Moser, is no longer outside of culture — a process of "acculturation" of waste is underway (Moser 2002, 89). In his essay, he combines Thompson's theory with Mary Douglas' insights on (im)purity, which I find useful in understanding what makes books in a trash can so unpleasant. Waste and impurity are, for Douglas, exogenous to the system, but they could easily become sources of revitalization of the system and a symptom of its interest in alterity (91). According to Douglas, rubbish is an "'in-between' state, both spatially and temporally", "a decayed object that finds itself 'out of place'", and as such it "endangers order" (97). It retains an identity as a result of its ties to the previous system. This is the moment when it constitutes a danger to the "purity" of the system. It somehow induces remembrance. And books seen in the garbage dump do exactly that; they endanger order because they do not belong there. More specifically, Douglas argues that when an order is being constituted, the rejected bits and pieces go through two phases. First, they are viewed as a threat to the good order and discarded. According to Douglas, it is at this stage that they are dangerous: they still retain some of their previous identity, and "the clarity of the scene in which they obtrude is impaired by their presence" (Douglas, 2001, 161). Once these rejected bits and pieces lose the last vestiges of their previous existence through rotting and dissolving, they are no longer to be feared. Once books are bulldozed or sold for pulp, they lose their identity as books: "So long as identity is absent, rubbish is not dangerous. It does not even create ambiguous perceptions since it clearly belongs in a defined place, a rubbish heap of one kind or another" (Douglas, 2001, 161). Thompson adds,

> "The discarded but still visible, because it still intrudes, forms a genuine cultural category of a special type—a rubbish category. That which is discarded but not visible, because it does not intrude, is not a cultural category at all, it is simply *residual* to the entire category system" (Thompson 1979, 92; italics in the original).

Inspired by what has been written so far and Thompson's line of reasoning, I would argue that discarded books also form a category of their own, the category of the discarded. And the discarded are not only books that no longer belong to a library and are marked with a "discarded" stamp. They are all of the books that lost currency, importance, actuality, or value with the breakup of Yugoslavia, not only those that were (un)officially discarded from libraries, but also those which readers identify as such. For instance, when the organizers of the exhibition "Discarded. On the occasion of the 20th anniversary of operation Storm" launched a call for citizens to bring books that were discarded in the 1990s, visitors brought books from their own personal libraries which did not necessarily come into their possession as discarded copies from a library. In other words, one can still find discarded books in libraries. One such book is *The Hedgehog's Home*, which is nowadays available in most libraries in Croatia, but continues being a discarded book. In subchapter 3.1, I will analyze the reasons for this and argue that because of the "name" acquired in the 1990s libraries in Croatia have to try harder to regain the confidence of their patrons. One example of how a better communication between libraries and their users can also be achieved through the medium of discarded books will be presented in section 3.2, followed by the examination of a donation story, namely from various libraries in Zagreb to the Central Library of Serbs in Croatia. In the remaining subchapters (3.3 and 3.4) a film and an exhibition will be scrutinized for their exploration of the potential of discarded books as vehicles for a critical examination of the recent past.

3.1. The Hedgehog in Search of a Home

Among the discarded books that have been attracting a lot of public attention is certainly *The Hedgehog's Home (Ježeva kućica)*. The fable was written in the form of a long poem by Branko Ćopić and first published in Yugoslavia in 1949. It tells the story of a hedgehog, Ježurka Ježić (Hedgemond the Hunter in the English translation by S. Curtis), who defends his humble home against a fox, a bear, a wolf and a wild boar. With its simple message—there is no place like home—and musicality achieved through rhyme, the book became very popular among children and their parents. The importance of the book for different generations of Serbo-Croatian-speaking Yugoslavs was perhaps best described by Goran Vojnović in his novel *Southern Scum, Go Home! (Čefurji raus!*, 2008):

> "There is no chance for us and the Slovenes. Everything starts when we are kids. Their parents read fucking Pedenjpeds and Slipper Cats to them, while ours read Hedgehogs' Homes and Grga Čvaraks to us. And from then on everything goes to hell. Everyone goes their separate ways and there is nothing that would put us together anymore. We can, like, hang out together, understand each other and pretend to be colleagues and all, but we cannot really get each other. Like brothers. We don't have the same things in our blood. We are Southerners and they are Slovenes, and that's it. Fuck it. Branko Ćopić and Jovan Jovanović Zmaj are to be blamed".[155]

Even if Vojnović uses this example to point to the difficulties a second-generation Bosnian immigrant might face when integrating into Slovenian society, I think this paragraph successfully conveys the presence of *The Hedgehog's Home* in one's childhood.

---

155 Vojnović, G. (2009). *Čefuri raus!*, Novi Liber, 57. Translated into Croatian by Anita Peti-Stantić and Jagna Pogačnik. I translated this paragraph from the Croatian edition.

The Hedgehog's Home has been successfully adapted into theatre plays and animated films, most recently in 2017.[156] The book was added to the list of recommended elementary school readings in Croatia in 1960. Compulsory and recommended readings lists have been continually published within the teaching plan and program for each school year since 1972 (Hameršak 2006, 99). They are frequently updated: in a thirty-year period around 500 titles were indexed, while only 22 were common to all lists (Hameršak 2006, 105-106). In the table of all the recommended individual readings in Croatian elementary schools between 1936 and 2011 compiled in 2018 by Smiljana Narančić Kovač and Ivana Milković within the BIBRICH (Building Intercultural Bridges through Children's Literature Translations: Texts, Contexts and Strategies) project, the number of titles rises to 1033.[157] As it can be seen in the table, The *Hedgehog's Home* was removed from the list in 1993. One of the proponents of the book's removal, the linguist Stjepan Babić, argued in his paper "*The Hedgehog's Home* as a Pedagogic and Linguistic problem" *(Ježeva kućica kao pedagoški i jezični problem*, 2006) that the poem, written in the Serbian language, is not suitable for first graders if left untranslated. Even if it has been partially adapted (or translated) to the Croatian language, it remains incomprehensible to Croatian pupils and/or would require too many additional explanations (Babić 2006, 146). In his article Babić actually refers to the book's removal "towards the end of last year" (Babić 2006, 139), that is, in 2005. On the other hand, the linguist Nives Opačić mentions in her paper published in the same year (but first presented at the international conference "Riječki filološki dani" in November 2004) that the book "will soon be placed on the list of readings" (Opačić 2006, 243). As two newspaper articles published in *Jutarnji list* in November 2005 testify, *The Hedgehog's Home* was supposed to enter the list in the 2005/2006 school year but it was decided not to

---

156 *Ježeva kuća/Hedgehog's Home*. Directed by Eva Cvijanović. National Film Board of Canada and Bonobostudio, 2017.
157 The table and more information about the project itself can be found on the following website: http://bibrich.ufzg.hr/reading-lists/. Last accessed on March 14, 2019.

include it after all.[158] In February 2019 it was announced again that *The Hedgehog's Home* was about to be removed from the reading list. However, in the BIBRICH table there is no mention that it was ever added to the list after 1993, and the same is confirmed in an interview given to *Novi list* by Marijana Hameršak in February 2019.[159] My assumption would thus be that the discussion about the list is still a work in progress. As reported in the press, this time the fable was to be removed together with internationally acclaimed works such as *The Little Prince, Peter Pan, Pippi Longstocking* and *Pinocchio*, just to name a few. The Croatian Writers Society and the Croatian Society of Writers of Children and Youth Books reacted with a statement saying that the country is again sliding into the 19th century, considering that only classics found themselves on the new list.[160] As Marijana Hameršak argues, these reading lists are rarely good indicators of the actual individual reading assignments in elementary schools (Hameršak 2006, 105), they do not always (at least not immediately) follow the sociopolitical changes in the country (104) and are of particular interest to publishers, who have an interest in seeing their (re)editions placed on the list. For instance, when in 2005 Stjepan Babić decided that *The Hedgehog's Home* should not be included in the reading list, the owner and director of the publishing house "Katarina Zrinski" reacted publicly, accusing Babić in the press of having caused considerable material damage to his company, which had received permission from the copyright owner, the

---

158 Ivana Kalogjera-Brkić, "'Ježeva kućica nije pisana hrvatskim'" ('Hedgehog's Home' is not Written in Croatian). *Jutarnji list*, 23 November 2005 and Ivana Kalogjera-Brkić, "'Ježeva kućica' ima fusnote na hrvatskom" ('Hedhehog's Home has Footnotes in Croatian). *Jutarnji list*, 26 November 2005.
159 Ljerka Bratonja Martinović. "Marijana Hameršak: Neodgovorno je što 'Ježeve kućice' već desetljećima nema na popisu lektire" (Marijana Hameršak: It is irresponsible that 'The Hedgehog's Home' is not on the reading list). *Novi list*, February 24, 2019. Retrieved on March 14, 2019, from: http://novilist.hr/Vijesti/Hrvatska/MARIJANA-HAMERSAK-Neodgovorno-je-sto-Jezeve-kuci ce-vec-desetljecima-nema-na-popisu-lektire.
160 More about it can be read in several online articles such as this one, published by the online portal Index.hr: "Iz lektire izbačeni Mali princ i Ježeva kućica". *Index.hr*, February 13, 2019. Retrieved on March 12, 2019, from: https://www.index.hr/vijesti/clanak/iz-lektire-izbaceni-mali-princ-i-jezeva-kucica/2 063852.aspx.

Branko Ćopić Endowment *(Zadužbina Branka Ćopića)*, to reprint the book with a glossary of less known words.[161]

The original *Hedgehog's Home* was written in a language that reflected the sociolinguistic background of its author, the Bosnian Serb Branko Ćopić, but also the cultural and political circumstances in Yugoslavia when it was first published in 1949.[162] In the multilingual, multiscriptual and multinational Yugoslavia the dominant tendency at the time was to create a unitary language for the whole country, which resulted in two models: Latin script and ekavian pronunciation or Cyrillic script and ijekavian pronunciation (Opačić 2006, p. 240). The first edition of the book was thus published by "Novo pokoljenje" in (Zagreb/Belgrade) in Ljubljana in ekavian and Latin script. In editions published in the following decades, the poem underwent minor changes that adapted it to the variants of Serbo-Croatian spoken in the respective regions.[163] It is after the breakup of Yugoslavia that *The Hedgehog's Home* was additionally reworked in Croatia. In her article "Spring Cleaning in Ježeva kućica of Branko Ćopić" (2006), the linguist Nives Opačić points to impermissible alterations in the text and illustrations in the 1999, 2001 and 2002 editions of the book published by "Naša djeca". Besides the replacement of certain words that the author examines in detail on pages 242–243, three examples clearly show that the changes were politically and ideologically motivated. Firstly, the word "drug" (friend, comrade) was replaced with "dragi" (dear), but also the corresponding illustration by Vilko Selan Gliha was whitewashed to hide the same noun. Finally, the book was printed without the name of the author on the cover, which appeared on the inside in all three editions mentioned before (1999, 2001, 2002). The anonymous "censors" acted in violation of the Copyright and

---

161 See second article mentioned in footnote 158.
162 It was originally published as *Ježeva kuća*, from 1953 as *Ježeva kućica*. Kalogjera-Brkić writes in her article from November 26, 2005, that the latter edition is nowhere to be found.
163 Opačić, for instance, mentions words such as *palata*, *odbrana* and *jagnje* (palace, defense and lamb) which were substituted with the Croatian *palača*, *obrana* and *janje*.

Related Rights Act *(Zakon o autorskom pravu i srodnim pravima)*[164], articles 15 and 16 and remained unsanctioned. This case demonstrates not only a lack of implementation of the existing laws but also the general nonchalant attitude of certain publishers towards literary works (Opačić 2006, 244).

Interestingly, in her article Opačić briefly touches upon what she calls the "spring cleaning" in Croatian libraries (241-242), where she mentions the "Korčula case". Her observation is triggered by the fact that in the Children's section of the Zagreb City Library she found only certain editions of *The Hedgehog's Home*: the one from 1949, 1983 *(Naša djeca*, Split), 1988 *(Veselin Masleša*, Sarajevo), 1988 *(Mladost*, Zagreb), 1999, 2001, 2002 *(Naša djeca*, Split) and 2003 *(Golden Marketing, Tehnička knjiga)*. The author concludes that the library should have more editions (surprising is the "gap" between 1949 and 1983), especially considering that some of the volumes represent the 5th or the 6th edition of the fable. Since they are missing, Opačić asks herself "what to think other than about an efficient 'broom', the kind of 'cleansing' on which the Croatian daily press was also reporting (the example of the library in Korčula etc.)" (242). Let us now briefly dwell upon the matter, since it might be helpful in understanding the complexity involved in establishing whether a book (or a set of books) was discarded for political and/or ideological reasons. In doing so, the professional guidelines on discarding and the information about public libraries presented in Chapter Two will be used. First of all, since the Zagreb City Library is not the National and University Library and *The Hedgehog's Home* is not a book that could be subsumed under the category of local studies, the library is not obliged to store all the available editions of Ćopić's poem. What is not clear from Opačić's account is whether the missing editions were not there at the moment of her research (some of them might have been borrowed) or in general? If it is the latter, the "gap" between 1949 and 1983 is indeed too long, especially if we consider that some of the available copies represent

---

[164] The currently valid Act is the one from 2018, while N. Opačić refers to the Act from 2003 (her article is from 2006), stating that the same text had been valid for twenty years, that is, at the time, when the mentioned editions were published.

later editions, which means that in the period between 1949 and 1983 various editions were published. Presumably, the library did possess at least some of these copies for a certain period of time. In order to be sure about that, the researcher/interested person would need to check the inventory book of the library, where it should also be stated if and when these copies were discarded. According to the Act on Librarianship (art. 10), libraries should prepare a review and weeding report, but these are usually not stored longer than ten years. If we do not have access to such a report, we can only guess which reasons might have induced librarians to discard them. Low circulation can be immediately excluded, since these were years in which the book was included in the reading list for elementary schools. This fact leads us to other potential reasons, including the possibility that some of the copies might have been lost due to greater circulation and were presumably physically damaged. This covers the "U(gly)" in the MUSTIE guidelines. "M" stands for misleading and/or factually inaccurate; the 1999, 2001 and 2002 editions fall under these categories, but they were not discarded. The next in line is "S" for superseded by a new edition, which could be the reason why some of the older editions are missing. But why was the 1949 edition not superseded? The remaining three letters, T, I, E (trivial, irrelevant and can be obtained elsewhere) do not seem to apply to this case. If the missing editions were discarded because Branko Ćopić is a Bosnian Serb, or because they were written in the Serbian language or published outside of Croatia, why was the 1949 edition (published in ekavian) kept? Or the one published in Sarajevo in 1988? In any case, I contacted the Children's Library in Zagreb by e-mail and by phone to find out. The head of the library answered by saying that detailed documents about discarding (e.g., the lists that are sent to the National and University Library) are archived for a maximum period of 11 years (a period set by the library). Based on an oral agreement with the State Archive in Zagreb, the library is only obliged to keep those until the completion of all the activities related to one financial year. Furthermore, inventories of books do not contain data about the reasons for discarding a particular volume. Finally, the Zagreb City Library is a public library and is not obliged to keep all the editions of a book, as I have already noted. The library head concluded her email by saying that all weeding and discarding are carried out based on professional regulations. These are all considerations that are not self-evident to a non-librarian, and it took me some time to understand, at least theoretically, how a library functions "behind the scenes". If this is put into the context of the cultural climate in Croatia (which also produced the abovementioned reworking of Ćopić's poem) in the 1990s and the various articles in the media on the destruction of books and cultural heritage to which professionals barely reacted, it is understandable that the public connects missing books with ideological cleansing. Most people, including highly educated professionals, are not at all acquainted with library policies, which is why libraries should reach out more to their readers, invite them to explore what librarians actually do and what the functions of a library are. Ideally this would add color to the dominant image of libraries as storage spaces for valuable books that can be borrowed from time to time. One such project that tried to bring the practice of discarding books closer to the users is *Odpisani (The Discarded)*, introduced in 2010 at the Maribor University Library.

3.2. Reusing Discarded Books

This section will first look at an example of what can be done with discarded books damaged beyond repair. This will be followed by an example of book donation. The project "Odpisani" (The Discarded), organized by the University Library in Maribor, shows that even books damaged beyond repair do not necessarily have to populate overcrowded landfills. Not only did the project save books from landfills, thereby benefiting the environment, but it will also be argued that the project had a positive role in presenting discarding to the public as a standard library procedure. The second example is the founding of the Serbian Central Library in Zagreb as a library of primarily discarded books.

3.2.1. The Book as Artistic Object: the Project "Odpisani" ("The Written-Offs") at the Maribor University Library

The University Library in Maribor *(Univerzitetna knjižnica Maribor)* has three functions: to act as a university, a local studies institution, and an archive. In its latter capacity and as one of the repositories of the so-called legal deposit, it has the task of preserving at least one copy of each publication published in Slovenian Styria, a region in northeastern Slovenia. These volumes are usually never deaccessioned, unless they are entirely damaged, in which case they have to be replaced by a new copy. In other words, what a university library like the one in Maribor usually discards are double or triple copies of an outdated scientific manual or monograph or severely damaged volumes. More specifically, the discarding criteria in the Maribor University Library foresee the discarding of damaged and incomplete volumes, double or triple copies, outdated books which were not part of the legal deposit, and incorrect or stolen volumes (Lončar 2010, 122). In 2010 the Library decided to use 2500 discarded volumes for the project "Odpisani" (The Discards or The Discarded) with the aim of donating the discarded volumes to the readers, while simultaneously promoting the activities of the University Library in Maribor and informing a wider audience on standard library procedures. Approximately 2 percent of the discarded volumes were too badly damaged to be donated, which is why they were turned into artistic objects as part of the same project. The only condition for their use was that they had to be functional and have an aesthetic value (122). Based on these considerations the idea was born to turn discarded materials into functional objects such as chairs and lamps that the patrons could use while consulting discarded volumes. In cooperation with partners including the students of the Department of Fine Arts at the Faculty of Education and of Art History at the Faculty of Arts, University of Maribor, two publishing houses, an electro installations company and a designer, the project was opened to the public in March 2010. Between March 16 and April 14, 2010, 3200 discarded volumes were offered to the users in an environment decorated by paper sculptures, lit by lamps and furnished with chairs all made with discarded books. At the end of the project, only 50 volumes were left undistributed. According to Nina Lončar, the librarian who together with her colleague Renata Močnik initiated the project, the fact that only 50 books remained undistributed is an indicator of the success of this multi-purpose project (Lončar 2010, 126). Discarded materials were given a new function and hence value, the art students had the chance to create and exhibit their art, while users could admire the artwork and enrich their personal libraries by taking home some of the books. The artistic project was well covered by the media, which not only popularized the event itself, but also presented to the wider public a standard library procedure which might have been unfamiliar to many. While some of the users enthusiastically embraced the project, there were those whose reaction could be summarized with the words "now even libraries are putting books away" (127). Indeed, libraries do not only acquire and borrow books, but from time to time they also need to discard them.

3.2.2. The Opening of the Serbian Central Library in Zagreb

In January 1996 the Central Library of the Serbian Cultural Society "Prosvjeta" was established in Zagreb. "Prosvjeta" itself, was founded in 1944 as a cultural, scientific and educational institution of the Serbs in Croatia. Together with the cultural institution "Matrix Croatica" *(Matica hrvatska)*, "Prosvjeta" was disbanded by the authorities in 1971 during the Croatian Spring but was re-established in 1993. The society's library also existed for a brief time between 1948 and 1953. The initial collection of the new library mostly comprised books in Serbian, in Cyrillic script, written by Serbian authors or published in Serbia that were discarded by other libraries in Zagreb. In an article in *Novosti* Velimir Sekulić enumerates the libraries that donated discarded books: Gornji grad (on two occasions), "Božidar Adžija", Samobor (on two occasions), Vrbovec, Velika Gorica, Otvoreno sveučilište (formerly "Moša Pijade"), "August Cesarec" (from two locations—Ravnice and Maksimirska street), Dubrava (on three occasions), "Marin Držić", "Vladimir Nazor", the musical and children's section of the Zagreb City Library, the library of the Parliament (Sabor), Staglišće (on two occasions), "Tin Ujević", Savski gaj, and "Silvije Strahimir Kranjčević" (on three occasions).[165] In total, around 15,000 volumes were acquired in this way (Čiča 2016, np). In his article Sekulić specifies the type of books that were donated: books in Cyrillic script (including Croatian authors like Matoš, Krleža and Ujević), books by Serbian authors regardless of the script and pronunciation (ekavian/ ijekavian), books in ekavian, books in ijekavian different from the Croatian variant (Bosnian and Montenegrin books), books formerly included on the reading list, the so-called "red" literature and the Croatian contemporary author Dubravka Ugrešić.

Due to the circumstances in which the library was founded, Lešaja describes it as an "extorted consequence and result of library cleansing" and a symbol of the definite separation between the Croatian and Serbian languages (Lešaja 2012, 312–328). In November 1996 the library entered the system of national minorities' libraries, becoming the Central Library of the Serbs in Croatia *(Centralna biblioteka/središnja knjižnica Srba u Hrvatskoj)*. The idea of establishing similar central libraries for national minorities started developing among librarians in the second half of the 1980s (the terminology that was used back then was that of "nationalities" rather than national minorities). The libraries were envisioned, however, not as separate entities but as units within larger libraries. Moreover, these plans did not foresee the creation of such libraries for nations speaking Serbo-Croatian (Serbs, Croats, Muslims and Montenegrins) (Lešaja 2012, 317). Since 2000 the central libraries of national minorities have been under the aegis of the Ministry of Culture, which took over the role previously held by the Government's office for national minorities. Today the Central Library of Serbs in Croatia comprises 25,000 volumes and is managed by two librarians. Their salaries and the acquisition of new volumes are financed by the Ministry of Culture. The library also receives books from the National Library of Serbia *(Narodna biblioteka Srbije)* and the Matrix Serbica Library *(Biblioteka Matice srpske)*. Its cultural activities are co-financed by the City of Zagreb *(Grad Zagreb)* and the Serbian

---

165 Velimir Sekulić. "Formiranje srpske biblioteke u Zagrebu", *Novosti*, September 2, 2005.

Ministry of Culture and Information *(Ministarstvo kulture i informisanja)*.

The examples from Maribor and the Central Library of Serbs in Zagreb demonstrate how the relocation of books within or to another library functions and what kind of projects it can generate in a library setting. The next step is to examine the potential of discarded books outside of this framework, that is, their intrinsic symbolism and alternative usage in varying contexts such as on screen and in an exhibition.

3.3. In War and Revolution: An Experimental Documentary Film by Ana Bilankov[166]

Almost a year before Ante Lešaja's book (briefly) brought into public focus the destruction of books in the 1990s, the multimedia artist and filmmaker Ana Bilankov completed her 15-minute-long experimental documentary film *In War and Revolution* (U ratu i revoluciji). Shot in Berlin and Zagreb, the film was co-financed by the Croatian Audiovisual Centre and premiered at Kino Arsenal in Berlin in autumn 2011. It was later shown at several locations in Zagreb, including the Museum of Contemporary Art and Kino Tuškanac, and abroad. In the film, Bilankov stays faithful to the central question of her *oeuvre*, namely, how to connect the poetic form and language with engaged topics[167], while at the same time telling stories about her life and the wider sociopolitical context of the narration. (Auto)biographical and historical events alternate with poetic and documentary language through the technique of parallel editing. The opening sequence of the film frames Micha Ullman's memorial to the Nazi book burning, consisting of a glass plate embedded in the cobblestone pavement at *Bebelplatz* in Berlin. Under the glass plate, white empty shelves commemorate the 20,000 volumes that

---

166 My scrutiny of this film has previously been published in Komnenović, D. (2021), "Remembering the 1990s in Croatia: The Potential of Discarded Books on and beyond Anniversaries," in Newman, J. P. and Apor, B. (eds.), *Balkan Legacies: The Long Shadow of Conflict and Ideological Experiment in Southeastern Europe*, West Lafayette, IN: Purdue University Press.
167 Artist's statement, available at: http://www.anabilankov.com/pdf/Ana_Bilankov_Artists_Statement.pdf. Last accessed on June 4, 2016.

were burned on the spot on May 10, 1933. The ghostlike reflections of the tourists visiting the memorial contribute to the sombre atmosphere of the ensemble—regardless of whether they are symbolically perceived as shadows of the past or what is left of humans who do not cherish their own literature and culture. In the background, the viewer hears the explanations of someone who is presumably a tourist guide and Bilankov's voice that echoes some syntagmas: empty shelves, burned books, antichristian, love of fellow men, literature, National Socialism, May 10, 1933.

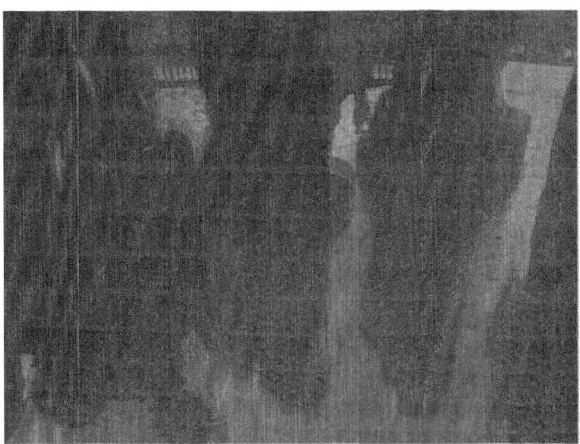

Figure 2. Ana Bilankov: In War and Revolution. Still frame.
© VG Bild-Kunst, Bonn 2022

The next scene takes place in Zagreb, in the apartment of Božica Žalac, Bilankov's 97-year-old grandmother, who is trying to remember her days as a teacher in a school set up on a hill by the partisans during World War II. With the help of a 1943 photograph published in her husband's (the artist's grandfather) book *School in War and Revolution (Škola u ratu i revoluciji*, Školska knjiga, 1988) and her granddaughter's questions, Mrs. Žalac is trying to recall some fragments from that period.

Figure 3. Ana Bilankov: In War and Revolution. Still frame.
© VG Bild-Kunst, Bonn 2022

As the focus of the camera moves from the retired teacher to the family library, her personal amnesia is juxtaposed to collective amnesia regarding the socialist past and the period of economic, political and social transformation that accompanied the dissolution of Yugoslavia and the ensuing wars. In fact, in the background the voices of a couple of intellectuals retrace the fate of unwanted books that disappeared from Zagreb libraries and bookstores during the 1990s. The personal story of the protagonist is thus interwoven with the larger context of history repeating itself—hence the reiteration of the *Bebelplatz* sequence towards the end of the film and the insistence on May 10, 1933—and the impossibility or unwillingness to deal with a shadowy past. The choice of filming in Berlin is not casual and only due to Bilankov's familiarity with the city where she is based, but Germany is often quoted as a role-model in the process of dealing with the past *(Vergangenheitsbewältigung)*. Moreover, Berlin is a recurrent *topos* in the post-Yugoslav literary imagination: partially because of the presence of a non-negligible ex-Yugoslav migrant community and as a symbol of (re)unification as opposed to the balkanization of former Yugoslavia. It is also the capital of Germany, an EU success story, and one of the principal interlocutors in post-Yugoslav countries' EU accession talks.[168]

The images that follow in the film, namely, a group of chanting people carrying a flag (presumably wedding guests) in front of the apartment building and a blossoming cherry tree, once again reaffirm the underlying dualities of the film: documentary vs. poetic; personal vs. collective; memory vs. forgetting, presence vs. absence. The documentaristic aspect is reinforced with a couple of lines of text about Bilankov's research appearing at the beginning and just before the end of the film. Inspired by her grandfather's claims that his book was banned after Tuđman came to power, the filmmaker did some research and found out that the volume disappeared from the publisher's register, as well as bookstores and libraries in the Croatian capital. Out of 49 libraries in the Zagreb area, seven had it, together with the National and University Library. On the other hand, the author's unwillingness to slide into a "purely" documentaristic dimension is observable in the choice of sometimes abstract frames, such as the empty space between and above books or the grandmother's profile reflecting on a black TV screen, black and white sequences, indiscernible shapes (achieved with exaggerated zooming) and sounds, including silences that render the setting less "ordinary". *In War and Revolution* almost ends where it began: the second to last scene is a bird's-eye view of Ullman's underground library and its empty, white bookshelves, carrying a

---

168 For a more detailed analysis see Vervaet (2016).

very explicit message: the necessity to remember the past "because those who cannot remember it are condemned to repeat it".[169]

The above-mentioned flag scene could be read along the same lines: it is a short but pungent reference to the time of filming, which coincided with the ICTY ruling against the Croatian Army generals Gotovina and Markač in April 2011. The ICTY indicted Croatian army generals Gotovina, Čermak and Markač for war crimes, specifically for the roles they played in Operation "Storm". Gotovina and Markač were found guilty and condemned to 24 and 18 years in prison, respectively, while Čermak was acquitted in April 2011. Gotovina and Markač were acquitted on appeal in November 2012. Such a ruling exonerated the generals and the Croatian political leaders (Tuđman, Šušak and Bobetko) from responsibility in an alleged joint criminal enterprise aimed at eliminating the Serbs from the Krajina region in Croatia.

The scene in the film points to the resurgence of nationalism (and its most banal manifestation: flag waving) partially resulting from the tabooization of the early 1990s that the artist became aware of while working on the project. Ana Bilankov in fact stated in a 2012 interview that she personally felt Croatia falling back into the 1990s, considering the vast display of nationalist kitsch, flags and war veterans' tears that the ICTY ruling provoked.[170]

---

169 Citation commonly attributed to the philosopher George Santayana (1863–1952). Here quoted from Santayana (2011), 172.
170 Full interview (in Croatian) available on the website of the artist: http://www.anabilankov.com/pdf/interview_kontura_12_2012.pdf. Last accessed on June 5, 2016.

Figure 4. Ana Bilankov: In War and Revolution. Still frame.
© VG Bild-Kunst, Bonn 2022

Bilankov also reiterated that she encountered difficulties in finding interlocutors willing to talk about the object of her research. Nevertheless, she provided a platform for those who wanted to do so, thus opening up new spaces to individual stories and testimonies not fitting into the official narrative. In such a way she (perhaps even unintentionally) paved the way for future discussions about the topic, which gained further impetus by Lešaja's book and the exhibition *Otpisane*.

3.4. The Discarding of Books in the 1990s in Croatia as an Inspiration for Artists: Exhibition-Action "Discarded"[171]

The present section will analyze the role of art in offering counter-hegemonic perspectives and breaching monolithic interpretations of history in the former Yugoslav space by focusing on an exhibition-action. Post-Yugoslav artistic practices as a new (Kirn, Kralj and Piškur 2009) and counter-public sphere that initiates discussions about war and postwar trauma (Dedić 2016) or questions the role of socialist heritage in official memory politics (Potkonjak and Pletenac 2011, 2016) have previously been objects of academic

---

171 Substantial parts of this text have been published in Komnenović (2021).

scrutiny. However, in this chapter attention will be given to an initiative that critically reflects upon the present sociopolitical constellation by examining the artists' and the collective's relationship with the past through the medium of discarded books. My contribution to the topic will consist of an analysis of the exhibition-action *Otpisane, povodom 20. godišnjice Oluje* (Discarded. On the occasion of the 20th anniversary of Operation Storm), a joint project of the artistic collective What, How and for Whom (WHW) *(Tko, kako i za koga)* and the non-profit association Multimedia Institute *(Multimedijalni institut MI2)*. Like in Ana Bilankov's film, (a) discarded book(s) acts as a "memory trigger" and propel(s) critical reflection about the 1990s and the present, thus underlying the inherent potential of discarded books in breaking taboos and rethinking the recent past. Such a critical thinking "exercise" also leads to the detection and better articulation of current issues, which is a precondition for an active participation in society. As a symbolical representation of the past that has been rejected in the name of promises for a better future, discarded books are regaining currency as it becomes clear that these promises have been broken. The public action-exhibition "Discarded. On the occasion of the 20th anniversary of Operation 'Storm'" *(Otpisane, povodom 20. godišnjice Oluje)* was opened in Gallery Nova in Zagreb on June 18, 2015. The exhibition was part of the project *Javna knjižnica* (Public Library), initiated by Tomislav Medak and Marcell Mars (Multimedia Institute), with the aim of promoting the universal right of access to knowledge by developing an infrastructure of digitalized collections. In cooperation with the curatorial collective WHW (What, How & for Whom), the Multimedia Institute has launched an open call for the collection and scanning of books that were removed from Croatian libraries in the 1990s, based on Ante Lešaja's "typology of exclusionism *(isključivost)*". In the wake of the action, 173 volumes were scanned and uploaded to the web page www.otpisane.org. Between June 18 and July 13, 2015, around 600 people visited the exhibition, and approximately 18–20 visitors brought books for scanning.[172]

---

172 The numbers were communicated to me by the organizers and are purely indicative and approximate.

The Afterlife of Discarded Books 157

Figure 5. Exhibition "Discarded". Zagreb, June 2015.
Photo by Dora Komnenović

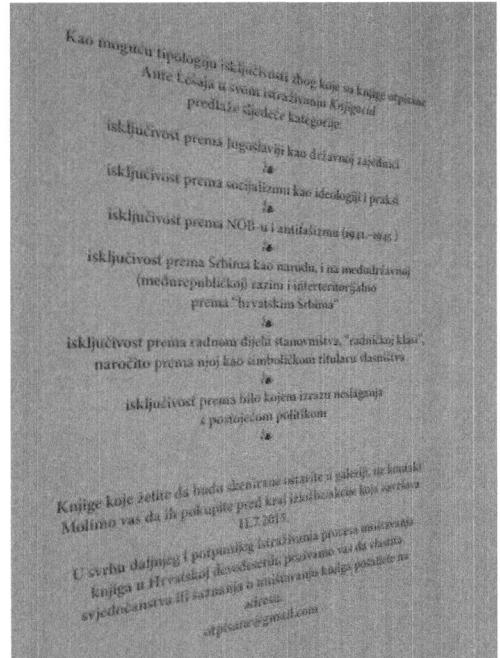

Figure 6. Ante Lešaja's categories of "exclusionism".
Photo by Dora Komnenović

The intention of the organizers was to

> "mark the anniversary of the military operation Storm with a collective action that, by referring to the book as a symbol of the famous 'knowledge society' in which knowledge becomes the location of a conflict engagement, tries to affirm the role of the exhibition and gallery as an institution that can be a platform for political and aesthetic experiments, a place of resistance and alternative to the current situation".[173]

The timing of the exhibition, which opened twenty years after the 1991-1995 war ended, was deliberately chosen to draw the public's attention to "the political logic behind the killing and expulsion of people"[174] during and in the immediate aftermath of the war and its last major battle, Operation "Storm".

By focusing on the destruction of books, the exhibition curators wanted to address the wider context, preceding or following operation "Storm", in which the simultaneous destruction of monuments, houses and the killing of people were made possible, both inside and outside the war zones. Consequently, the background questions that the action raises pertain to post-conflict, but also postsocialist transformation, that is, the writing of history, what constitutes the official narrative, the nature of war, justice and the status of victims, refugees, ethno-nationalism as an aspect of neoliberalism, etc.

The exhibition took place in the relatively small gallery "Nova" in the center of Zagreb. A large photo print of books scattered around the floor covered an entire wall of the gallery, dominating the room. Two long desks, which looked like school desks, were covered with books placed in such a way that the photo visually continued the series.

---

173 Quoted from the exhibition brochure.
174 Quoted from the exhibition brochure.

The Afterlife of Discarded Books 159

Figure 7. The exhibited books. Photo by Dora Komnenović

Figure 8. The scanner with which the books were scanned during the exhibition. Photo by Dora Komnenović

Right across the desks stood a professional scanner that was used to scan all the volumes *in situ*. To the left from it, there was a small table with a couple of chairs, where the visitor could consult some of the data, principally newspaper articles, that Lešaja gathered during twenty years of research. On the same side of the wall, Siniša Ilić painted *Zidna kompozicija s motivom usmenog predanja, grupe za učenje napamet i grupe za neučenje napamet* (Wall composition with the motive of oral tradition, learning by heart groups and non-learning by heart groups).

Figure 9. Siniša Ilić's wall painting. © Ivan Kuharić, 2022

His wall painting addresses societal divisions, knowledge production and the (im)possibility of articulating a coherent critique of the system. Ilić's "ghostlike figures are wandering in the whiteness of the wall (or paper), reflecting the fragility of knowledge and the complexities involved in understanding history".[175] Some of the figures are easily identifiable as bureaucrats, fighters, administrators, as well as a worker in the field,[176] who are trying to utilize, organize and imagine a space alternative to the existing one.[177] Some of them (critical groups) are trying to escape a homogenizing system (populated by inert groups) that recognizes only its own unifying

---

175 Quoted from the exhibition brochure.
176 This was inspired by the French realist painter Jean-François Millet (1814–1875).
177 E-mail correspondence with the author, as well as in the following paragraphs.

The Afterlife of Discarded Books   161

principles, national belonging *in primis*, and perceives everything foreign as a threat. The title of the composition evokes notions connected with education, autodidacticism or transfer of knowledge, including oral tradition. At least for an instant, Ilić argues, the latter appears to be safer, more reliable and efficient than what is methodologically elaborated, controlled and written by the winners.

Additionally, "Discarded" included the performances and installations of five artists at three different locations in Zagreb. As stated above, these interventions

> "reaffirm the role of art as a potential space of a change of perspectives and hegemonic view, even if it is clear that art itself is caught in the processes of the socioeconomic transformation of the 'knowledge society' and various forms of neoliberal co-optation and surveillance".[178]

The common denominator of all artistic interventions is that they point to current problems, inspired by past controversies, but at the same time look to the future.

At the center of Siniša Labrović's performance *Svjetlost knjige* (The Light of the Book) is the difficult position of books in the former Yugoslav space. In fact, according to annual studies conducted by the GfK—Centre for Market Research, fewer and fewer people are reading and buying books. Only 47 percent of the population read at least one book in 2016 (51 percent in 2015), compared to 56 percent in 2011. Moreover, 52 percent of people who did not buy a single book that year indicated that they were not interested in books or did not need them.[179] In his act, Labrović is reading a book in flames. *Svjetlost knjige* was first performed in Belgrade in 2011, when he read a burning copy of *The Palanka Philosophy (Filosofija palanke)* by Radimir Konstantinović.

---

178 Quoted from the exhibition brochure. My translation.
179 Source: GfK Research of the bookmarket: https://issuu.com/modernavre mena/docs/gfk_-_istra__ivanje_tr__i__ta_knjig. Last accessed on July 4, 2016.

Figure 10. Siniša Labrović's performance. © Ivan Kuharić, 2022

Reading aloud transforms the intimate act of reading into a performative one. With this gesture, violent but at the same time affectionate, Labrović wishes to enlighten the dark in which books are relegated to in the region. Reading a book in flames is a race against time, trying to catch a flash of light before it is swallowed by darkness. Each time the artist reads a different book, depending on the occasion and the context; this time his selection was the Serbian poet Branko Miljković (1934–1961), known for his anti-system behaviour and bohemian lifestyle.

In her performative installation *Revizija obiteljske biblioteke* (Review of the family library), Božena Končić Badurina juxtaposes individual and collective memories, as well as a private and a public library. The artist was struck by the discrepancy between the tacit public rejection of books and the private stance of her family (and probably other families, too), positing that they are something valuable that should be never thrown away, not even when they are old and damaged.[180] Consequently, Končić Badurina translated her initial shock into concrete action: based on the criteria outlined by Lešaja, she meticulously carried out an assessment of her family's library. The "discarded" volumes were later exhibited in the public library "Bogdan Ogrizović", where visitors could have a look at

---

180 E-mail correspondence with the author.

them and listen to an audio recording about the history of some of the titles, what they meant to the family and how they got to the library in the first place. Some of them were, for example, saved from "burning", which for Končić Badurina is a way of defending the right to identity and remembrance, to one's own relationship with legacy and culture. On the other hand, argues the artist, Croatian society has an immature, non-critical relationship towards its own past. Attempts at completely erasing the memory of socialism are counter-productive and are obstructing a more objective examination of the period, of its bad and good sides, as well as their integration into the present, that could only enrich and further develop Croatian society.

Figure 11. Performative installation by Božena Končić Badurina.
© Ivan Kuharić, 2022

What is more, two performances took place in an outdoor public space, namely at the main square in Zagreb, *Trg bana Josipa Jelačića*, that in Yugoslav times bore the name of Republic Square *(Trg Republike)*. Antonio Grgić's performance addresses the issue of the gulf that is created whenever individual memories need to adapt to the newly imposed ideological memory. *Čitanje misli Karla Marxa konju bana Josipa Jelačića na bivšem Trgu Republike* (Reading Karl Marx's thoughts to Ban Jelačić's horse on the former Republic Square) wishes to connect Marx's theory about the role of fetishism with the ideological role of culture as a fetish, where culture is considered, an ideological war aimed at covering up class antagonism. It is not possible to read to the *ban (governor)*, as he is too high on his pedestal, where he was put by official historiography, and is thus too detached from ordinary people.

Figure 12. Antonio Grgić's performance. © Ivan Kuharić, 2022

The text that Grgić selected for this occasion was *Capital* and Marx's notes about *ban* Jelačić and the Croats, particularly his thesis about "non-historic peoples", counter-revolutionary by their very nature. Grgić's performance is a cry against the violent inscription of "history" into memory. In his view, history is an ideological construct, which can be only dealt with.

Similarly, Luiza Margan's *Osluškivanje* (Listen) examines the potential of a joint action in the public space and calls for critical awareness, an artistic and socially engaged consciousness of the citizens. Twenty performers are reading out loud the works of two Yugoslav writers, Miroslav Krleža (1893–1981) and Danilo Kiš (1935–1989), on different locations at Zagreb's main square. With this performative sculpture the artist criticizes the structures of power and the construction of national identities. This critique is articulated through the act of reading that, as in Labrović's case, from an individual becomes a public and performative, political and cultural act.

Figure 13. One of the readers in *Osluškivanje*. © Ivan Kuharić, 2022

"Discarded" as a project relies on the symbolic capital of (discarded) books in order to address present problems that might equally inform the future. It is a collective brainstorming "before and after" session that compares Croatia as it was in the 1990s, what it wanted to become and what it has become. The defeating results of this diachronic analysis inevitably lead to a reconsideration of the legacy that was massively discarded at the beginning of the 1990s. Was everything even vaguely connected with Yugoslavia that bad?

The discarding of books is approached as a synecdochic representation of (cultural) politics in the 1990s that is still awaiting proper scrutiny outside of alternative circles. Aware that art and education are not independent of the sociopolitical reality they operate in and are thus subject to all kinds of compromises, the authors emphasize the role of art in offering counter-hegemonic perspectives and of education in breaching monolithic interpretations of history. Nevertheless, they are far from singing the "education gospel", by which education is a panacea that will solve all problems. On the contrary, knowledge in a "knowledge society" is a platform for engagement that should expose the contradictions of the system and deconstruct myths such as the inevitability of capitalism. In addition, the inconsistencies of neoliberalism, democracy and freedom of speech, in the name of which independence was sought, are also implicitly questioned. One such contradiction is censorship, which, even if it may not be as straightforward as the index of prohibited books or a decree signed by the Ministry, it does not mean it is absent from the logic of the market. Similarly, fascistic tendencies in a society are not always easily recognizable. Nationalist legacies are to be coped with by supporting self-investigative and critical societal discourse that transcends round anniversaries (Zakošek 2007, 42). In this respect the exhibition-action Discarded is a contribution towards critically dealing with the past, which is still an exclusive prerogative of nongovernmental organizations. During our interview the journalist IL described it as follows:

> "This is an example of an initiative where the input does not come from the state, but from a smaller circle of interested cultural workers, who decided to enlighten this aspect of the whole issue of the so-called liberation and disassociation from Yugoslavia, which is worth mentioning. It is precisely these kinds of initiatives that could save the public, the collective conscience about what happened [...] It is a qualitative breakthrough, since the action was supported by public money, and I am not sure whether something like that could have happened 10 years ago, not in that way" (IL, journalist, personal interview, Zagreb, October 7, 2015).

Even though it was launched on a round anniversary, the "Discarded" project was soon transferred online (www.otpisane.org), where it continues to exist. The intention of the authors was to "act against the normalization of scandal"[181] by making the discarded books available to everyone in an open online archive.

As previously mentioned, the exhibition "Discarded" was a continuation of the project "Public Library" *(Javna knjižnica)*, a platform which gathers hackers and activists who are creating tools for the digitization and sharing of books that wishes to enable access to those resources that are unavailable due to commercial and copyright related issues. The exhibition organizers, the curatorial collective WHW and the Multimedia Institute, connected what they considered a current form of censorship — namely, restrictive copyright laws and the commercialization of culture — with a period when a similar limitation to the access to information and knowledge was

---

181 Quoted from the exhibition brochure.

imposed by the indiscriminate discarding of "unsuitable" books. In this way "discarded" books acted as a bridge between the recent past and the present and revealed their potential as "triggers" of change. By scanning and uploading the books to a web page, the organizers of the exhibition returned them to the library, albeit digitally, while making a provocative statement on copyright and the infringement thereof. Finally, through the medium of the exhibition the "Public Library" presented itself to a wider audience, aiming to initiate a discussion and question the "natural order", a precondition for an active citizenship and the basis of emancipatory politics (Fisher 2009, 17).

4. In Lieu of Conclusions: On Discarded Books, Memory and Dealing with the Socialist and Yugoslav Legacy Thirty Years Later

While Europe was getting ready to celebrate the 30th anniversary of the fall of the Berlin Wall, new walls are being built around the world: in 1989 there were eleven walls worldwide, today there are 70 ("Border Walls"). Indeed, the world has changed a great deal in the past thirty years and not always for the better. Globalization and informatization have had a major impact on society, as did the reconfiguration of the distribution of power in world politics. Postsocialist transition is over, and the triumph of neoliberalism is eroding democracy. Voters are increasingly turning to right-wing populist movements and parties to find a solution to their precarity or are voting with their feet. Between 2013 and 2016 2 percent of the Croatian population left the country, mostly to live in Germany and Ireland. As a side note, more people are leaving Croatia, Romania and Bulgaria now than were leaving the German Democratic Republic (GDR) immediately before the wall, which was supposed to prevent it, was built.[182] But that Wall is history, at least physically. Thirty years have passed since 1989, and now even events that happened in that year or shortly afterwards are slowly finding their way into museums, as temporary projects aimed at commemorating the round anniversary of the fall of the Wall, or as permanent exhibitions. Photography exhibitions seem to be prevailing in the first case: at the time of writing in 2019 I visited two of the probably countless exhibitions that in that year opened in Berlin and

---

182 About the emigration dynamic in Croatia and new EU member states, see Draženović, Kunovac and Pripužić (2018). On page 418 the authors write that the current annual population outflow in Croatia is 2 percent; proportionally similar is the situation in Romania and Bulgaria. Two years before the Wall was built 143,917 people fled from the GDR and East Berin, 199,188 in 1960, and 207,026 in the first eight months of 1961, which is a bit more than 1 percent of the population each year considering that the number of inhabitants amounted to 17.83 million in 1955. Source: Hertle (2016) and https://de.statista.com/.

elsewhere to celebrate the 30th anniversary of the fall of the Wall. The first was "Umbrüche (Turns): 1980–1995. Photographs by Ann-Christine Jansson," shown at the Fotogalerie Friedrichshain between November 2018 and January 2019, followed by "After the Fall of the Berlin Wall. Daniel Biskup Photographs 1990–1995", which opened in the GDR Museum in the *Kulturbrauerei* in February. Both exhibitions featured at least one photo of garbage dumps, landfills or municipal trash cans filled with state and party insignia, mass-produced furniture, Soviet or GDR-made cars etc. One of Biskup's photographs, together with an interview with the artist, was printed in the *Museumsmagazin* of the foundation "House of the History of the Federal Republic of Germany" *(Haus der Geschichte der Bundesrepublik Deutschland)* to which the GDR museum belongs. On the photograph a "graveyard" of Trabant cars could be seen, and underneath it was the caption, "with the reunification a society that previously knew no garbage became a throwaway society".[183] In fact, many products could no longer compete with the Western ones and became throwaway objects. These objects included books, too. In the recently opened permanent exhibition "Our History. Dictatorship and Democracy after 1945" at the "Forum for Contemporary History" *(Zeitgeschichtliches Forum)* in Leipzig, there is a small section on rescuing books that publishing houses and cultural institutions in the GDR were throwing away in 1990. Thousands of these books were rescued by the pastor Martin Weskott of Katlenburg, who offers them to interested people in exchange for a donation to *Brot für die Welt* (Bread for the World), a relief agency of the Protestant churches in Germany. For his action *weitergeben statt wegwerfen* (passing on instead of throwing away), the pastor was awarded the Order of Merit of the Federal Republic of Germany in 1993 and the Karl Preusker Medaille in 2008.[184]

---

[183] "Die Kamera war und ist ein Teil von mir". Interview with Daniel Biskup conducted by Ulrike Zander. Museumsmagazin 1/2019, Stiftung Haus der Geschichte der Bundesrepublik Deutschland.
[184] More about the project can be found here: http://www.buecherburg.de/index.html. Last accessed on February 27, 2019.

In Lieu of Conclusions 171

Figure 14. Rescuing books. A small section of the exhibition in Leipzig, February 2019. Photo by Dora Komnenović

The tag next to the photograph and small bookshelf explains that in the spring of 1990, publishing houses were dumping massively produced volumes that no one wished to buy in order to make room for new, western publications. It is also mentioned that many of the more than 1000 cultural centers needed to close due to a lack of funds. The

> "biggest book destruction in the postwar period" is clearly framed in economic terms. Even if this is not explicitly mentioned in the exhibition, between 50 and 70 percent of public libraries' collections were simultaneously replaced, and with the help of federal funds the libraries that kept operating in the former GDR could quickly rebuild their collections" (Wimmer and Seadle 2014, 206).

The fact that this story made it into the museum means that someone (the exhibition curators) must have considered it relevant for the understanding of the sociocultural climate immediately after German reunification. It would be interesting to examine similar situations in other Soviet bloc countries, without disregarding the specific context in each. How were Soviet books treated in the

Baltics or in the Caucasus, for instance? Did the Czechoslovak "Velvet Divorce" have any consequence for library collections in these two countries? Among socialist states, Yugoslavia was often counted as a special case because of its non-alignment and unique blend of planned and market socialist economy. In the group of postsocialist states, the former Yugoslav area continues to stick out, mostly due to negative (economic) indicators. Although in this book I focused mainly on the former Yugoslav context, I tried not to lose sight of the bigger picture, which reveals that thirty years after the end of state-socialism the political will to approach the period in a less divisive manner is still lacking. Round anniversaries such as the one in 2019 usually serve as a good "pretext" for novel and insightful scholarly publications and gatherings, but in mainstream discourse celebratory tones prevail.

A festive atmosphere also characterized the 20th anniversary of Operation "Storm", the last major military operation in the Croatian War of Independence (1991–1995). While the main state celebration consisted of a military parade in the Croatian capital on August 5, 2015, honoring the victory of the Croatian army, a couple of fringe events laid emphasis on the wrongdoing of the victorious Army and the darker side of the nation-building process. One of these events was the exhibition "Discarded. On the Occasion of the 20th Anniversary of Operation Storm" held in Zagreb. By inviting visitors to reflect upon and to actively search for and bring books that were discarded in the 1990s in Croatia, the exhibition makers wanted to raise awareness of the politics that made the killing and expulsion of people and the removal of books possible. The occasion to do so was not chosen randomly: it was an attempt at making a contribution, albeit symbolic, to the ways in which the recent past is being dealt with. The organizers wished in fact to emphasize the importance of enabling a public "dialogue on interpretations", rather than insisting on a constant discussion of the facts, which is what civil society organizations have been trying to do in the past quarter century. During the exhibition the volumes were scanned and uploaded to a web site where they are still accessible. In this way, the once discarded books were reinserted into the library, this time digital, and are now accessible to an even greater number of

In Lieu of Conclusions 173

potential users, at least until someone removes them on the basis of copyright infringement. The creators of the "Discarded" exhibition thus drew a connection between what they consider as current forms of censorship, namely, restrictive copyright laws and the subjugation of culture to the logic of the market, and the discarding of "unsuitable" books from Croatian libraries in the 1990s, which equally corresponded to a limitation of the access to information. The aggressive nationalism and warmongering that characterized the public space in the (early) 1990s put the professional ethics of librarians (and others) to the test. However, although the often-proclaimed neutrality and objectivity of librarians are ideals that might find enthusiastic adherents, they are often contradicted in practice. In the words of a librarian that I interviewed in Ljubljana:

> "A librarian needs to be above nationalist motives. It is not that you are apolitical in the library and something else at home. In Sarajevo[185] once the topic was how a librarian can distance him/herself from politics, how to step out of it? When there is no war, it is easier" (TPČ, librarian, personal interview, Ljubljana, March 24, 2015).

Ideally, a librarian should be neutral, but how to disassociate oneself from personal political beliefs and the overall sociopolitical context?

The pressure that librarians were exposed to was great, and it came not only from "above", that is, from local and/or state authorities, but also from the patrons, who wished to see certain books displayed and others less so. The "Binding Instruction on the Usage of School Library Book Inventories" and the memorandum that preceded it are probably the most illustrative examples of a directive from "above", directed, however, at school libraries. When it comes to the local level, the letter that the President of the Steering Committee sent to the Head of the "Ivan Vidali" Library in Korčula is a case in point. Some of my interviewees and the people I had informal conversations with claim that these were not isolated cases and do not exclude the circulation of other, secret instructions. After all, the 1992–1994 Minister of Education, Culture and Sport

---

185 The reference here is to the International Convention of Slavicist Librarians in Sarajevo, which my interlocutor attended a number of years in a row.

Vesna Girardi-Jurkić herself would later state that she was exposed to pressure. Even if the state did not directly request the removal of Serbian or socialist books from public libraries, the hiring of "suitable" people, political statements encouraging the persecution of the Serbs and political opponents, and a general atmosphere of fear made it increasingly hard to keep "a cool head". Nevertheless, the numerous public libraries across the country are heterogeneous entities, which suggests the use of caution in making general observations. Despite the pressures coming from different sides, most decisions were taken at an individual level or in agreement with a few colleagues. Once the first newspaper articles on inappropriate discarding appeared, such as the one in Slatina or the reaction of the citizen Anton Lukežić to the statement of a librarian on TV, who had said that her library was completing the process of removing "unsuitable" books, professional librarians failed to react. An even greater failure is the tepid reaction of professional librarians' associations, like the Croatian Library Association and the Croatian Council on Libraries, as well as state authorities, to the so-called "Korčula case". The latter acquired a grotesque dimension with the lawsuits against the main critics of "libricide", the philosopher Milan Kangrga and the weekly *Feral Tribune*. As the IFLA/FAIFE 2001 report on Croatia argues, what happened in Korčula harmed the overall reputation of librarians, who did not even try to reach out to the public and to present their work to citizens, who, for their part, in many cases do not know that even libraries discard books from time to time. With this "let them talk" approach, professionals left the debate but were at the same time not able to provide concrete inputs which would have ended mystifications and further politicization. Since similar debates keep resurfacing even today, be it in the form of endless discussions about school readings or book "destruction", it is indispensable that professionals take their share of responsibility and that data about publicly relevant issues and services be made available to citizens.

The collapse of communism and the dissolution of Yugoslavia were "disjunctive moment[s]", in which "relations of power are transformed through reformulations of ideology that combine theory with myth" (Denich 1994, 382) and in which "spectators,

In Lieu of Conclusions 175

citizens, participants, are forced to take sides ... Events of confrontation take on metaphorical and meto-nymical significance" (David Apter, as quoted in Denich 1994, 383). In such a polarized setting, criticizing "libricide" became a platform for expressing disagreement with the dominant political option. In other words, "libricide" as a phenomenon is a product of the specific Croatian context, characterized by an intense national homogenization process, which reached its peak once the institutional and discursive frameworks that distinguished socialist Yugoslavia disappeared, and of the limited possibilities of publicly expressing disagreement with the ruling party. The role of critically minded intellectuals and the few independent media outlets was crucial in providing a voice and some space to the expression of dissent. "Weeding controversies" have happened and are likely to arise again whenever considerable amounts of discarded library material are disposed publicly. These controversies are mainly due to the different meaning attached to books by professionals and non-librarians and the incongruencies in the understanding of the function of the public library. In order to avoid such misunderstandings, libraries should intensify their communication with the patrons and involve them, when possible, in the "behind the scenes" activities. If museums can open their storage rooms and show visitors how exhibitions are being made, why would a public library not do something similar? This is particularly advisable in a country like Croatia, where libraries carry the reputation of unprofessional and controversial handling of books and where trust in librarians has been shaken. Nevertheless, examples from the 2000s show that discarded books are still being massively disposed in visible paper bins, instead of through one of the other available options. Suffice it to mention an episode from 2013 when the Director of the Vrgorac City Library organized the transfer of a number of discarded moldy books to the local landfill. This decision was announced in the newspaper as follows: "No one wanted them in Vrgorac. The Director of the Library threw Tito and Kardelj into the garbage: If it was Pavelić, it would be the same."[186]

---

186 "Nitko ih nije htio u Vrgorcu. Ravnatelj knjižnice bacio Tita i Kardelja u smeće: Da je i Pavelić, isto bi bilo". *Slobodna Dalmacija*, September 27, 2013. Retrieved

Again, this potentially explosive headline could have inflamed passions, but in a context different from the one mentioned above it did not attract great attention. On a more provocative note, it was precisely the throwing of books into the garbage in Korčula that initiated a broader debate on the discarding of books in Croatia. It is what Mary Douglas would call "endangered order" that made the public aware of the hasty increase in discarding, which otherwise could have been presented as a "natural sequence of events" and passed relatively unnoticed. With that, I am not saying that the discarding of books that no longer reflected the needs and wishes of the patrons (be it books in ekavian, dealing with socialist topics or those removed from the list of school readings) should not have happened, but that it should have happened by respecting the rules of the profession and by making sure that no book is permanently lost. Discarding is a much more complex process than simply removing books which lose currency once a state ceases to exist. It has to take into consideration the needs of the users (or members, as they are called in Croatia) and the general orientation of the library expressed in its mission statement. Above all, it has to be done by considering the collection as a whole, with the aim of improving and renewing it instead of potentially impoverishing it. Also, it is important to cooperate with other libraries in order to make sure that a rare book does not get lost, as well as to balance discarding with the acquisition of new volumes. There is plenty of professional literature, as well as legal and less binding legislation, that provide detailed guidelines on how to proceed. The problem was and remains implementation. Empirical evidence has shown that in some cases discarding in Croatia was much more "improvised" than it should have been. Furthermore, some of of the structural problems that libraries had to face in the 1990s are still present: insufficient funding, lack of professional staff, inexistence of a unified catalogue used on a national level which would render the communication between libraries easier, etc.

---

on April 1, 2015, from: https://www.slobodnadalmacija.hr/novosti/hrvatska/clanak/id/213368/ravnatelj-knjiznice-bacio-tita-i-kardelja-u-smece-da-je-i-pavelic-isto-bi-bilo.

The comparison with the Slovenian situation was significant in understanding how a standard library practice was mismanaged and turned into a political scandal in Croatia, in that respect a *unicum* in former Yugoslavia. Several factors led me to focus on Slovenia. Firstly, the two countries share large chunks of (pre-Yugoslav) past, were the most developed part of Yugoslavia, declared independence on the same day, and saw themselves as more "European" than their southern neighbors. Furthermore, since Slovenia did not go through a protracted war and its path after Yugoslavia did not feature as many discontinuities as that of Croatia, I was curious to test the assumption that the war contributed to the frenzy and the destruction of cultural artefacts even outside the war zones. Finally, articles about "bookicide" in Croatia appeared relatively early in the Slovenian press (the integral text of the "Instruction on the Procedure for Elementary School Libraries" was published in Slovenia earlier than in Croatia, but also Mihaljević's three articles in January 1993), which inevitably led to comparisons and to the "pointing of fingers". Tomislav Sabljak's assertion about the "great discarding" in Ljubljana in 1989 not being labelled as cultural genocide echoed in my ears as I sat on a train towards the Slovenian capital. Apart from the said discarding (to which professionals immediately reacted), there were no publicly recorded cases of politically motivated discarding, and the librarians that I interviewed confirmed it. Hearsay stories do circulate, of Slovenians doing things in a covert manner, of the unlikely probability that a country which erased people would not erase/discard books, of book burnings ordered from Ljubljana... Nevertheless, the statistical data collected at the National and University Library also confirms that in Slovenia collections kept growing. The problem with these data is, however, that being limited to the numbers of discarded copies it is not possible to establish which books were discarded and why. In any case, Slovenian collections kept growing immediately after independence; the same cannot be said about Croatia.

What the increased discarding from public libraries and ensuing debate brought about as a result in Croatia is the emergence of the category of the "discarded". These are not only books that were (un)officially discarded from libraries, but also all volumes that lost currency after the dissolution of Yugoslavia, be it because of their content, because they are no longer included in the school program, or simply because they are written in a language that no longer exists (Serbo-Croatian). Many of these books are still to be found in private, family libraries, but are also publicly available again, or never stopped being so. As such, they act as metonyms of memory and have a certain potential as "discussion triggers". Two such examples are *The Hedgehog's House* and *School In War and Revolution*" in Ana Bilankov's experimental documentary, the vicissitudes of which have been analyzed here. Books have once again survived the powerful detergents of nationalist exclusion and ideological mystifications. But what does the future hold for them?

One of my interviewees expressed his scepticism towards e-books:

> "A bigger damage is being created by e-books than physical destruction. We now have an absolute culturecide [...] Those that are publishing the so-called e-books, this lalala. This is the problem. Do you know what happened? It happened that there is a total campaign against the book. And books are ending up in massive numbers in the dump. What happened in the 1990s is a "little baby" compared to what is happening now!" (TV, antiquarian, personal interview, Rijeka, March 14, 2015).

Those less pessimistic, such as Stephen Fry, would argue that "books are no more threatened by Kindle than stairs by elevators".[187] And what about libraries? In 2018 an op-ed piece by economics professor Panos Mourdoukoutas appeared in *Forbes* under the title "Amazon Should Replace Local Libraries to Save Taxpayers Money". As it can be assumed from the title, the article created a certain commotion, in particular among librarians. In fact, it was later removed from the *Forbes* website and can now be found online on the web page of the American Library Association (ALA).[188] A

---

187 Stephen Fry on Twitter. March 11, 2009. https://twitter.com/stephenfry/stat us/1312682218. Last accessed on April 1, 2019.
188 Panos Mourdoukoutas. "Amazon should replace local libraries to save taxpayers money". Retrieved from: http://www.ala.org/yalsa/sites/ala.org. yalsa/files/content/AmazonShouldReplaceLocalLibrariestoSaveTaxpayersM oney.pdf. Last accessed on April 4, 2019. The *Forbes* version was saved at https://web.archive.org/web/20180722033527/https://www.forbes.com/

Forbes spokesperson stated that "Libraries play an important role in our society. This article was outside of this contributor's specific area of expertise, and has since been removed."[189] In the article, Mourdoukoutas argues that libraries should be replaced by Amazon, "which combines a library with Starbucks". Even if he admits that based on library surveys the number of users is "fairly stable", the author is of the opinion that libraries are losing their value because "third places" like Starbucks, online bookstores such as Amazon, or streaming services like Netflix offer a replacement for library services — borrowing books, free WiFi or video rental. In addition, the development of digital technology "has turned physical books into collectors' items". The latter point is something that my interviewee RG also observed:

> "in the 1980s or 1970s books were for everyone and everyone knew how to use them, while the computer was for those with money and who knew how to use it. Today it is the other way around" (RG, antiquarian, personal interview, Ljubljana, March 11, 2015).

Those more pessimistic than Stephen Fry would argue that Panous Mourdoukoutas succinctly expressed what shall happen to libraries unless a corrective is found to neoliberal policies.

The privatization of public institutions like libraries could in fact drastically impact their function and mission. A first step towards privatization is creating a legal framework that makes it possible. This is, for instance, the case with the new Croatian Law on Libraries and Library Activities (NN 17/2019), which came into effect in February 2019. The act foresees, among other things, the creation of private libraries with access to public funds, which was severely criticized by librarians because it is unclear how they should operate, considering that libraries are traditionally non-profit institutions.[190] Having in mind the selective interpretation of the law

---

sites/panosmourdoukoutas/2018/07/21/amazon-should-replace-local-libra ries-to-save-taxpayers-money/.
189 Quoted from Thu-Huong Ha. "Forbes deleted a deeply misinformed op-ed arguing Amazon should replace libraries". *Quartz*, July 23, 2019. Retrieved on April 4, 2019, from: https://qz.com/1334123/forbes-deleted-an-op-ed-arguing-that-amazon-should-replace-libraries/.
190 Maja Tisaj. "Još jedan zakon podiže prašinu: 'Štetan je za razvoj društva'; 'Rade sve da ponize struku'" (Another law raises a dust: "It is harmful for the

that has revealed itself as a constant in Croatia and is discussed in this research, the question is how and whether the new Law will affect libraries. So far two articles of this act concerning the responsible bodies for libraries have been amended (October 2019), and what has unavoidably had a more pronounced impact on libraries than the said law is the Coronavirus pandemic. Once highly controversial calls for "clean" and hygienized libraries have now become the norm, worldwide.

Figure 15. A book sterilizer in the Rijeka City Library, March 2021.
Photo by Dora Komnenović

---

development of society"; They are doing everything to humiliate the profession"). *Dnevnik.hr*, October 9, 2018. Retrieved on March 20, 2019, from: https://dnevnik.hr/vijesti/hrvatska/tragikomican-prijedlog-novog-zakona-o-knjiznicama---533279.html.

Bibliography

Abazović, D. and Velikonja, M. (2017) (Eds.). *Post-Yugoslavia. New Cultural and Political Perspective*. London: Palgrave Macmillan.
Ambrožič, M. and Žumer, M. (2015). "Libraries and the Library System of Slovenia." *Library Trends* 63 (4): 725–744.
Aparac-Gazivoda, T. and Katalenac, D. (1993) (Eds.). *Wounded Libraries in Croatia*. Zagreb: Croatian Library Association.
Assmann, A. (2002). "Beyond the Archive." In Neville, B. and J. Villeneuve (Eds.). *Waste-Site Stories. The Recycling of Memory*, 71–83. New York, NY: State University of New York Press.
Assmann, J. (2008). "Communicative and Cultural Memory." In Errl, A. and Nünning, A. (Eds.) in collaboration with Young, S., Cultural Memory Studies. *An International and Interdisciplinary Handbook*, 109–118. Berlin/New York: De Gruyter.
Babić, S. (2006). "Ježeva kućica kao pedagoški i jezični problem." *Jezik* 53: 139–146.
Báez, F. (2008). *A Universal History of the Destruction of Books: From Ancient Sumer to Modern-Day Iraq*, New York: Atlas & Co.
Bailyn, J.F., Jelača, D. and Lugarić, D. (2018). *The Future of (Post)Socialism. Eastern European Perspectives*, Albany: State University of New York Press (SUNY).
Baker, C. (2015). *The Yugoslav Wars of the 1990s*. London: Palgrave Macmillan.
Bakić-Hayden, M. (1995). "Nesting Orientalisms: The Case of Former Yugoslavia." *Slavic Review* 54 (4): 917–931. Retrieved on November 6, 2021, from: https://www.academia.edu/26546254/Nesting_Orientalisms_1_.pdf
Bell, Duncan S.A. (2003). "Mythscape: Memory, Mythology, and National Identity." *British Journal of Sociology* 54 (1): 63–81.
Beronja, V. and Vervaet, S. (2016) (Eds.). *Post-Yugoslav Constellations. Archive, Memory, and Trauma in Contemporary Bosnian, Croatian, and Serbian Literature and Culture*, Berlin: De Gruyter.
Biggins, M. (2000). "Publishing in Slovenia." In Biggins, M. and Crayne, J. (Eds.). *Publishing in Yugoslavia's Successor States*, New York: The Haworth Press Inc.

Booher, E. (1975). "Publishing in the USSR and Yugoslavia." *The Annals of the American Academy of Political and Social Science*, vol. 421, Perspectives on Publishing: 118-129.

Borneman, J. (1997). *Settling Accounts. Violence, Justice and Accountability in Postsocialist Europe*, Princeton: Princeton University Press.

Brailo, N. (1998). "Librocide: Destruction of Libraries in Croatia 1991-1995." Master's Thesis. 1688. Retrieved on April 4, 2019, from: https://scholarworks.sjsu.edu/etd_theses/1688/.

Buchli, V. and Lucas, G. (2001) (Eds.). *Archaeologies of the Contemporary Past*, New York: Routledge.

Buden, B. (2010). "Children of postcommunism." *Radical Philosophy*, issue 159, series 1. Retrieved on April 24, 2016, from: https://www.radicalphilosophy.com/article/children-of-postcommunism.

Bugarski, R. (2002). *Lica jezika – sociolingvističke teme*. Beograd: Biblioteka XX. vek.

Bugarski, R. (2005). *Jezik i kultura*. Beograd: Biblioteka XX. vek.

Bugarski, R. (2010). *Jezik i identitet*. Beograd: Biblioteka XX. vek.

Bugarski, R. (2012). *Portret jednog jezika*. Beograd: Biblioteka XX. vek.

Carothers, T. (2002). "The End of the Transition Paradigm." *Journal of Democracy* 13 (1): 5-21. Retrieved on November 6, 2021, from: https://issuu.com/hernandezcortez/docs/the_end_of_the_transition_paradigm_/14

Carrière, J.C. and Eco, U. (2011). *This is Not the End of the Book. A conversation curated by Jean-Philippe de Tonnac*. London: Harvill Secker.

Chelcea, L. and Druță, O. (2016). "Zombie Socialism and the Rise of Neoliberalism in Post-Socialist Central and Eastern Europe." *Eurasian Geography and Economics* 57 (4-5): 521-544. Retrieved on November 6, 2021, from: https://www.tandfonline.com/doi/pdf/10.1080/15387216.2016.1266273

Čiča, S. (2016). "Centralna biblioteka Srpskog kulturnog društva 'Prosvjeta' – centar ulture Srba u Hrvatskoj." *Novosti* (Hrvatsko knjižničarsko društvo) n. 69.

Dalbello-Lovrić, M. (1993). "Review of Hrvatske knjižnice na meti: vodič and Wounded Libraries in Croatia." *Journal of Croatian Studies* 34: 290-294.

Dedić, N. (2016). "Yugoslavia in Post-Yugoslav Artistic Practices: Or, Art as ..." In Beronja, V. and Vervaet, S. (Eds.). *Post-Yugoslav Constellations. Archive, Memory, and Trauma in Contemporary Bosnian, Croatian, and Serbian Literature and Culture*, 169–190. Berlin: De Gruyter.

Denich, B. (1994). "Dismembering Yugoslavia: Nationalist Ideologies and the Symbolic Revival of Genocide." *American Ethnologist* 21 (2): 367–390.

Doll, C. and Barron, P. (2002). *Managing and Analyzing Your Collection: A Practical Guide for Small Libraries and School Media Centers*, Chicago: American Library Association. Chapter 3. Weeding. Retrieved on November 6, 2021, from: https://www.ala.org/aboutala/sites/ala.org.aboutala/files/content/publishing/editions/samplers/doll_mayc.pdf.

Douglas, M. (2001). *Purity and Danger. An Analysis of the Concepts of Pollution and Taboo*, London and New York: Routledge.

Draženović, I., Kunovac, M. and Pripužić, D. (2018). "Dynamics and Determinants of Emigration: The Case of Croatia and the Experience of New EU States." *Public Sector Economics* 42 (4): 415–447.

Dular, J. (2001). *Article on the Slovenian Language prepared on the occasion of the European Year of Languages*. Retrieved on March 3, 2019, from: http://www.vlada.si/en/about_slovenia/slovenian/historical_overview/.

Fisher, M. (2009). *Capitalist Realism. Is there no Alternative?*. Winchester: Zero Books.

Gabrič, Aleš. 2006. "The Transformation of Values in the Cultural Sector." In Ramet S. and Fink-Hafner, D. (Eds.). *Democratic Transition in Slovenia: Value Transformation, Education and Media*, 148–167. College Station, Texas: Texas A&M University Press.

Ghodsee, K. (2017). *Red Hangover. Legacies of Twentieth Century Communism*. Durham and London: Duke University Press.

Gille, Z. (2010). "Is there a Global Postsocialist Condition?" *Global Society* 24 (1): 9–30. Retrieved on November 6, 2021, from: https://f021c784-68e4-4691-9eb2-5a7d932b2783.filesusr.com/ugd/87303d_bf1e6931252f4073a757e8307cc1f7ac.pdf.

Gorup, R. (2013) (Ed.). *After Yugoslavia. The Cultural Spaces of a Vanished Land*, Stanford: Stanford University Press.

Gow, J. and Carmichael, C. (2000). *Slovenia and the Slovenes. A Small State and the New Europe*. London: C. Hurst & Co.
Greenberg, R. (2004). *Language and Identity in the Balkans. Serbo-Croatian and its Disintegration*. Oxford: Oxford University Press.
Griffith, W. (1964) (Ed.). *Communism in Europe. Continuity, Change and the Sino-Soviet Dispute*, vol. 1, London: Pergamon Press.
Groys, B. (1997). "The Role of the Museum when the National State Breaks Up." In *Proceedings of the ICOMON meetings held in Stavanger, Norway (1995) and Vienna, Austria (1996)*, Madrid: Museo Casa de la Moneda.
Hertle, H.-H. (2016). *The Berlin Wall Story. Biography of a Monument*. Berlin: Christoph Links Verlag.
Hitzke, D. (2014). "Nomadisches Schreiben nach dem Zerfall Jugoslawiens: David Albahari, Bora Ćosić und Dubravka Ugrešić." *Slavische Literaturen* Band 46, Bern: Peter Lang.
Horvat, S. and Štiks, I. (2015). *Radical Politics in the Desert of Transition*, Retrieved on October 24, 2016, from: https://www.versobooks.com/blogs/1905-radical-politics-in-the-desert-of-transition.
Hrženjak, J. (2002) (Ed.). *Rušenje antifašističkih spomenika u Hrvatskoj 1990–2000*. Zagreb: Saba RH.
Ignatieff, M. (1998). *The Warrior's Honor: Ethnic War and the Modern Conscience*. New York: Henry Holt & Co.
Irvine, J. (2008). "The Croatian Spring and the Dissolution of Yugoslavia." In Cohen, L.J. and Dragović-Soso, J. (Eds.). *State Collapse in South-Eastern Europe. New Perspectives on Yugoslavia's Disintegration*, 149–178. West Lafayette, IN: Purdue University Press.
Ivančić, V. (2000). *Točka na U. Slučaj Šakić: Anatomija jednog skandala*. Split: Feral Tribune biblioteka.
Jacoby, R. (1975). *Social Amnesia. A Critique of Conformist Psychology from Adler to Laing*. Boston: Beacon Press.
Jelušić, S. (2004). "Book Publishing in Croatia Today." *The Public* 11 (4): 91–100.
Jović, D. (2001). "The Disintegration of Yugoslavia. A Critical Review of Explanatory Approaches." *European Journal of Social Theory* 4 (1): 101–120.
Jović, D. (2009). *Yugoslavia: A State that Withered Away*. West Lafayette, IN: Purdue University Press.

Kapović, M. (2011). "Language, Ideology and Politics in Croatia." *Slavia Centralis* 2: 45-56.
Katalenac, D. (1994). "Narodne knjižnice između narodnog preporoda i knjige za sve: osvrt na stanje fondova narodnih knjižnica—slavonsko baranjsko iskustvo." *Vjesnik bibliotekara Hrvatske* 3-4: 53-66.
Kernel, I. (1999). "Kam z izločenim knjižničnim gradivom?" *Knjižnica* 43 (1): 23-49.
Kirn, G., Kralj, G. and Piškur, B. (2009) (Eds.). *New Public Spaces: Dissensual political and Artistic Practices in the Post-Yugoslav Context*. Ljubljana/Maastricht: Radical Education Collective and Jan Van Eyck Academie.
Kirn, G. and Burghardt, R. (2012). "Yugoslavian Partisan Memorials: Between Memorial Genre, Revolutionary Aesthetics and Ideological Recuperation." *Manifesta Journal* MJ 16: 66-74.
Kiš, D. (2001). *A Tomb for Boris Davidovich*. Champaign: Dalkey Archive Press.
Knuth, R. (2003). *Libricide: The Regime-Sponsored Destruction of Books and Libraries in the Twentieth Century*. Santa Barbara, CA: Greenwood Publishing Group.
Knuth, R. (2006). *Burning Books and Leveling Libraries: Extremist Violence and Cultural Destruction*. Santa Barbara, CA: Greenwood Publishing Group.
Kolstø, P. (2007). "The 'Narcissism of Minor Differences'-Theory. Can it Explain Genocide and Ethnic Conflict? A Review Article." In Karlsson, K., Dietsch, J., Törnquist-Plewa, B. and Zander, U. (Eds.). *Historia mot strömmen: Kultur och konflikt I det moderna Europa*, Carlsson bokförlag. Retrieved on March 1, 2019, from: https://www.duo.uio.no/bitstream/handle/108 52/25227/86810_kolstoe.pdf?sequence=1.
Kolstø, P. (2014) (Ed.). Strategies of Symbolic Nation-Building in South Eastern Europe. London; Ashgate.
Komnenović, D. (2017). "The 1990s: A Decade that Never Ended?" *Der Donauraum* 1-2: 51-61.
Komnenović, D. (2018). "The "Cleansing" of Croatian Libraries in the 1990s and Beyond or How (Not) to Discard the Yugoslav Past." In Bevernage, B. and Wouters, N. (Eds.). *The Palgrave Handbook of State-Sponsored History After 1945*, London: Palgrave Macmillan.

Komnenović, D. (2021). "Remembering the 1990s in Croatia: The Potential of Discarded Books on and beyond Anniversaries." In Newman, J. P. and Apor, B. (Eds.). *Balkan Legacies: The Long Shadow of Conflict and Ideological Experiment in Southeastern Europe*, West Lafayette, IN: Purdue University Press.

Kordić, S. (2010). *Jezik i nacionalizam*, Zagreb: Durieux.

Kuljić, T. (2007). "Was Tito the Last Habsburg? Reflections on Tito's Role in the History of the Balkans." *Balkanistica* 20: 85–100.

Langston, K. and Peti-Stantić, A. (2014). *Language Planning and National Identity in Croatia*. London: Palgrave Macmillan.

Larson, J. (2012). *CREW: A Weeding Manual for Modern Libraries*. Austin, TX: Texas State Library and Archives Commission. Retrieved on November 6, 2021, from: https://www.tsl.texas.gov/sites/default/files/public/tslac/ld/ld/pubs/crew/crewmethod12.pdf

Lešaja, A. (2010). "Kulturocid. Sudski process protiv Milana Kangrge" (Culturecide. The Court Case against Milan Kangrga). *Republika*, n. 490–491. Retrieved on February 2, 2017, from: http://www.republika.co.rs/490-491/23.html.

Lešaja, A. (2012). *Knjigocid. Uništavanje knjiga u Hrvatskoj 1990-ih*, Profil & SNV, Zagreb.

Lešaja, A. (2019). "Odjeci (Recepcija) knjige i fenomena uništavanja knjiga (i spomenika NOBe/socijalističke revolucije) (od objavljivanja knjige polovicom 2012. do 2018)" (Reception of the book *Knjigocid. Uništavanje knjiga u Hrvatskoj 1990-ih* and of the phenomenon of the destruction of monuments to the People's Liberation Struggle/the socialist revolution from its publishing in mid-2012 to 2018). Unpublished paper.

Lindstrom, N. (2003). "Between Europe and the Balkans: Mapping Slovenia and Croatia's Return to Europe." *Dialectical Anthropology* 27: 313–329. Retrieved on November 6, 2021, from: https://sites.google.com/site/nrlindstrom/fulltext.pdf

Lončar, N. (2010). "Projekt 'Odpisani' in odpis gradiva v Univerzitetni knjižnici Maribor." *Knjižnica*, 54 (3): 117–128.

Macdonald, S. (2009). *Difficult Heritage. Negotiating the Nazi Past in Nuremberg and Beyond*. London and New York: Routledge.

Mencinger, J. (nd). *Privatization in Slovenia*, Retrieved on March 3, 2019, from: http://www.pf.uni-lj.si/media/mencinger.privatization.pdf.

Mesić, Đ. (1991). "Narodna knjižnica—prilog određenju pojma." *Journal of Information and Organizational Sciences* 15: 145–159.
Moser, W. (2002). "The Acculturation of Waste." In Neville, B. and Villeneuve, J. (Eds.). *Waste-Site Stories. The Recycling of Memory*, 85–105. New York, NY: State University of New York Press.
Müller, J.-W. (2004) (Ed.). *Memory and Power in Post-War Europe. Studies in the Presence of the Past*. Cambridge: Cambridge University Press.
Najbar-Agičić, M. and Agičić, D. (2007). "The Use and Misuse of History Teaching in 1900s Croatia." In Ramet, S.P. and Matić, D. (Eds.). *Democratic Transition in Croatia: Value Transformation, Education & Media* (pp.193–223). College Station: Texas A&M University Press.
Narančić Kovač, S. and Milković, I. (2018). *Lektira u hrvatskoj osnovnoj školi: popis naslova*. BIBRICH, Retrieved on February 20, 2019, from: http://bibrich.ufzg.hr/reading-lists/.
Nebesny, T. (nd). *Otkup knjiga kao način nabave u narodnim knjižnicama*. Retrieved on April 22, 2019, from: http://dzs.ffzg.unizg.hr/text/nebesny_otkup.htm.
Norkus, Z. (2012). *On Baltic Slovenia and Adriatic Lithuania. A Qualitative Comparative Analysis of Patterns in Post-Communist Transformation*. Budapest: Central European University Press.
Opačić, N. (2006). "Veliko pospremanje u Ježevoj kućici Branka Ćopića." In Srdoč-Konestra, I. and Vranić, I. (Eds.). *Riječki filološki dani: zbornik radova s Međunarodnoga znanstvenog skupa Riječki filološki dani održanoga u Rijeci od 18. do 20. studenoga 2004*, 237–246. Rijeka: Filozofski fakultet.
Ožegović, N. (2018). "(Ne)vjerodostojnost medijske reprezentacije culture: od političke manipulacije do strategije skandala." *In Medias Res* 7 (3): 2101–2114.
Pavelić, B. (2014). *Smijeh slobode: uvod u Feral Tribune*. Rijeka: Adamić.
Pehar, I. (1994). "Nestali, uništeni, oštećeni fondovi 1991–1994." *Vjesnik bibliotekara Hrvatske* 3/4: 119–121.
Petrović, T. (2014) (Ed.). *Mirroring Europe. Ideas of Europe and Europeanization in Balkan Societies*, Balkan Studies Library, vol. 13. Leiden: Brill.

Pogačar, M. (2010). "Mnemonautica: Online Representations of the Yugoslav Past." In Riha, D. (Ed.). *Humanity in Cybernetic Environments*, 23–34. Oxford: Inter-Disciplinary Press.

Pogačar, M. (2016). *Media Archaeologies, Micro Archives and Storytelling: Re-presencing the Past*. London: Palgrave Macmillan.

Polastron, L. (2007). *Books on Fire: The Destruction of Libraries throughout History*. Rochester: Inner Traditions.

Poličnik-Čermelj, T. and Sešek, I. (2006). "Bosanskohercegovačka, hrvatska, makedonska i srpska građa u Nacionalnoj i univerzitetskoj biblioteci u Ljubljani: analitički izvještaj za novi milenijum." *Yearbook of International Convention of Slavicists Librarians in Sarajevo (ICSL)*, vol. 2.

Poličnik-Čermelj, T. and Žagar, V. (2007). "Otpis građe u bibliotekama Slovenije kao način popunjavanja fonda Narcionalne i univerzitetne biblioteke u Ljubljani." *ICSL Yearbook*, vol. 3.

Popescu, M. (2007). "Imaging the Past: Cultural Memory in Dubravka Ugrešić's 'The Museum of Unconditional Surrender'". *Studies in the Novel* 39 (3): 336–356.

Potkonjak, S. and Pletenac, T. (2011). "Kada spomenici ožive — 'Umjetnost sjećanja' u javnom prostoru." *Stud. Ethnol. Croat.* 23: 7–24.

Potkonjak, S. and Pletenac, T. (2016). "The Art and Craft of Memory: Re-Memorialization Practices in Post-Socialist Croatia." In Beronja, V. and Vervaet, S. (Eds.). *Post-Yugoslav Constellations. Archive, Memory, and Trauma in Contemporary Bosnian, Croatian, and Serbian Literature and Culture*, 65–81. Berlin: De Gruyter.

Radonić, Lj. (2012). *Standards of Evasion: Croatia and the "Europeanization of memory"* http://www.eurozine.com/articles/2012-04-06-radonic-en.html. Last accessed on April 7, 2015.

Ramet, S. (2007). "The Dissolution of Yugoslavia: Competing Narratives of Resentment and Blame." *Südosteuropa. Zeitschrift für Politik und Gesellschaft* 55 (1): 26–69.

Ramet, S. and Matić, D. (2007) (Eds.). *Democratic Transition in Croatia. Value Transformation, Education & Media*. Texas: A&M University Press.

Repe, B. (2012). *Slovenes and their Identity after the Disintegration of Yugoslavia*, Lecture held at the Faculty of Arts, Charles University Prague on April 11, 2012. Retrieved on November 6, 2021, from: http://oddelki.ff.uni-lj.si/zgodovin/wwwrepe/Micro soft%20Word%20-%20Slovenci%20in%20njihova%20identitet a%20po%20razpadu%20Jugoslavije%20-%20Praga_ANG.pdf.

Roksandić, D. (2015). "Krležina Enciklopedija Jugoslavije između euroskepticizma i euronormativizma: prilog poznavanju početaka Krležina projekta Enciklopedije Jugoslavije." *Studia lexicographica* 8 (2) (15): 5–22.

Santayana, G. (2011). *The Life of Reason or The Phases of the Human Progress. Introduction and Reason in Common Sense.* Volume VII, Book One. Co-edited by Marianne S. Wokeck and Martin A. Coleman. Critical Edition. Cambridge and London: MIT Press.

Skender, D. (Ed.) (1992). *Hrvatske knjižnice na meti: Vodič* (Croatian Libraries on Target: Guide), Zagreb: National and University Library.

Skrbiš, Z. (2017). *Long-Distance Nationalism. Diasporas, Homelands and Identities.* London and New York: Routledge.

Stolac, D. (2014). "Expressing Croatian Identity through Language Designations." *Croatian Studies Review* 10: 105–132. Retrieved on November 6, 2021, from: https://www.academia.edu/15 742230/Expressing_Croatian_identity_through_language_de signations.

Strićević, I. and Pehar, F. (2015). "Libraries in Croatia: Developments and Trends in the Postsocialist Period." *Library Trends* 63 (4): 675–696.

Subotić, J. (2011). "Europe is a State of Mind: Identity and Europeanization in the Balkans." *International Studies Quarterly* 55: 309–330.

Subotić, J. (2017). "Building Democracy in Serbia: One Step Forward, Three Steps Back." In Ramet, S., Hassenstab, C. and Listhaug, O. (Eds.). *Building Democracy in the Yugoslav Successor States. Accomplishments, Setbacks, Challenges since 1990*, 165–191. Cambridge: Cambridge University Press.

Šuvar, S. (2004). *Hrvatski karusel – prilozi političkoj sociologiji hrvatskog društva*, Zagreb: Razlog.

Taylor, A.J.P. (1976). *The Habsburg Monarchy, 1809–1918: A History of the Austrian Empire and Austria-Hungary.* Chicago: University of Chicago Press.

Thompson, M. (1979). *Rubbish Theory: The Creation and Destruction of Value*. Chicago: University of Chicago Press.
Todorova, M. (1993). "Ethnicity, Nationalism and the Communist Legacy in Eastern Europe." *East European Politics and Societies*, 7 (1): 135-154.
Todorova, M. (2005). "Spacing Europe: What is a Historical Region?" *East Central Europe* 32 (1): 59-78.
Todorova, M. (2009). *Imagining the Balkans*. Oxford: Oxford University Press.
Tuđman, F. (1989). *Bespuća povijesne zbiljnosti*. Zagreb: Nakladni zavod matice Hrvatske.
Turk, M. and Opašić, M. (2008). "Linguistic Borrowing and Purism in the Croatian Language." *Suvremena lingvistika* 65 (1): 73-88.
Ugrešić, D. (1998). *Museum of Unconditional Surrender*. London: Phoenix.
Ugrešić, D. (1999). *Kultura laži. Antipolitički eseji*. Zagreb: Biblioteka bastard, Arkzin.
Ugrešić, D. (2015). "Esej koji putuje već pune 23 godine." *Peščanik*, May 30, 2015. Retrieved on June 4, 2015, from: https://pescanik.net/esej-koji-putuje-vec-pune-23-godine/.
Valencia, M. (2002). "Libraries, Nationalism, and Armed Conflict in the Twentieth Century." *Libri* 52: 1-15.
Vegh, Ž. (2015). "Sudbina hrvatskih knjiga kršćanske tematike i nadahnuća u Gradskoj knjižnici u Zagrebu u doba komunizma." *Kroatologija* 6 (1-2): 27-93.
Velikonja, M. (2017). "When Times were Worse, the People were Better: The Ideological Potentials and Political Scope of Yugonostalgia." *Nostalgia on the Move*. Belgrade: Museum of Yugoslavia, 7-13.
Verdery, K. (1996). *What Was Socialism, and What Comes Next?*. Princeton: Princeton University Press.
Vervaet, S. (2011). "Whose Museum? Whose History? Whose Memories? Remembering in the Work of Dubravka Ugrešić." *Comparative Critical Studies* 8 (2-3): 295-306.
Vervaet, S. (2016). "Intersecting Memories in Post-Yugoslav Fiction: The Yugoslav Wars of the 1990s through the Lens of the Holocaust." In Beronja, V. and Vervaet, S. (Eds.). *Post-Yugoslav Constellations. Archive, Memory, and Trauma in Contemporary Bosnian, Croatian, and Serbian Literature and Culture*, 99-126. Berlin: De Gruyter.

Vlašić, M. (2010). "Tradicija purizma u hrvatskom jezikoslovlju." PhD dissertation. Retrieved on April 5, 2019, from: https://dspace.cuni.cz/handle/20.500.11956/31177.
Vodovnik, Ž. (2017). "Democratisation and New Social Movements." *World Political Science* 13 (1): 2363–4782.
Wachtel, A. (1998). *Making a Nation, Breaking a Nation: Literature and Cultural Politics in Yugoslavia*, Stanford: Stanford University Press.
Wimmer, U. and Seadle, M. (2014). "A Friendly Conquest: German Libraries after the Fall of the Berlin Wall." *Library trends* 63 (2): 197–211.
Wischenbart, R. and Popović, N. (2000). *Re-Inventing Publishing in the War-Torn Balkans*. Retrieved on February 25, 2019, from: https://homepage.univie.ac.at/ruediger.wischenbart/03_ce ntral-Europe-balkan/03_artikel-allgem/03_publishing-in-YU _engl.htm.
Zajc, M. (2015). "The 70th Anniversary of the End of WWII in Slovenia." *Cultures of History Forum*. Retrieved on March 1, 2019, from: http://www.cultures-of-history.uni-jena.de/debates/slovenia/the-70th-anniversary-of-the-end-of-wwii-in-sloven ia/.
Zakošek, N. (2007). "The Heavy Burden of History: Political Uses of the Past in the Yugoslav Successor States." *Croatian Political Science Review* (Politička misao) 44 (5): 29–43.
Žanić, I. (2009). "Titlovanje 'Rana' – pokušaj načelnog pristupa." In Badurina, L., Pranjković, I. and Silić, J. (Eds.). *Jezični varijeteti i nacionalni varijeti. Prilozi proučavanju standardnih jezika utemeljenih na štokavštini*, 457–472. Zagreb: Disput.
Živković, D. (2008). "Publishers and Libraries in the Information Society – Allies or Rivals?" Retrieved on December 20, 2017, from: https://bib.irb.hr/datoteka/365173.zivkovic-final-Ma rch08.doc.
Žnideršič, M., Podmenik, D., Kocijan, G. (1999). *Knjiga in bralci IV*, Bibliothecaria 5. Ljubljana: Filozofska Fakulteta, Oddelek za bibliotekarstvo.
Žuvić, M. (2016). "'Jugolinija': The Myth and the Truth." *Transactions on Maritime Science* 5 (1): 69–81. Retrieved on December 20, 2017, from: https://www.toms.com.hr/index.php/toms/article/view/143.

Newspaper articles

Adriana Piteša. "Lešaja: Devedesetih smo uništili 2,8 mil. 'nepoćudnih' knjiga". *Jutarnji list*, July 13, 2012. Retrieved from: https://www.jutarnji.hr/kultura/knjizevnost/lesaja-devedesetih-smo-unistili-28-mil.-%E2%80%98nepocudnih%E2%80%99-knjiga/1540434/ on April 18, 2019.

Andrew Osborn. "Disappearing Books: How Russia is shuttering its Ukrainian library". *Reuters*, March 15, 2017. Retrieved from: https://www.reuters.com/article/us-ukraine-crisis-russia-library-idUSKBN16M0PW.

Ante Talijaš. "Umjesto cvijeta vidjeli petokraku". *Jutarnji list*, April 26, 2018. Retrieved on April 20, 2019.

Anton Lukežić. "Tko pali knjige, palit će i ljude" (Who burns books, will burn people, too). *Novi list*, July 12, 1994.

"Border Walls: 'turnkey' answer to threats real and imagined" (February 27, 2017). *Mail online*. Retrieved from: https://www.dailymail.co.uk/wires/afp/article-4263692/Border-walls-turnkey-answer-threats-real-imagined.html on March 17, 2019.

Boris Dežulović. "Gdje ste bili devedeset prve?". *Globus*, September 24, 2014. Retrieved from http://www.6yka.com on November 25, 2014.

Branimir Donat. "Informatorova lažna dostava". *Večernji list*, February 7, 1993.

Branka Džebić. "Otpor librocidu". *Vjesnik*, October 16, 1991. "Catholic priests burn 'sacrilegious' Harry Potter books and Twilight novels in Poland". *Mail online*, April 1, 2019. Retrieved from: https://www.dailymail.co.uk/news/article-6874121/Catholic-priests-burn-sacrilegious-Harry-Potter-books-Twilight-novels-Poland.html.

"Chief librarian in Feodosia (Crimea) fined for displaying books on Holodomor". *Euromaidan Press*, January 17, 2015. Retrieved from: http://euromaidanpress.com/2015/01/17/chief-librarian-in-feodosia-crimea-fined-for-displaying-books-on-holodomor/#arvlbdata.

"Cirkus u otvorenom zbog prijevoda srpskih filmova". *Net.hr*, January 25, 2012. Retrieved from: https://net.hr/danas/hrvatska/cirkus-u-zbog-prijevoda-srpskih-filmova/.

"Confirmed: Czech Republic is in Western Europe, says US textbook". *Expats.cz*, February 4, 2019. Retrieved on February 5, 2019, from: https://news.expats.cz/weekly-czech-news/confirmed-czech-republic-is-in-western-europe-says-us-textbook/.

Damijana Hainz and Brane Čop. "Knjige na odpadu". *Delo*, November 22, 1989.

Danilo Hinič. "Zaradi prostorske stiske Mestne knjižnice deset ton knjig na odpadu". *Dnevnik*, November 21, 1989.

Darko Brdarić. "Tatarski biftek od sirove mržnje". *Vjesnik*, January 30, 1993.

Davorka Vukov Colić. "Knjižnice grada Zagreba. Miševi u koricama". *Zarez* I/V, April 16, 1999.

Davorka Vukov Colić. "Sudstvo i kultura. Šutnjom u bezbolno društvo". *Zarez*, I/16, October 15, 1999.

Dejan Vodovnik. "Slovanski knjižnici ostaja staro ime". *Delo*, June 8, 1999.

Denis Derk. "Hrvatska pisana mržnjom". *Večernji list*, January 26, 1993.

Denis Derk. "I Balzac na smetlištu?". *Večernji list*, April 3, 1993.

"Die Kamera war und ist ein Teil von mir". Interview with Daniel Biskup conducted by Ulrike Zander. *Museumsmagazin* 1/2019, Stiftung Haus der Geschichte der Bundesrepublik Deutschland.

Dimitar Anakiev. "Omarska, pakao za ljude". *E-novosti*, January 15, 2011. Retrieved on April 20, 2019, from: http://www.e-novine.com/stav/43912-Omarska-pakao-ljude.html." Disintegration in the Balkans could be foretaste of things to come in the USSR". *The Economist*, vol. 317, n. 7676, October 13, 1990.

Dubravka Ugrešić. "Saubere kroatische Luft". *Die Zeit*, October 23, 1992.

Dušan Cunjak. "Kje so knjige?". *Mladina*, May 7, 2011. Retrieved on March 20, 2015, from: http://www.mladina.si/87893/m-knjige/?utm_source=tednik%2F200118%2Fclanek%2Fm-knjige%2F&utm_medium=web&utm_campaign=oldLink.

Đurđica Jureša. "Akademik Kangrga brani knjige na srpskom, ali nije izustio ni slova dok su gorjele hrvatske knjige". *Vjesnik*, April 21, 1998.

"Hoćete li dopustiti ulazak slikovnice o tzv. istospolnim obiteljima u vrtiće i škole? (Will you allow the entry of the picture book about the so-called same-sex families into kindergartens and schools?). *Večernji list*, January 4, 2018. Retrieved from: https://www.vecernji.hr/vijesti/udruga-vigilare-blazenka-divjak-istospolne-zajednice-1217836.

Igor Lasić. "Djevojčica sa žigicama". *Feral Tribune*, March 1, 1999.

Igor Lasić. "Sjećanje na 'otpis': uništavanje knjiga devedesetih". *Bilten*, June 30, 2015.

"I knjige se mogu ubiti". *Novi list*, May 10, 1999.

Ivana Kalogjera-Brkić. "'Ježeva kućica nije pisana hrvatskim'" ('Hedgehog's Home' is not Written in Croatian). *Jutarnji list*, November 23, 2005

Ivana Kalogjera-Brkić. "'Ježeva kućica' ima fusnote na hrvatskom" ('Hedhehog's Home' has Footnotes in Croatian). *Jutarnji list*, November 26, 2005.

"Iz lektire izbačeni Mali princ i Ježeva kućica". *Index.hr*, February 13, 2019. Retrieved on March 12, 2019, from: https://www.index.hr/vijesti/clanak/iz-lektire-izbaceni-mali-princ-i-jezeva-kucica/2063852.aspx.

Jasmina Kuzmanović. "Epoha na smetlištu" (Epoch on the Junkyard). *Danas*, December 4, 1990.

"Javio se predsjednik udruge koja je pred djecom spalila gay slikovnicu, probao je biti duhovit" (The president of the association that in front of children burned a gay picture book comments the event trying to be witty). *Index.hr*, February 4, 2018. Retrieved from: http://www.index.hr/vijesti/clanak/javio-se-predsjednik-udruge-koja-je-pred-djecom-spalila-gay-slikovnicu-probao-je-biti-duhovit/1023773.aspx?fb_comment_id=1730524903635295_1730577726963346#f35eaa6a66190d8.

Ljerka Bratonja Martinović. "Marijana Hameršak: Neodgovorno je što 'Ježeve kućice' već desetljećima nema na popisu lektire" (Marijana Hameršak: It is irresponsible that 'The Hedgehog's Home' is not on the reading list). *Novi list*, February 24, 2019. Retrieved on March 14, 2019, from: http://novilist.hr/Vijesti/Hrvatska/MARIJANA-HAMERSAK-Neodgovorno-je-sto-Jezeve-kucice-vec-desetljecima-nema-na-popisu-lektire.

Maja Tisaj. "Još jedan zakon podiže prašinu". *Dnevnik.hr*, October 9, 2018. Retrieved on March 20, 2019, from: https://dnev nik.hr/vijesti/hrvatska/tragikomican-prijedlog-novog-zako na-o-knjiznicama---533279.html.

Micha Haarkötter. "In aller Stille abgewickelt. Vom verschwinden der DDR-Betriebs-Bibiotheken". *Die Tageszeitung*, August 10, 1994.

"Milan Kangrga proglašen krivim" (Milan Kangrga declared guilty). *Novi list*, March 30, 1999.

Milan Kangrga. "Hrvatski knjigocid — barbarizam i renesansa" (Croatian libricide: Barbarism and Renaissance). *Feral Tribune*, March 30, 1998.

Miran Čubic. "Poblazneli svet". *Dnevnik*, November 22, 1989.

Mirjana Jurišić. "Kome služe izmišljotine o vandalizmu hrvatskih knjižničara. Knjige srpskih pisaca nitko ne baca s polica". *Večernji list*, May 23, 1998.

Mojca Kaučič. "Na stotine knjig komaj rešili pred uničenjem". *Delo*, November 21, 1989.

Mojca Kaučič. "Knjige z odpada bodo dobile nove lastnike v Bukvarni". *Delo*, December 6, 1989.

Mourdoukoutas, P. "Amazon Should Replace Local Libraries to Save Taxpayers Money". *Forbes*, July 21, 2018. Retrieved on April 4, 2019, from: http://www.ala.org/yalsa/sites/ala.org. yalsa/files/content/AmazonShouldReplaceLocalLibrariesto SaveTaxpayersMoney.pdf.

"Na Kaštelanskom dječjem karnevalu spaljena slikovnica duginih boja". *Večernji list*, February 4, 2018. Retrieved on April 2, 2019, from: https://www.vecernji.hr/vijesti/na-kastelanskom-djec jem-karnevalu-spaljena-slikovnica-duginih-boja-1224175.

Nataša Latković. "Ministar besan što 'Srbija uvozi' GEJ SLIKOV-NICE IZ HRVATSKE [capitalized in the original]: 'Nije u redu da Roko ima dve mame, a Ana dvojicu tata' (Minister furious about 'Serbian import' of CROATIAN PICTURE BOOKS: It is not OK that Roko has two moms, and Ana has two dads). *Blic*, May 4, 2018. Retrieved from: https://www.blic.rs/vesti/ drustvo/ministar-besan-sto-srbija-uvozi-gej-slikovnice-iz-hr vatske-nije-u-redu-da-roko-ima/nl7nlsd.

Nikica Mihaljević. "Miroslav Krleža je vedel: Gorje nam, ki smo vaši pesniki: književno življenje v 'stari' in 'novi' Hrvaški" (Miroslav Krleža knew: Woe to us, who are your poets: literary life in 'old' and 'new' Croatia). *Delo* 35 (4) (7 Jan. 1993): 13; (10) (14 Jan. 1993): 14–15; and (16) (21 Jan. 1993): 14–16.

Nina Domazet. "Nacionalni čistunci haraju policama" (National cleaners are pillaging shelves). *Novi list*, April 11, 1998.

"Nitko ih nije htio u Vrgorcu. Ravnatelj knjižnice bacio Tita i Kardelja u smeće: Da je i Pavelić, isto bi bilo". *Slobodna Dalmacija*, September 27, 2013. Retrieved on April 1, 2015, from: https://www.slobodnadalmacija.hr/novosti/hrvatska/clan ak/id/213368/ravnatelj-knjiznice-bacio-tita-i-kardelja-u-sme ce-da-je-i-pavelic-isto-bi-bilo.

"Otvorena nova zgrada NSK u Zagrebu" (New building of the NSK opens). Retrieved March 28, 2019, from: https://povij est.hr/nadanasnjidan/otvorena-nova-zgrada-nsk-u-zagrebu-1995/ and https://www.zagreb.info/ritam-grad/nadanasnji dan/otvorena-nova-zgrada-nacionalne-sveucilisne-knjiznice-zagrebu-1995/129960.

Panos Mourdoukoutas. "Amazon should replace local libraries to save taxpayers money". Retrieved from: http://www.ala. org/yalsa/sites/ala.org.yalsa/files/content/AmazonShould ReplaceLocalLibrariestoSaveTaxpayersMoney.pdf. Last accessed on April 4, 2019.

Petrit Çollaku. "Kosovo activists overturn Serbian truck in schoolbook protest". *Balkan Insight*, March 3, 2016. Retrieved from: http://www.balkaninsight.com/en/article/serbia-s-truck-rolled-over-as-response-to-refused-school-books-03-03-2016.

"Pijani 50-godišnjak pretukao 19-godišnju konobaricu: Gdje si bila '91.?" (Drunken 50-year-old beats up 19-year-old waitress: Where were you in 1991?). *Slobodna Dalmacija*, September 20, 2014. Retrieved on November 25, 2014, from: https://slobodn adalmacija.hr/dalmacija/dubrovnik/clanak/id/247302/pija ni-50-godisnjak-pretukao-19-godisnju-konobaricu-gdje-si-bil a-91.

"Poništena presuda Kangrgi". *Novi list*, September 10, 1999.

Ratko Čangalović. "Hrvatske knjižnice otpisuju nepodobnu literaturu. Kad gore knjige, pucaju kosti". *Novi list*, April 29, 1998.

Ratko Čangalović. "Zagrepška šepetanja. Nazor in Krleža na smečišču". *Delo*, March 12, 2004.

"Russia: Conviction of librarian for holding 'extremist books' demonstrates utter contempt for rule of law". *Amnesty International*, June 5, 2017. Retrieved from: https://www.amnesty.org/en/latest/news/2017/06/russia-conviction-of-librarian-for-holding-extremist-books-demonstrates-utter-contempt-for-rule-of-law/.

Sanja Stapić. "Jedina knjižnica bivše 'JNA' koja je preživjela rat. Knjige za HRM". *Slobodna Dalmacija*, May 5, 1992.

Stephen Engelberg. "Breakup of Yugoslavia Leaves Slovenia Secure, Croatia shaky". *The New York Times*, January 16, 1992.

Thu-Huong Ha. "Forbes deleted a deeply misinformed op-ed arguing Amazon should replace libraries". *Quartz*, July 23, 2019. Retrieved on April 4, 2019, from: https://qz.com/1334123/forbes-deleted-an-op-ed-arguing-that-amazon-should-replace-libraries/.

Tihomil Maštrović. "Zločin ćiriličnog uma". *Večernji list*, October 1, 1995.

Tomislav Sabljak. "Moj prijatelj terorist". *Vjesnik*, March 6, 1993.

Velimir Sekulić, "Formiranje srpske biblioteke u Zagrebu" (The Creation of the Serbian Library in Zagreb). *Novosti*, 2 September 2005.

"Verbalno napao Josipovića: Stidite se i vi i Milanović! Gdje ste vi bili '91?" (Verbally assaults Josipović: Shame on you and Milanović! Where were you in 1991?). *Večernji list*, August 5, 2014. Retrieved on November 27, 2015, from: http://www.vecernji.hr/hrvatska/verbalno-napao-josipovica-stidite-se-i-vi-i-milanovic-gdje-ste-vi-bili-91-954182.

"Zagovora knjižničarjev ne sprejmemo": Odgovor Slovenskega bibliografskega (pravilno bibliofilskega!) društva na poziv delavcev Knjižnice Oton Zupančič, naj novinarji in javnost zaupajo njihovi "strokovni presoji". *Delo*, November 28, 1989.

"Zagreb Pride, Lori, Dugine obitelji i Roda kazneno prijavili organizatora karnevala" (Zagreb Pride, Lori, Dugine obitelji and Roda report the organizers of the carnival to the police). *Večernji list*, February 6, 2018. Retrieved from: https://www.vecernji.hr/vijesti/spaljivanje-slikovnica-zagreb-pride-lori-dugine-obitelji-roda-karneval-1224669.

Zlatko Vidačković. "Gruntovnica će iseliti iz NSK. Razgovor s Tihomilom Maštrovićem" (The Land Registry will move out of the National and University Library.Interview with Tihomil Maštrović). *Vijenac* 359, 6 December 2007.

Official Documents

Civil and Political Rights in Croatia, Human Rights Watch 1995. Retrieved on January 18, 2019, from: https://www.hrw.org/legacy/reports/1995/Croatia.htm.
European Commission. 25 Years After the Fall of the Iron Curtain. The State of Integration of East and West in the European Union, European Union 2015. Retrieved on February 1, 2019, from: https://web.archive.org/web/20201111205956/https://ec.europa.eu/research/social-sciences/pdf/policy_reviews/east-west_integration.pdf.
IFLA/UNESCO Public Libraries Manifesto 1994. Retrieved on April 4, 2019, from: https://repository.ifla.org/bitstream/123456789/168/1/pl-manifesto-en.pdf.
Memory of the World: Lost Memory – Libraries and Archives Destroyed in the Twentieth Century (1996) / prepared for UNESCO on behalf of IFLA by Hans van der Hoeven and on behalf of ICA by Joan van Albada, UNESCO, Paris.
Naputak za provođenje revizije i otpisa građe u knjižnicama Republike Hrvatske, Vjesnik bibliotekara Hrvatske 3–4/92
Navodilo za izločanje in odpis knjižničnega gradiva, Narodna in univerzitetna knjižnica (NUK), 0007-7/2012
Pravilnik o matičnoj djelatnosti knjižnica u Republici Hrvatskoj, Narodne novine (NN 43/2001)
Pravilnik o reviziji i otpisu knjižnične građe, Narodne novine (NN 21/2002)
Rješenje trgovačkog suda u Zagrebu Tt–97/84-2
Ustav Republike Hrvatske (NN 56/1990)
Ustavni zakon o pravima nacionalnih manjina (NN 155/2002)
"War damage to the cultural heritage in Croatia and Bosnia and Herzegovina presented by the Committee on Culture and Education", doc. 6869, Strasbourg: Council of Europe, Parliamentary Assembly, July 17, 1993. Retrieved on January 21, 2019, from: https://assembly.coe.int/nw/xml/XRef/X2H-Xref-ViewHTML.asp?FileID=7222&lang=EN.
Zakon o autorskim i srodnim pravima, Narodne novine (NN 96/18)

Zakon o elektroničkim medijima, Narodne novine (NN 153/2009)
Zakon o knjižnicama i knjižničnoj djelatnosti, Narodne Novine (NN 17/19)
Zakon o knjižničarstvu, Uradni list Socijalističke republike Slovenije 27/1982
Zakon o knjižničarstvu (Zknj-1), Uradni list Republike Slovenije 87/2001

Statistical data and reports

Croatia in figures 2016. Zagreb: Croatian Bureau of Statistics. Retrieved on April 5, 2019, from: https://www.dzs.hr/Hrv_Eng/CroInFig/croinfig_2016.pdf.

GfK istraživanje tržišta knjiga u Hrvatskoj 2016. (GfK Research of the Book Market in Croatia in 2016), https://issuu.com/modernavremena/docs/gfk_-_istra__ivanje_tr__i__ta_knjig. Last accessed on May 10, 2018.

IFLA/FAIFE World Report: Libraries and Intellectual Freedom. Slovenia. Retrieved on March 18, 2019, from: https://www.ifla.org/files/assets/faife/publications/ifla-world-report/slovenia.pdf.

IFLA/FAIFE World Report: Libraries and Intellectual Freedom. Croatia. Retrieved on March 18, 2019, from: https://www.ifla.org/files/assets/faife/publications/ifla-world-report/croatia.pdf.

Novljan, S. (1991). *Splošnoizobraževalne knjižnice v letu 1990 (Posnetek po vprašalniku)*. Ljubljana: National and University Library.

Novljan, S. (1992). *Splošnoizobraževalne knjižnice v letu 1991 (Posnetek po vprašalniku)*. Ljubljana: National and University Library.

Novljan, S. (1993). *Zgovornost številk: splošnoizobraževalne knjižnice v letu 1992*. Ljubljana: Nacionalna in univerzitetna knjižnica.

Novljan, S. (1994). *Pogoji dela zaostajajo za rastjo potreb (Splošnoizobraževalne knjižnice v letu 1993)*. Ljubljana: Nacionalna in univerzitetna knjižnica.

Novljan, S. (1995). *Vam lahko pomagam?: splošnoizobraževalne knjižnice v letu 1994*. Ljubljana: Nacionalna in univerzitetna knjižnica.

Novljan, S. (1996). *Splošnoizobraževalne knjižnice v letu 1995: posnetek po vprašalniku*. Ljubljana: Nacionalna in univerzitetna knjižnica.

Novljan, S. (1997). *Slovenske splošnoizobraževalne knjižnice: poročilo za leto 1996*. Ljubljana: Nacionalna in univerzitetna knjižnica.
Novljan, S. (2000). Splošnoizobraževalne knjižnice v letu 1999. *Knjižničarske novice,* 10(2000)10.
Obvestila republiške matične službe 1990, n. 1-2. Ljubljana: Nacionalna in univerzitetna knjižnica.
"Population by ethnicity, 1971/2011 censuses". Data published by the Croatian Bureau of Statistics. Available online at: https://www.dzs.hr/Eng/censuses/census2011/results/htm/usp_0 3_EN.htm. Last accessed on May 24, 2018.
"227. Slovenia since 1990". Report by Sabrina P. Ramet. *Wilson Center,* July 7, 2011.Retrieved on February 5, 2019, from: https://www.wilsoncenter.org/publication/227-slovenia-1990.
Slovenske splošnoizobraževalne knjižnice: poročilo za leto 1997 (Ed. by Eva Kodrič-Dačić). Ljubljana: Nacionalna in univerzitetna knjižnica, 2000.
Slovenske splošnoizobraževalne knjižnice: poročilo za leto 1998 (Ed. by Eva Kodrič-Dačić). Ljubljana: Nacionalna in univerzitetna knjižnica, 2000.
Slovenske splošnoizobraževalne knjižnice: poročilo za leto 1999 (Ed. by Silva Novljan). Ljubljana: Nacionalna in univerzitetna knjižnica, 2001.
Slovenske splošnoizobraževalne knjižnice: poročilo za leto 2000. Ljubljana: Nacionalna in univerzitetna knjižnica, 2003.
Slovenske knjižnice v številkah. Splošne knjižnice. Poročilo za leto 2015. Edited by Eva Kodrič-Dačić. Ljubljana: Nacionalna in univerzitetna knjižnica, 2016.
Statistični podatki o knjižnicah 2000–2017: https://bibsist.nuk.uni-lj.si/statistika/. Last accessed on February 28, 2019.
"25 Years of Reforms in Ex-Communist Countries. Fast and Extensive Reforms Led to Higher Growth and More Political Freedom". Policy Analysis by Oleh Havrylyshyn, Xiaofan Meng and Marian L. Tupi. *Cato Institute*, July 12, 2016, n. 795. Retrieved on April 19, 2019, from: https://object.cato.org/sites/cato.org/files/pubs/pdf/pa795_2.pdf.

Websites

Ana Bilankov Website. www.anabilankov.com. Last accessed on July 27, 2016.

Bookocide in Croatia. Retrieved on April 2, 2019, from: https://en.wikipedia.org/wiki/Bookocide_in_Croatia.
Border Walls. Borders, Fences and Walls. Text by Élisabeth Vallie 2015, September 1. Retrieved on March 28, 2019, from: https://borderwalls.hypotheses.org/date/2015/09.
Bücher weitergeben statt wegwerfen. http://www.buecherburg.de/index.html. Last accessed on February 27, 2019.
Citizens in Southeast Europe. Citizens of "Yugosphere" and "United Kingdoms"? — An Interview with Tim Judah, March 14, 2012. Retrieved on November 25, 2014, from: http://www.citsee.eu/interview/citizens-%E2%80%98yugosphere%E2%80%99-and-%E2%80%98united-kingdoms%E2%80%99-interview-tim-judah.
Dugine obitelji Website: https://www.dugineobitelji.com/slikovnica/. Last accessed on May 24, 2018.
German History in Documents and Images (GHDI). Chancellor Kohl's Television Address on the Day the Currency Union took Effect, July 1, 1990. Retrieved on November 27, 2018, from: http://ghdi.ghi-dc.org/sub_document.cfm?document_id=3101.
Jezik i nacionalizmi. Declaration on the Common Language. Retrieved on April 5, 2019, from: http://jezicinacionalizmi.com/deklaracija/.
Merriam-Webster Dictionary. Retrieved March 27, 2019, from: https://www.merriam-webster.com/.
Nakladništvo. Retrieved on March 30, 2019, from: http://www.enciklopedija.hr/natuknica.aspx?id=42840.
Otpisane: www.otpisane.org. Last accessed on April 17, 2018.
Platform of European Memory and Conscience: https://www.memoryandconscience.eu/. Last accessed on April 19, 2019.
Spaljivanje knjiga. Retrieved on April 2, 2019, from: https://hr.wikipedia.org/wiki/Spaljivanje_knjiga.
Spomenik Database. Retrieved on March 6, 2019, from: https://www.spomenikdatabase.org/.
Statista — Das Statistik-Portal. https://de.statista.com/. Last accessed on April 4, 2019.
Stephen Fry on Twitter. March 11, 2009. https://twitter.com/stephenfry/status/1312682218. Last accessed on April 1, 2019.

Targeting history and Memory. The ICTY and the investigation, reconstruction and prosecution of the crimes against cultural and religious heritage. Retrieved on April 2, 2019, from: http://www.heritage.sense-agency.com/.

Documentary films

Biti ili ne, Ivan Hiti (To be or not to be, Ivan Hiti). Directed by Branko Lazić. Radio televizija Republike Srpske, 2015.

Bosnien und Kosovo – Europas vergessene Protektorate (Bosnia and Kosovo. Europe's Forgotten Protectorates). Directed by Rüdiger Rossig and Zoran Solomun, Arte, 2016.

Neželjena baština (Unwanted Heritage). Directed by Irena Škorić. Artizana film, 2016.

The Destruction of Memory. Directed by Tim Slade. Icarus Films, 2016.

The Love of Books: A Sarajevo Story. Directed by Sam Hobkinson. Oxford Film & Television, 2011.

Udar na sjećanje (Damnatio Memoriae). Directed by Bogdan Žižić. Gama Studio, 2001.

U ratu i revoluciji (In War and Revolution), Directed by Ana Bilankov. Hrvatski filmski savez (HFS), 2011.

Vraćaju li se devedesete (Are the 1990s Coming Back) 10 Buka TV interviews by Aleksandar Trifunović: http://www.6yka.com/novosti/deset-buka-tv-intervjua-vracaju-li-se-devedesete-video. Last accessed on May 25, 2017.

Feature films

Rane (Wounds). Directed by Srđan Dragojević. RTS & Cobra Films, 1998.

Žikina dinastija (Žika's Dynasty). Directed by Zoran Čalić. TRZ film i ton & Morava film, 1985.

Animated film

Ježeva kuća (Hedgehog's Home). Directed by Eva Cvijanović. National Film Board of Canada and Bonobostudio, 2017.

Exhibitions and performances

After the Fall of the Berlin Wall. Daniel Biskup photographs 1990–1995. Photography exhibition. Museum in der Kulturbrauerei, Berlin, February 14–August, 25, 2019.

Čitanje misli Karla Marxa konju bana Josipa Jelačića na bivšem Trgu Republike (Reading Karl Marx's thoughts to Ban Jelačić's horse on the former Republic Square). Performance by Antonio Grgić on Ban Jelačić Square, Zagreb, July 9, 2015.

Naši heroji. Socialistični realizem revidiran (Heroes we Love. Socialist Realism Revisited). Maribor Art Gallery (*Umetnostna galerija Maribor UGM*), March 20–August 30, 2015.

Odpisani (The Written-Offs). University Library Maribor, March 16–April 14, 2010.

Osluškivanje (Listen). Performative sculpture by Luiza Margan on Ban Jelačić Square, Zagreb, July 8, 2015.

Otpisane, povodom 20. Godišnjice Oluje (Discarded, on the Occasion of the 20th Anniversary of Oluje). Galerija Nova, Zagreb, June 18–July 13, 2015.

Previjanje ranjenika ("Bandaging the Wounded"). Performance by Siniša Labrović on June 22, 2000 in Sinj, Croatia.

Revizija obiteljske biblioteke (Revision of the Family Library). Installation by Božena Končić Badurina in the Bogdan Ogrizović Library in Zagreb on July 9, 2015.

Svjetlost knjige (The Light of the Book). Performance by Siniša Labrović on July 8, 2015 in Galerija Nova, Zagreb.

Umbrüche (Turns): 1980–1995. Photographs by Ann-Christine Jansson. Photography exhibition at Fotogalerie Friedrichshain, November 30, 2018–January 26, 2019.

Literatur und Kultur im mittleren und östlichen Europa

herausgegeben von Reinhard Ibler

ISSN 2195-1497

1 *Elisa-Maria Hiemer*
  Generationenkonflikt und Gedächtnistradierung
  Die Aufarbeitung des Holocaust in der polnischen Erzählprosa des 21.
  Jahrhunderts
  ISBN 978-3-8382-0394-2

2 *Adam Jarosz*
  Przybyszewski und Japan
  Bezüge und Annäherungen
  Mit einem Vorwort von Hanna Ratuszna und Quellentexten in Erstübertragung
  ISBN 978-3-8382-0436-9

3 *Adam Jarosz*
  Das Todesmotiv im Drama von Stanisław Przybyszewski
  ISBN 978-3-8382-0496-3

4 *Valentina Kaptayn*
  Zwischen Tabu und Trauma
  Kateřina Tučkovás Roman *Vyhnání Gerty Schnirch* im Kontext der
  tschechischen Literatur über die Vertreibung der Deutschen
  ISBN 978-3-8382-0482-6

5 *Reinhard Ibler (Hg.)*
  Der Holocaust in den mitteleuropäischen
  Literaturen und Kulturen seit 1989
  The Holocaust in the Central European Literatures and Cultures since 1989
  ISBN 978-3-8382-0512-0

6 *Iris Bauer*
  Schreiben über den Holocaust
  Zur literarischen Kommunikation in Marian Pankowskis Erzählung *Nie ma Żydówki*
  ISBN 978-3-8382-0587-8

7 *Olga Zitová*
  Thomas Mann und Ivan Olbracht
  Der Einfluss von Manns Mythoskonzeption auf die karpatoukrainische Prosa
  des tschechischen Schriftstellers
  ISBN 978-3-8382-0633-2

8   *Trixi Jansen*
    Der Tod und das Mädchen
    Eine Analyse des Paradigmas aus Tod und Weiblichkeit in ausgewählten
    Erzählungen I.S. Turgenev
    ISBN 978-3-8382-0627-1

9   *Olena Sivuda*
    "Aber plötzlich war mir, als drohe das Haus über mir
    zusammenzubrechen."
    Komparative Analyse des Heimkehrermotivs in der deutschen und russischen
    Prosa nach dem Zweiten Weltkrieg
    ISBN 978-3-8382-0779-7

10 *Victoria Oldenburger*
    Keine Menschen, sondern ganz besondere Wesen ...
    Die Frau als Objekt unkonventioneller Faszination in Ivan A. Bunins Erzählband
    Temnye allei (1937–1949)
    ISBN 978-3-8382-0777-3

11 *Andrea Meyer-Fraatz, Thomas Schmidt (Hg.)*
    „Ich kann es nicht fassen,
    dass dies Menschen möglich ist"
    Zur Rolle des Emotionalen in der polnischen Literatur
    über den Holocaust
    ISBN 978-3-8382-0859-6

12 *Julia Friedmann*
    Von der Gorbimanie zur Putinphobie?
    Ursachen und Folgen medialer Politisierung
    ISBN 978-3-8382-0936-4

13 *Reinhard Ibler (Hg.)*
    Der Holocaust in den mitteleuropäischen Literaturen und Kulturen:
    Probleme der Politisierung und Ästhetisierung
    The Holocaust in the Central European Literatures and Cultures:
    Problems of Poetization and Aestheticization
    ISBN 978-3-8382-0952-4

14 *Alexander Lell*
    Studien zum erzählerischen Schaffen Vsevolod M. Garšins
    Zur Betrachtung des Unrechts in seinen Werken aus der Willensperspektive
    Arthur Schopenhauers
    ISBN 978-3-8382-1042-1

15   Dmitry Shlapentokh
     The Mongol Conquests in the Novels of Vasily Yan
     An Intellectual Biography
     ISBN 978-3-8382-1017-9

16   Katharina Bauer
     Liebe – Glaube – Russland:
     Russlandkonzeptionen im Schaffen Aleksej N. Tolstojs
     ISBN 978-3-8382-1182-4

17   Magdalena Baran-Szołtys, Monika Glosowitz,
     Aleksandra Konarzewska (Eds.)
     Imagined Geographies
     Central European Spatial Narratives between 1984 and 2014
     ISBN 978-3-8382-1225-8

18   Adam Jarosz
     Der Spiegel und die Spiegelungen
     Über Geschlecht und Seele im Werk von Stanisław Przybyszewski
     ISBN 978-3-8382-1246-3

19   Šárka Sladovníková
     The Holocaust in Czechoslovak
     and Czech Feature Films
     ISBN 978-3-8382-1196-1

20   Julia Spanberger
     Grenzen und Grenzerfahrungen in den Texten Viktor Pelevins
     Eine Analyse seiner frühen Prosa
     ISBN 978-3-8382-1460-3

21   Magda Dolińska-Rydzek
     The Antichrist in Post-Soviet Russia: Transformations of an Ideomyth
     ISBN 978-3-8382-1545-7

22   Martina Napolitano
     Sasha Sokolov: The Life and Work of the Russian "Proet"
     ISBN 978-3-8382-1619-5

23   Astrid Maria Ottilie Shchekina-Greipel
     Deutsch-sowjetischer Kulturtransfer unter totalitären Bedingungen
     Heinrich Böll und Günter Grass in der Sowjetunion (1953–1985)
     ISBN 978-3-8382-1660-7

24 *Dora Komnenović*
    Reading between the Lines:
    Reflections on Discarded Books and Sociopolitical Transformations in
    (Post-)Yugoslavia
    ISBN 978-3-8382-1643-0

25 *Reinhard Ibler und Andreas Ohme (Hg.)*
    Holocaustliteratur
    Überlegungen zu Reichweite und Grenzen eines literaturwissenschaftlichen
    Konzepts
    ISBN 978-3-8382-1673-7

26 *Marie Brunová*
    Die faktualen und fiktionalen Texte Jiří Weils
    ISBN 978-3-8382-1656-0

ibidem.eu